Drink from the Well

Fred C. Plumer

St. Johann Press
Haworth, New Jersey

ST. JOHANN PRESS

Published in the United States of America
by St. Johann Press
P.O. Box 241
Haworth, NJ 07641
www.stjohannpress.com

Copyright © 2016 Fred Plumer

All Rights reserved. No part of this publication may be reproduced,
stored in a retrieval system, or transmitted in any form or by any means
electronic, mechanical, photocopy, recording, or otherwise without the
prior written permission of the publisher.

The paper used in this publication meets the minimum requirements of
the American National Standard for Information Sciences—Permanence
of Paper for Printed Library Materials, ANSI/NISO Z39/48-1992

Composition and interior design by Susan Ramundo
(susan@srdesktopservices.com)
Cover design by G&H SOHO, Inc., Elmwood Park, NJ

ISBN 978-1-937943-33-2

Manufactured in the United States of America

Contents

Acknowledgments

I would like to thank the people who have kept me focused, and directed enough so that this publication was possible. I want to thank Karyn Lindberg for her contribution to both this book, and for making me a better writer. It was her idea that starting this ball rolling, and it was her encouragement that got me to finish it. I would like to thank the rest of my staff for supporting and working tirelessly on this project. Special thanks to Deshna Ubeda whose efforts to complete another project never cease to amaze me. I want to thank the literally thousands of people who support our organization, who have contributed financially, or through their valued writings. This was really for all of you.

And finally I want to thank my wife of over forty years, Charron. She has been my rock and my supporter the entire time, regardless of what I was doing. Without her, none of this would have happened.

Preface

I have always been a seeker. I still am. This is not a pejorative term. I am aware that some of the conservative, mega-churches use this term for hesitant or non-believers but are still coming to the church. Many of these churches have separate services for "seekers," those who have not made the big commitment to the beliefs of that particular church.

However, I use the word here as someone who keeps searching for the "truth," knowing that they probably will not find it. As a seeker, I have always had a thirst that is probably insatiable. But frankly, it is because of that thirst, that my life has taken me to some wonderful and exciting places. I have had the opportunity to drink sweet water all along the journey.

When I look over my life, as one tends to do as they reach their 75th birthday, I am amazed at the teachers, the thinkers and the committed people I have had the opportunity to work with, to study with and in many cases to be friends with. Each and every one of these people offered me a chance to drink from the well.

I was once very active as a youth, in a Presbyterian Church in the community my family lived in for nearly 18 years. It was a wonderful, foundational experience. I was given so much freedom to question and to doubt, I had nothing I needed to purge as I matured. It was truly sweet water.

Years later I met with a group that studied G.I. Gurdjieff. I was part of a discussion group and we pondered such words as: "Conscious faith is freedom. Emotional faith is slavery. Mechanical faith is foolishness." We had many discussions about how we might create conscious faith. I don't think I made it, but it was a wonderful part of my journey. Some years later, I joined a P. D. Ouspensky group. His study of the miraculous fascinated me. Both teachings of Gurdjieff and Ouspensky tasted like sweet water. I drank of it fully.

Over 30 years ago, I spent three years in seminary and could not have attended at better time. The lodging above our apartment was reserved for the schools guest lecturer, usually for one semester. In my second semester of my first year, I became friends with the husband and his wife upstairs. He was the new minister in residence of the semester. He introduced me to some of the people who started the Jesus Seminar when it was only in the planning stages. He gave me several books from some of the early founders of the Jesus Seminar. I was so excited about this new information and the direction they were going. This introduction impacted my entire study. I felt like I was going to two seminaries at the same time. One that challenged me and the other gave me direction. I was given a great amount of freedom to search for the historical Jesus. The people I met, the sincerity of their work, was like a drink from the freshest water in the world.

The second year, the guest lecturer who stayed in that room, was Paulos Gregorious. He was born, Paul Varghese but years later when he was named Bishop by the India Orthodox Church, his name was changed. As a very young man, while traveling through Ethiopia, he made in contact with Hailie Selassie. He worked with him early on as an assistant. Selassie was so impressed with this young man, he sent Paulos back to school in India, where he received a Master's in theology and then returned to Ethiopia. There he served as the Emperor's personal aide and advisor. In 1975, he was elevated as a bishop in the Orthodox Church and he took charge of the newly formed Diocese of Delhi, of the India's Orthodox Church. It was a position he held until his death. When I met him, he had been in a leadership role in the World Council of Churches for years, becoming President in 1983.

Paulos was a wonderful man who taught me in the strangest but effective ways. When he first moved into the apartment above us, I was called into the Seminary President office. President, Neely McCarter explained to me who Paulos was and asked if I would be willing to help him if he needed anything. Then he said, "Please call him, Your Holiness, or Father." My reaction was obvious. I was a 41 year old, Southern California boy. I did not call anyone His Holiness or Father except for my dad. Neely pleaded his case, and I said I would do what I could.

The next day I dropped by to see if Paulos needed anything. He said he would love a ride to the store. I avoided calling him anything. While we were driving he said, "Fred, I know you are having a problem knowing how to address me. So I want to be clear. You can call me Paulos or Paul. You can call me buddy or hey you. You can call me anything you like and it won't bother me. But when the people from my church are here, if you call me anything other than Your Holiness or Father, they will probably be offended. They will get over it and I will chuckle. But I thought you should know."

By the time Paulos left six weeks later, I would have called him anything he wanted. And I certainly did not call him anything but Your Holiness when his people were there.

Paulos had dinner with my family on a regular basis and used to bring our five year daughter little presents. We talked about everything, frequently taking long walks up and down the Berkeley streets. What I found interesting was he seemed far more curious about my life than his own. Frequently I would ask him a question about his life and before I knew it had turned it into a question about my own life. I remember thinking when we said goodbye that I had a thousand questions I wanted to ask him. I always thought I would do that sometime but never did.

Paulos Gregorious had a huge influence on my life. He was one of a very few people I have come to know in my life, I would call a "holy man." His well was deep, and the water he fed me was wonderful. And yet he left me thirsty for more.

The third year, the guest lecturer upstairs was the Reverend Reuben Sheares. Reuben was an executive with the United Church of Christ and was there to finish up his book on spirituality. We had many long talks about my future, since I was still not certain if I was going to accept a job at a church, at least a white church.

For the past two years I had been working in the Potrero Hills Neighborhood Center which was an interfaith organization. It primarily served the 95% black population of the Housing Projects. I loved that job and continued to visit the center long after I had graduated. I was one of two whites on the staff of twenty-seven at the time. I worked primarily with a bunch of fourteen year olds and loved each and every one of them. For the brief period I worked there I virtually forgot what color I was. I am guessing I was going through somewhat of an identity crisis at the time. Reuben happened to be black.

One day toward the end of my seminary days I received a call from the head of the search team in Irvine, Southern California, informing me that I was their choice. I told her I would call her back after my wife and I talked about it. Then I ran up the stairs and pounded on Reuben's door. He had been taking a nap until I woke him.

I was practically yelling when I told him that I had been selected at the Irvine church, and I thought I had made a huge mistake. My heart was pounding. I was practically in tears and I know I was babbling. He gently took my face in his hands and looked me in the eyes and slowly said: "Fred, just love them . . . just love them . . . just love them . . ." over and over. Each time he would say it a little slower until my heart stopped pounding and I relaxed. And suddenly I realized, I can do that. I can love them.

For a little over twenty years as a pastor at that church, I never forgot those words or that experience. And every time things started to unravel after our church had gone through another of its growth spurts and the ensuing tension, I would find a quiet place and ponder his words. Sometimes I would actually chant, "Just love them" and things always seemed to settle down. It was indeed a sweet drink of living water that has stuck with me after all of these years.

And then finally, there are the authors of many of the over 500 theological books I have read in the last 35 years. Some I know personally and some I never met but each and every one of them has touched me, has coached me, tested me and informed me. Each one of them has fed me. And each one of them has allowed me the opportunity to drink from their wells. And I drank.

All of these experiences, and literally dozens of others have led me to where I am today. In some ways most of those are somehow represented in the writings I now offer each of you. I do not think I have found the answer or the "truth." But what I do know is that I have tapped into something that has made my life more meaningful, joyful and fulfilling.

I now offer them to you, hoping you might drink from the well.

Introduction

Publishing anthologies is always challenging. First, you never know who may have already read the material and may find it in a reprinted form redundant. The second reason is the subject material may be dated. Something one might have written after a major world event, or before a major event, may seem irrelevant and meaningless in a new context. And finally if the articles have been written over a period of time, the author may have changed his or her perspectives, as hopefully they always do. But it could be a little confusing to some people.

It is for these reasons, and a few others, I have been reluctant to publish this anthology. If it had not been for the numerous requests from our readers, and supporters, and from the constant harassment from my beloved staff, this collection would not have happened. I certainly need to acknowledge and thank one staff member in particular, Karyn Lindberg. Karyn does most of the editing for just about anything I publish anymore. She worked tirelessly to pull this book together. She was relentless in her efforts to convince me this was an important project, and she hounded me when I fell behind in my rewrites. I also want to thank her publically for her constant coaching. I believe I have become a better writer because of her patient persistence.

The material for this publication was written over of a period of approximately six years. Most of the included articles were selected from articles we published in our eBulletins and other assorted publications over the same time period. A few of the articles were lifted, in part, from speeches I have given over the last few years. All of them have been edited and revised for this publication.

I found it interesting to reread some of my own writing from nearly six years ago and realize how my descriptive language has changed. Some of that change is reflected here. Our team discussed the option of sanitizing the language of all of it, so it would be consistent. However, we finally decided it might be good for you, the reader, to understand we are all in flux. Things change, including us. There were some places I did make changes and there were others I left alone. It seemed like something would be lost. It is my main hope is that you will find yourself more comfortable with your own changes and even transitions as you read through these articles.

One of our goals here was to organize the material into chapters which focus on a particular subject, so it might shed more light on that subject or theme. We hope we have achieved at least some of this goal by the articles we chose and the way they are assembled.

Ever since I was a very young man, I have viewed my life as a journey, always wondering what interesting, or even exciting event was around the corner. My journey has always had a spiritual component in it, but for most of my life, I viewed that spirituality as the sauce on the omelet. It was first and foremost about living life fully and completely with some spirituality poured over the omelet, like a spicy sauce. I wanted to enjoy the banquet of life. Over the last decade I have come to realize my journey was always a spiritual journey, with a human life component. My goal became to discover who I am as spirit. I am reminded of the wonderful line in the song, *Shine* by Alexi Murdoch, from the album *Time Without Consequence*. "I am a spirit trying to learn how to be human."

Obviously I have been influenced by some of the great scholars of our time, the late Marcus Borg, Bishop John Shelby Spong, John Dominic Crossan, Lloyd Geering, Joan Chittister, Don Cupitt. Elaine Pagels and Val Webb to name just a few. But what you are reading is mine and mine alone. I take full responsibility for anything you may read.

Yes, this is my journey and to the many of you who have been part of that journey, I want to thank you. It has been quite the ride.

CHAPTER ONE

Who We Are

A Search for the Real

One day, nearly 40 years ago, I hiked up to the edge of the tundra at the base of a glacier lake on a 14,000-foot mountain in Colorado. I went up there in part because I was terribly depressed and needed to be alone. I was not certain I would come down off that mountain. I had come to realize I had pretty much messed up just about everything that was important in my life. My marriage to my soul mate appeared to be on the rocks. My two businesses were in a mess and I assumed we would have to close them and lose everything. My two business partners, one of them an older brother, were no longer speaking to me.

With a sense of helplessness, I went over and over my life wondering how all of this could have happened. After all, I had always been successful. I had always come out on top. Things always had seemed to go my way. But none of that was true anymore. I clearly was not successful. I had lost the respect of all of the people who were important to me. I was broke and broken. I did not know who I was anymore. I have never experienced such utter loneliness in my life.

Emotionally and physically exhausted, I finally laid down on the edge of the tundra. As I laid there I realized I was weeping. My weeping turned into sobbing until I was literally out of tears and out of breathe. Then I fell into a deep sleep, face down in the mud I had created with my tears. I have no idea how long I slept in that situation and I have no explanation for what happened next.

I felt like I was dreaming but everything was so vivid it did not seem like a dream. My adult life starting flashing by like a slide show on fast forward—faces, places and situations in no special order. I was horrified to see the pain and suffering my insensitivities, thoughtlessness and self-centeredness had caused others over the years. I may have thought I was having fun but it became abundantly clear my shallow fun had often created deep pain in others. I felt like was looking at a trail of bloody body parts along a path of people I had wounded with my insensitivity. I was horrified and remember trying to say I was sorry but nothing came out of my mouth. I was trying to wake up when I whispered, "I give up." And the horror movie seemed to end.

When I woke up I still could not move. I was not entirely clear about where I was when I noticed a gentle breeze blowing across my face. It felt like the loving caress from a gentle hand. I laid there in silence except for the breeze whispering in the trees. I had the sensation I was being cradled as a mother might cradle her child. I was surrounded with a Presence. Without voice I "felt" these words: "I am with you, I have always been with you."

More importantly, I experienced a sense of unconditional love I had never before experienced. Interestingly, I no longer felt the sense of lingering loneliness I had experienced off and on all my life. It was as if I was connected, part of something so big, so awesome that it defied words or logic as I understood it.

When I hiked back down the mountain the next day everything looked different. Colors were brighter, more effervescent. I saw and heard more birds that I ever have. I imagined that they were all coming out of hiding to welcome me. I wondered what they were trying to tell me. I felt a connection to every tree, every bird, and every small animal. The gentle breeze that followed me down the mountain felt like another caress. I became part of a beautiful, forest symphony.

As weeks passed, in spite of the fact that little had changed in my marital or business situation, everything else seemed different. I was still working eighteen hour days and coming home to a cold house. However, I continued to experience this new awareness wherever I went. I became more attentive to the feelings and the needs of others. I felt a sense of love for people I had never known, the people I did know, including those I had battled with. I felt that same love with those who were angry with me. That sense of love, connectedness and awe has seldom left me ever since.

Frankly, I was not certain what happened on that mountain or what it meant. I rarely spoke to anyone about it. But I wondered if I had a nervous breakdown. Was it altitude sickness? Had I done too many drugs in the '60s? Eckhart Tolle would suggest my ego dissolved. I prefer to think of it as a forced journey of *kenosis*, a radical self-emptying. Whatever it was, it was a life changing experience that has never left me.

As I tried to put my life back together again, I was still curious what had happened to me. I studied the great mystics and spiritual teachers from many different religions, cultures and time periods. I paid special attention to these spiritual giants during my seminary years in the early '80s. I found they all had experienced something most of them referred to as a profound sense of connectedness, oneness and unity. They all seemed to have experienced a dissolving of tribal boundaries, of the concept of enemies, of any lines of demarcation between different people and a sense of equanimity.

Today we find a tremendous interest in these same spiritual teachers and some new ones. The fastest growing religious group in the nation is made up of those people who say they are spiritual but not religious. But what do they mean by spiritual?

A few years ago I did a web search on the subject of spirituality. We did not have search engines when I was in seminary or I might have saved myself a lot of time back then. Here are a few quotes I found. Spirituality is:

- An inner sense of something greater than oneself. Recognition of a meaning to existence that transcends one's immediate circumstances.

- In a narrow sense, that what concerns itself with matters of the spirit. The spiritual, involving (as it may) perceived eternal verities regarding humankind's ultimate nature, often contrasts with the temporal, with the material, or with the worldly. A sense of connection forms a central defining characteristic of spirituality—connection to something greater than oneself.

- That part of us which, while anchored in biology, is non-local, universal and timeless, and which yearns for connection with what might be called the mind universal, or God, or whatever term you prefer.

- "This we know, all things are connected like the blood which unites one family. Whatever befalls the earth befalls the sons and daughters of the earth. Man did not weave the web of life; he is merely a strand in it. Whatever he does to the web, he does to himself."—Chief Seattle

A defining characteristic then, of the spiritual or a spiritual event or of life, is the experience of some strong connection—a connection to something greater than oneself beyond ego as well as a connection to others.

I would like to posit that this experience of connectedness is a thing most humans, consciously or unconsciously hunger for. If the book sales in this country are any indication, then it is a big, multimillion dollar hunger. And I would also suggest it is one thing our mainline churches across the country tend to ignore.

Today we know the concept of something we call progressive Christianity covers a wide spectrum of Christological and theological thinking. However, I believe it is this understanding of the connectedness, the interdependency or Oneness, that provides the spiritual foundation of progressive Christianity.

Some progressives have reached that perspective on a more intellectual basis. It may depend on their interpretation of scripture or on their idea of the real, historical Jesus they choose to emulate. Others have come to that position through science and their understanding of the interconnected universe. Others have empirically discovered we live in an interconnected world sharing our trash as well as our economy. We are never more aware of it than we are today. For some, it may be an awakening to what is being called an ecological theology.

It is this understanding—for some a very spiritual one—that leads us to an alternative way of seeing and experiencing reality. It creates a very different starting point in the way we see and relate to our fellow human beings.

If we take it seriously and try to live as progressive Christians, we must view all living things as part of one pulsating, vibrant creation, constantly trading cells and breath. Unlike our conservative and Orthodox cousins, progressives start with the assumption that every person is a precious creation—a child of God—regardless of their color, sexual orientation, religious conviction, and yes, even their political party of choice.

Most progressives Christians today reject the Augustinian concept of Original Sin. Aside from all the psychological damage it has done over the centuries because of its interpretation of the Pauline text, the whole idea continues to be terribly divisive. It means some are in and some are out. Some are saved and some are not. It is another form of ancient tribal divisiveness that still haunts most religious expressions in the world.

The truth is, based on this definition, progressives have been around for a long time. We live in the long tradition of progressive prophets like Amos, Hosea and third Isaiah who overlooked the tribal and ethnic issues of their time. They saw and experienced their world differently. They were often considered crazy by their peers.

I would argue Jesus was indeed a progressive. Something happens when we begin to relate to the entire world as being infused with God's Spirit (not withstanding that we may not know what we mean when we say God). Something changes when we begin to see every human being as a child of God—a creation of the Creator. That something can be a spiritual phenomenon beyond explanation.

I would like to suggest that the teachings of Jesus offer us a path for one of those spiritual experiences of inter-connectedness that can be life changing. It is something that can give us eyes to see and ears to hear like no other. I know I have a bias but I can make a strong case based on the best biblical scholarship. What Jesus was doing, when he offered his teachings, was to provide us with a path to experience what he might have called the Kingdom of God or the Oneness of All Life.

It was not just about social justice. It was not about reforming Judaism. It was not about the zealots' tactics to overcome the Romans. It is not just about end times or about life after death. It is the path to experience the Oneness in God. As Neal Douglas-Klotz translates it, it is a path to experience Sacred Unity, the divine nature that imbues all living things.

5

Frankly, I suspect Jesus himself had one of those profound experiences of the eternal, of this Sacred Unity. According to Bruce Chilton, in his book, *Rabbi Jesus*, this experience could have been a result of his difficult childhood as a member of the Mamzer caste, his early discipleship of John the Baptist, and his own intense meditative practices.

Whatever happened, it is clear he experienced something he called the Kingdom of God or Sacred Unity in all things. He felt connected to something that he experienced as love. He lived so fully in the moment that he may have referred to something he called the Eternal life, an experience of timelessness. He experienced reality as one interconnected whole. The experience or experiences most likely changed him, offering a new, profound awareness. He became a teacher and practitioner of Oneness.

According to the Gospel of Thomas, Jesus told his listeners, *"Look for the Living One while you are alive, lest you die and then seek to see him and be unable to see."* (Saying 59)

"On the day when you were One, you became two. But when you have become two, what will you do?" (Saying 11:4)

And finally: *"When you make the two One, and when you make the inner as the outer and the outer as the inner, and the above as the below . . . then will you enter the Kingdom."* (Saying 22:4-7)

John Dominic Crossan writes of the unique nature of Jesus' radical egalitarianism that broke down all barriers, all tribal boundaries and hierarchies. I am suggesting these actions and mindsets were part of his experience of the Sacred Unity or the Oneness that was for him experiential and existential.

If such an event occurred, his friends would have noticed and might have asked what happened. When he explained to the best of his ability to describe what he was experiencing he said he was experiencing the One or The Oneness.

"How do we experience what you are experiencing?" his friends and followers must have asked.

"You follow the laws and you treat others kindly," he said.

"But you know we do those things. What else can we do?" they may have responded.

It was from here that we have gained the teachings of Jesus. There were lessons or steps for each of us to experience the One, the Oneness or Sacred

Unity. They can lead to a life changing experience of the Kingdom of God that Jesus suggested could bring such joy.

But the path Jesus gave each of us in order to experience this sacred connectedness, Oneness, or Sacred Unity is not necessarily easy. It is learning to care for our neighbor. It is learning what it means to take in the stranger. It is even being willing to love our enemy. It means to reach out and serve, to have the same kind of compassion for another as a mother has for the child in her womb. It is being willing to stand in solidarity with the less fortunate even when it means a risk.

Whether it is loving, healing, feeding, holding, resisting, forgiving, trusting, it seems clear we were instructed to "go and do likewise." Go! Do! These are two of the most common instructions placed in the mouth of Jesus that we find in our texts.

For too long however, we have treated Jesus' teachings as something we ought to do if we want to be a good Christian. If we do not do them, or we do not do them long enough or well enough, we feel guilty.

We also risk the danger of being obsessed about a particular injustice we think we are supposed to make right. I have met far too many people who identify themselves as progressives Christians who are single issue people. They know who the enemy is—the one who disagrees with them. These folks can offer a lot of energy to a campaign for change and most of the time I am in complete agreement with their positions. But they often grow angry, self-righteous and indignant. They usually burn out quickly often leaving a bloody trail behind.

Progressive assumes change or what I would like to assume is progress. Without a spiritual foundation and spiritual practices to support and ground us, trying to be a progressive Christian can be a very difficult challenge. It risks causing internal and external warfare.

But what if we viewed these teachings not as oughts but as opportunities to experience the Realm of God? What if we think of Jesus' teachings as a response to the question, "How do I find and experience the Realm of God?" Do you want to want to experience the Kingdom of God? Then love your neighbor with compassion. Do you want to experience the Realm of God? Then forgive the unforgivable. Do you want to feel connected to the Sacred Unity? Then do not judge another. We are searching for real experiences of that radical egalitarianism John Dominic Crossan writes about so eloquently. What if we actually developed the eyes to see and the ears to hear every living being as a precious child of God just the way they are?

What a very different kind of Christianity we would experience. What a very different life we would lead. What a very different kind of world we would live in.

You cannot love and serve with a compassionate heart without eventually seeing those whom you are serving as your brother, your sister, your mother, your father, or eventually as yourself, even if it is the least of these whom you serve. But if we do our serving because we feel it is something we are supposed to do because the Bible says we should or because that is what Jesus did according to scripture, or because it is our duty, we only separate ourselves more from others.

On the other hand, if we see our compassionate service as an opportunity to experience the Realm of God or Sacred Unity, then our compassionate actions or practices become golden opportunities.

Felix Adler, the Jewish philosopher, once wrote, *"The unique personality which is the real life in me, I cannot gain unless I search for the real life, the spiritual quality, in others. I am myself spiritually dead unless I reach out to the fine quality dormant in others. For it is only with the god enthroned in the innermost shrine of the other, that the god hidden in me, will consent to appear."*

I was at a forum one time when the Dalai Lama was the speaker. Someone from the audience made a comment that went something like this, "It sounds like you are suggesting that living compassionately can lead to a type of enlightenment and certainly happiness. Isn't it then self-serving?"

The Dali Lama looked at him, smiling. He hesitated for a moment and then responded, *"Yes I suppose it is. Is there something wrong with that?"*

I am convinced every spiritual journey must include a time for silence and reflection whether one is a progressive Christian or not. We need to create the time, the space and the practices to help us remove the egoic chatter from our heads; to reflect upon what we have learned; and to open ourselves to that healing/guiding Spirit we call God. It is also helpful to be part of a community that supports and celebrates with us. But it is by nurturing our deep compassion for others without conditions or restraints that ultimately leads to a progressive Christian spirituality. It is not an easy path and it requires commitment, practice and patience. But it can be a wonderful journey.

Today Progressive Christians have the opportunity to teach a different kind of Christianity. Not as a method to experience heaven after we die, but as a path to experience heaven on earth. Not something to off-set our original sin, but a chance to get in touch with the divine that is within. We have a path to the kingdom, to eternal life. Right now that path is covered with weeds, brambles and thick brush. I believe it is time to clear that path and show people the Yeshua Way once again. May we joyfully become self-serving?

Becoming President in 2006: Into the Future

I wonder why I occasionally reread the letter I sent to the Progressive Christianity.org board nearly ten years ago. In that letter I agreed to assume the role of board president as of January 1, 2006 with a few minor conditions. I had been active with the organization since 1996. At that point I should have had a pretty good idea about what assumptions I should make.

Since taking on this responsibility was going to cut into my retirement time, I wanted to be clear about how I was going to protect that time. After all, I was planning to write a book and I just spent a lot of money setting up a woodworking shop. I was planning to make beautiful furniture in my more quiet years. I wrote that I would volunteer to take on this part-time responsibility but only if we could move the office to a nearby location in the state of Washington. If my travel could be minimal and if it did not take more than 20 hours a week, I was ready to go.

I think I keep the letter around so I can have a good laugh now and then. We did move the office to Washington State where my wife and I had already located to start my retirement. The beautiful table saw that was to have been the center for my budding woodworking skills is still in the crate. The book, maybe half done, has moved through two generations of computers with nary a word added since I left Southern California.

For the last eight years I have achieved MVP status with Alaska Airlines because of the number of miles I travel. Needless to say there never was a 20-hour week. Today I suspect I am much closer to three times that amount although I refuse to count so I really do not know.

So what happened? I suppose my personality—some would say personality flaw—has something to do with it. I am a workaholic and have been for as long as I can remember. I like to create new things or make them better. When things are running smoothly or simply require management, I am quickly bored. My brain is constantly asking, "How can we change this or do this better?" But there is a price for change and all of my experience over the years indicates the price is hard work and diligence.

Secondarily, somewhere along the way as I began to read more Progressive Christianity.org emails from people I had never met, I discovered there was a real hunger for serious dialogue about faith, spirituality and religious beliefs. I lost count a long time ago of the number of people who asked, "Why haven't I heard this before?" The more often this happened, the more I realized there were a lot of people who were counting on ProgressiveChristianity.org to initiate and foster this kind of discourse. I tend to take things personally so it became a call of sorts to see that this continued. I have assumed some responsibility to see that it does.

Finally there really is a progressive religious movement in itself. Just in the last few years we have seen an explosion of organizations, scholars and even lay people using the term progressive Christianity. Of course there is still a lack of clarity about what the term means. At least the dialogue is out in the open and not in the back rooms of seminaries or the religious departments of some universities. We assume one of our mandates is to provide resources and a forum to help each other clarify what we mean by that term. The basic understanding is it will always be changing; it will always be evolving.

The impact on ProgressiveChristianity.org would have been unimaginable a few years ago. Our web activity has increased ten-fold; our email has grown five-fold. The demand for speakers and workshops continues to exceed our expectations.

We have learned there is a hunger in our society today for a tangible, viable and compelling spiritual path. More and more people want to talk openly and frankly about faith, belief and spirituality. They get excited about finding a place where they can talk freely about a religious experience that no longer works for them. Most of them want not only a healthy dialogue but they want to find solid information about the religion of their tradition so they can make choices knowing they are making informed decisions.

So we work, most of us as volunteers with a couple others who are willing to work for less than they could earn elsewhere, because we believe in the purpose and the call. We read the emails. We hear the phone calls. We know why people are saying, "Why haven't I heard this before?"

We do not need to be the leader or number one. We just need to do what we apparently have been called to do and to keep doing it better. That means finding more effective ways of sharing the progressive Christian message.

What is Progressive Christianity Anyway?

In the early 1990s Jim Adams, the founder of ProgressiveChristianity.org, gathered with a few friends and colleagues to discuss the possibility of starting an organization that might help network more liberal and open churches. The conversation led to a discussion about what that organization might be called. As you might imagine a multitude of ideas were bantered around. Over the next 18 months or so, the term Progressive Christianity came up more and more. It seemed to fit Jim Adams' vision better than anything else. Although in 1993 the internet search engines were not what they are today, there appeared to be no scholarly papers, or book titles at the time using the term progressive Christianity. Certainly there were no non-profit organizations using that term in their name or self-description.

This is not to suggest progressive Christianity has no history. At the end of the 19th century there was a group of Christians historians today sometimes refer to as Progressive Christians. Although there is not a direct lineage with the contemporary progressive movement, there is more than one indirect link.

According to Gary Dorrien, professor at Union Theological Seminary, the 19th century progressive Christians asserted that *"Christianity is essentially a life, not a doctrine."* According to Dorrien most of these same founders of progressive Christianity were *"leading exemplars of religious speech as imaginative metaphorical expression."* (*The Making of American Liberal Theology: Imagining Progressive Christianity*)

Another excellent study of these early progressives has been written by Richard Gamble, professor of history at Hillsdale College. In his fascinating book, *The War for Righteousness*, Gamble writes about progressive Christians of the era: *"Traditional Christianity, with its biblical literalism and notions of eternal retribution and individual redemption, seemed dangerously ill-equipped for the modern world. Progressive Christianity, in contrast, was to be intellectually respectable, credible, relevant and liberating. In short it would be a suitable spiritual companion to modern man as he entered the twentieth century."*

Both Gamble and Dorrien referred to this 19th and 20th century movement as progressive Christianity. Although my research was limited, I found it interesting, after reading several of the original texts cited by these two excellent scholars, I was unable to find one theologian who referred to himself as a progressive Christian. Nor was there one who suggested his views represented something called progressive Christianity. It is true that the word even progressivism was used by these theologians and preachers when they described their understanding of God's will or plan for the world. It is easy to see how both Gamble and Dorrien were able to categorize these Christians as progressive. But it appears progressive Christianity was not a common self-identifying factor among these Christians in their lifetimes.

In a telephone interview, Gamble explained that he wanted to identify a particular group of theologians and preachers of the era who shared the perspective that progress was visible in every facet of life and was a demonstration of God's will. They envisioned a history leading toward a definite goal. It was this perspective, when merged with a political agenda, which had a tremendous influence on the politics of their time. Gamble chose the term progressive Christian, he explained, in order to distinguish these theologians and preachers from the social gospel adherents as well as other liberal Christians.

Dorrien also suggested he had thought of the term progressive Christian as a category to identify a segment of the liberal Christians of the time. He admitted he was in some way looking through the lenses of the late 20th and early 21st centuries in his desire to give this unique group a common identity.

My point here is that by the beginning of the 21th century, progressive Christian had become so familiar that historical scholars were using the term as if it had a known quality. This is in spite of the fact that the term *progressive* had fallen out of favor by the 1920 with the failure of the Wilsonian world view, the downfall of the progressive political parties and the horrors of WWI. In the mid-20th century the term seemed to be virtually non-existent in public dialogue.

Today the term progressive Christianity has become common in the church culture. Do a Google search for progressive Christianity and you will discover pages of related sites and links. Scholars, media, and clergy use the term regularly. We receive an average of eight to ten books a month from scholars, publishers and clergy who have written a book they believe is about progressive Christianity. You know something is happening when articles and blogs from the religious conservative commentators are increasingly attacking and ridiculing progressive Christians.

Is it a movement? In recent years the web activity has exploded. Our church affiliates grow slowly every year and our individual affiliates continue to grow exponentially. I have talked with the leadership of most other progressive organizations and almost all of them are reporting similar phenomenon.

You would think all of this would make those of us who helped guide the development of our organization downright giddy. And certainly there is some of that. But it has become clear this rush toward something called progressive Christianity is going to require a lot more work to clarify what we mean and maybe more importantly what we do not mean.

From the very beginning those of us who were part of The Center for Progressive Christianity, our original name, assumed that if we were going to identify and represent a certain type of Christianity, there would need to be a theological/Christological foundation for that perspective. When you use a term like progressive as an adjective, it seemed obvious you are describing a type of Christianity. It is therefore important to state what that means.

Not only do we believe there needs to be a common theological foundation for what we mean by that that term, but by its nature progressive Christianity must always be actively engaged in theological development relevant to the times. I would also argue that one of the responsibilities of the progressive Christian movement is to engage in redefining what we mean by Christ in relationship to the historical Jesus.

The late Delwin Brown, former Dean Emeritus of Pacific School of Religion, once wrote in the web page, *Progressive Christian Witness*, that progressive Christianity is not so much about theology as it is about practice. In a paper he stated, *"Progressive Christianity today is not a single party line; it is a family of perspectives and practices that seek to be faithful to Christ. It is diverse because it draws from a variety of Christian expressions rooted in the biblical witness."*

Eminent theologian John Cobb, co-founder of Progressive Christians Uniting, wrote: *"[Progressive Protestantism] is the liberal tradition transformed first by its rejection of the dualism of commitment to the tradition and commitment to new insights in the present. It wants to be deeply continuous with the Bible and tradition and believes that this continuity requires openness to new insights."*

Although our leadership has much in common with these two organizations and their highly respected and qualified founders, I do not think we would put the same emphasis on tradition and continuity with the Bible. Nor do we believe progressive Christianity is something made up out of family of perspectives.

The matter has been further confused by the addition of well-known evangelicals like Jim Wallis of Sojourners and Brian McLaren both of whom now refer to themselves as progressive Christians. In a blog, for example, Wallis wrote about a talk he gave to students at Bethel University. *"It was clear from the response in chapel that a new generation of evangelical Christians want to be, like Jesus, good news to the poor. And because of that their agenda is now much broader and deeper than just the two things the Religious Right continues to talk about as the only moral values issues—abortion and gay marriage. The Bethel students, like me, still believe that the sanctity of life and healthy family values are indeed important issues."*

Once again there is much about the new social agenda of both of these evangelical leaders that our organization appreciates. However their emphasis on the authority of the Bible, the exclusive nature of the high Christology, and more importantly, their apparent disregard for the plight of the entire GLTB community, separates them from what I believe are the common building blocks of the new progressive Christian movement.

Although we have made an effort to spell out what we mean by progressive Christianity as an organization with our Eight Points, it seems to me there are at least five essential components for anyone who considers to be a Progressive Christian today:

- To see oneself as a follower of Jesus or Jesus' teachings rather than a believer in a creed;

- To recognize that Christianity is not the only way;

- To search the great mysteries of life with an open theology and an intellectual integrity;

- To recognize that ecology and social justice are interlinked and part of your faith;

- And to understand that gays, lesbians, transgenders and bi-sexuals are full participants in our world as a natural part of God's creation.

I have always assumed the progressive perspective was a response to the unfolding of the awesome scientific secrets of the universe that continue to expand our understanding of this incredible and often unfathomable creation. It is a response to the ongoing scholarship that has recently expanded our understanding of biblical times, the historical Jesus and the way religions in the world have developed historically. It is a response to our growing and changing information about human nature. A progressive attitude is both a response to and the search for truth while accepting we are almost always looking at horizons.

I would suggest here that the foundational tenet of progressive Christianity is the ontological understanding that pre-dates Bible, tradition and even religion. That is, all living beings are created by one force, one Spirit, one God and are inter-related and interdependent. This is a universal truth revealed in Jesus and other enlightened teachers and prophets over the centuries. It is one science makes more of a reality for us every day. But it makes no difference whether one comes to that understanding of reality through Biblical teachings, some scientific revelation or some existential spiritual experience. Once you begin to see the creation this way, everything changes.

It is out of this understanding that we are compelled to work for social justice; it is out of this insight that we begin to see others as we would like them to see us; it is out of this awareness that we can no longer let others suffer without interceding; it is out of this recognition that our compassion for others grows without limits; and it is out of this consciousness that we are even willing to die on behalf of others.

Progress by definition is to move forward. Obviously this implies movement, transition and usually the need to let go or revise. Progress always means change and change is seldom easy, especially when we are dealing with issues that are so subjective and even sacred in our lives.

It is not my purpose here to judge the propriety of the positions by other organizations and individuals but only to point out the confusion one can have when they attempt to get a clear answer to the simple question, "What do you mean when you say progressive Christianity?"

Are these differences and the confusion they sometimes cause a bad thing for the progressive movement or for Christianity? Not necessarily. One of the most positive things about these differences is that they have already forced many of us to begin a dialogue about what we mean, not only when we say progressive, but also what we mean when we say Christian. Not only are theologians, biblical scholars, sociologists and clergy discussing these issues today, but so are people in the pews. I suggest you take a look at the message boards on our website and our extremely active Facebook pages. There are ongoing discussions between young people primarily, that astound me at times with the depth of their thinking, education and the quality of exchanges that transpire every day.

One thing is clear. There are spiritually hungry people all over the country who are looking for a safe place to discuss these religious and spiritual issues. For over a decade, the media has made rethinking what we mean when we say Christian a front page issue. Yet all too often, according to the literally thousands of emails we receive every year, when seekers walk into one of our mainline churches, they hear milk toast, muddled sermons filled with dead theology and an impotent Christology. They are looking for courageous clergy to open a discussion about a fresh new, rational way to approach their Christian faith. According to my mail, they usually walk away feeling empty. They come looking for spiritual transformation and they leave feeling stagnant institution. They come because they are spiritually hungry and they leave thinking no one rang the dinner bell.

Matthew Fox writes, *"Yes, at this time in history Protestantism, like Catholicism, needs a radical overhaul—a New Reformation and new transformation. Both need to move from religion to spirituality."*

Phyllis Tickle in a PBS interview stated: *"Every 500 years the church has a giant rummage sale. Christianity is in the midst of a new Reformation that will radically remake the faith."*

I believe literally millions of people in this country are hungry for a new face on Christianity. They are looking for a rational and informed theology, a compelling Christology and a healthy and vital spirituality. A growing number of people are now finding those things in their own ways outside the church walls. Others have just given up. Church statistics are telling the tale and it is not a pretty picture. Every denomination is losing members and closing churches at a growing rate. We can only reorganize our denominations so many times before they become meaningless. Some commentators are predicting the end of the mainline Christian church. If we continue to do what we have always been doing, and expect something different to happen, the end result seems pretty clear.

I believe Progressive Christianity *is* a movement and it is gaining energy and voice. For churches to be part of that movement today, it will require creativity, hard work, willingness to change, and courage by members and church leaders alike. Only time will tell if we have the will to progress to something new. If not, I suspect something new will come to us.

What Do We Mean When We Say, I am a Christian?

Over ten years ago I heard the startling comment, "I don't think of myself as a Christian anymore, but I do think of myself as a follower of Jesus." It was not the comment in itself that was so startling but rather the source. The individual who said those words was a well-known professor of early Christianity and a biblical scholar. He was also a teacher in a seminary training students for the ministry. He had just finished a keynote on early Christianity at a conference I was attending and had opened the microphone to questions from the audience. His talk covered an overview of the first 350 years of Christianity with an emphasis on the political and economic powers influencing the development and nature of the Christian church. It was a fascinating and revealing lecture.

At one point someone from the audience had asked: "With all you have covered here, do you still call yourself a Christian?"

It was interesting to listen to the comments on the professor's response later that evening when several of my colleagues and I gathered for a dinner conversation. With a couple of exceptions we were all clergy. It was a gathering of self-proclaimed progressive Christians so there was a degree of selective process in those who were there. However, a couple of people were put off by the remarks. They begged the question about the propriety of someone who did not consider himself a Christian preparing seminarians for work in the church. But for the most part, the majority of us found ourselves sympathetic with the professor and were struggling with some of same issues.

After a couple of glasses of wine we even began to question if we would call ourselves Christian when push came to shove. We admitted we seldom did so in most of our secular settings. Further, almost every one of us discovered we at least hesitate to tell a stranger we are clergy when on vacations away from home or traveling on airplanes. We all seemed to have funny stories about that.

We spent more than a few minutes wondering what we would call ourselves if we were free to change. We agreed that a follower of Jesus was a bit wordy and would probably give the wrong impression without a lot of explanation. We pondered calling ourselves Jesuits for a moment but realized that would not work. Christist might work following the Buddhist tradition, but someone mentioned there was already a Christist sect. It is very fundamental and conservative, so we let that go as well.

Although there was a lot of bantering and even levity throughout the evening, when I left that night we all agreed it had been an interesting conversation. I would guess over half of us turned our conversation into a sermon or two over the next few weeks. I believe it was a good exercise for most of us that led to deeper thinking about the faith we claimed to represent.

I also believe the world will be well served in the same way as the result of the very public statement by well-known author, Anne Rice. She said she was *"quitting Christianity and renouncing any claim to the title Christian."* However, she added, *"I remain committed to Christ as always but not to being Christian or to being part of Christianity. It's simply impossible for me to belong to this quarrelsome, hostile, disputatious, and deservedly infamous group. For ten years, I've tried. I've failed. I'm an outsider. My conscience will allow nothing else."*

Over the last 15 years I have listened to a growing number of troubled clergy who are in conflicted and or dying churches. (I believe there is a connection.) Sometimes the battles are over LBGT issues. Other times it may be about politics. But far more often, the conflict is rooted in theology, Christology and ideology. Frankly, with rare exceptions, clergy cannot freely teach what they learned in seminary or more importantly, what they have come to believe about their own understanding of the Christian religion, the Bible or their faith. The resultant message is often mixed or muddled and almost always without passion.

Maybe that is why, according to several recent polls, mainline churches continue to decline at an increasing rate, Maybe it's why the number of people who consider themselves spiritual but not religious appears to be growing exponentially. Sadly, more and more of these individuals are leaving organized religion and are finding other ways to satisfy their spiritual needs.

Many of us who consider ourselves progressive have been frustrated over the years because it seemed as if the religious right had co-opted our perspective on Christianity. Somehow our liberal, progressive Christianity was stolen from us. One colleague suggested the media attention of the religious right made him feel like a dog with a can on his tail. He is not alone.

In his recent article published on the *Huffington Post*, Michael Rowe writes, *"Like Rice, our belief in the purity of Christ's teachings has chained us to a body of believers who no longer represent anything of what we believe, and indeed represent the very opposite of what Christ's teachings are. There seems to be precious little Christ in Christianity as it's understood in America today."*

It would be nice to blame it on them, whoever the *them* might be. But at some point we must take some responsibility in this uncomfortable situation. I suspect it has a lot to do with courage of our convictions. I am afraid too many pastors have tried to somehow stay in the middle of the road over the years in order to maintain peace in their respective congregations. Although they seem to know what they are against, pastors have had a hard time articulating what they believe. It appears we are all being forced to confront that confusing weakness from many different directions.

A couple of ago, Richard Dawkins, a leader in the New Atheist movement wrote an article about some of the pain and confusion Christianity continues to cause in our world. And he did not let us mainline folks off the hook. He writes: *"You nice, middle-of-the-road theologians and clergymen, be-frocked and bleating in your pulpits, you disclaim Pat Robertson's suggestion that the Haitians are paying for a pact with the Devil. But you worship a god-man who—as you tell your congregations, even if you don't believe it yourself—'cast out devils.'"* You even believe (or you don't disabuse your flock when they believe) that Jesus cured a madman by causing the devils in him to fly into a herd of pigs and stampede them over a cliff. Charming story, well calculated to uplift and inspire.

It has been interesting to read some of the responses to the Anne Rice statements, both in articles and letters to the editors. Some people discount her comments because she is coming out of a Roman Catholic tradition. But the most frequent type of comment I have seen has been that "Anne Rice should have come to our church. We do not have those issues in our church."

This may be a nice start and I am certain someone felt better about their church by writing it. But a really tough question remains: what do we really mean when we say I am a Christian? What about our worship of a god-man and our reliance on the Bible for the truth? What about substitutionary atonement? How do we respond to those types of questions today . . . honestly?

The good news is that like my experience with the seminary professor and the critiques of the New Atheist movement, the Anne Rice event is stirring things up. People are reading, writing and hopefully having serious conversations in their homes and in their churches. Maybe this will be an opportunity for more church leaders and people in the pews to have honest dialogue about the meaning of Christianity in the 21st Century. It is about time.

Words Do Matter

Scholar, Sallie McFague, begins her classic 1987 book, *Models of God*, with the children's taunt, "Sticks and stones may break my bones but names will never hurt me." She goes on to claim this childhood bravado has always been a lie. Names do matter and names do hurt, she explains. *"What we call something, how we name it, is to a great extent what it is to us. We are preeminent creatures of language, and though language does not exhaust human reality, it qualifies it in profound ways. It follows then, that naming can be hurtful, and that it can also be healing or helpful. The ways we name ourselves, one another, and the world cannot be taken for granted: we must look at them carefully to see if they heal or hurt."*

Although McFague was primarily concerned in this book in the ways we refer to God in our churches, her critique challenged the whole of the Christian spectrum. She called the language we use as anachronistic and hurtful. This book was written over a quarter of a century ago. In spite of prophets and sages like McFague, with some wonderful exceptions, it seems little has changed when I visit churches across the country.

A few years ago I attended a conference being held in a progressive Episcopal Church on the West Coast. The keynote speakers were well known published progressive Christians. One scholar in particular is considered one of the most important leaders of the progressive movement. After the two-day event, several of us attended the Sunday worship service in the church the next morning. I happened to end up sitting next to this same scholar. I was surprised when he stood up at one point, along with the rest of the congregation, and recited something that sounded to me like the Nicene Creed. After the service, while standing with him in the hallway, I asked him if it made him feel uncomfortable reciting something he had refuted in his own scholarly publications. He explained that for him the creeds were just metaphors. He added there was something very special about reciting words with such a long and powerful history. I seem to recall him saying it made him feel connected.

I was frankly stunned and did not know how to respond. I remember saying something like: "What about your six-year old grandchild who is holding your hand and listening to you. Do you explain to her that it's just metaphor? What about the new couple who walked into the church for their first Sunday. Do you state in the bulletin, "We don't really mean it folks. It's just metaphor?" Our conversation ended there.

Admittedly, I have spent most of my life attending something other than high church communities but it was a little baffling to me. Language matters.

When we speak we cannot use footnotes with our words, letting people know we are being metaphorical or are just connecting to the ancients of the past. It seems to me, when we start off with what we believe in a church, what follows should be something we actually believe without footnotes or explanations.

The fact is, Christian creeds were created to divide Christians into those who were right and those who were deemed wrong about what they believed. Christian creeds represent some very serious battles throughout history. If you ended up on the losing side, you may have ended up dead, tortured or in prison. These may have been meaningful metaphors for my scholar friend, but they were never a metaphor for hundreds of thousands of innocent people who died because of them throughout history.

Unfortunately, I do not find this issue only in Anglican churches which are bound to some degree by the *Book of Common Prayer*. I visit a lot of other mainline churches referring to themselves as progressive. Frequently I find myself surprised by the language used throughout the service. Some mainline denominational churches may be progressive on social justice issues but it does not keep them from using language that is, in McFague's words, anachronistic and hurtful. That does not keep them from using theologically regressive language, even when they claim to be progressive.

With some notable exceptions, I regularly hear words like Redeemer, Lord, Savior and sin sprinkled throughout the service. They are used in everything from the call to worship to the benediction. I often wonder what the people in the pews are thinking when they hear me preach and then stand up and recite something completely contrary to the sermon they just told me was inspiring.

I once attended an installation service for a dear friend. Throughout the entire service, I heard most of these words being used in readings, music and even by an executive of the denominational staff. This special event was attended by several visitors. I wondered what they were thinking about the language and what it reflected about the nature of the church. My initial reaction was critical.

I have come to realize, however, that most folks in the pews have probably attended churches like these for most of their lives. They do not hear the language the same way I do. For them, these words are familiar and comfortable sounds that may even bring back warm childhood memories. These folks are unlikely to give thought to the theological meanings or the sociological implications they represent. For them, it is just church and church language has always been there. For many of them, there is a separation between church and the rest of their lives. They probably do not want to spend a lot of time thinking about the meaning and derivation of these words or their impact on society, the church, or their grandchild for that matter. It takes time and energy to educate oneself and education often demands a change. Few people come to church for change. Rather they come for comfort and community. Certainly these good people, both clergy and those in the pews, intend no harm.

I do believe if someone took the time to delve into these anachronistic words with many of these folks, they might very well be surprised or even shocked. I have experienced this phenomenon often when teaching a class or doing a workshop. Talk to any of the progressive Christian scholars who speak in local churches across the country and they will probably share a similar story.

The reality is, many of these words and their theological constructs were created in large part by men struggling for leadership in the evolving Christian movements. These same words have undergirded and have helped create patriarchal societies for far too long. These societies were too often guided more by men seeking power than by sincere spiritual experiences or the teachings of Jesus.

Joan Chittister writes in her wonderful book, *Heart of Flesh*, "*The downward spiral of woman in patriarchal culture, a culture given to the preeminence of father figures over mother-god of earlier civilizations, dizzies the mind.*" How many women have suffered or have been held back because we have used male terms for a deity no one can really define? How many suffer the consequences today?

I believe that same mindset led to the Crusades, the Inquisitions, the so-called witch hunts, misogyny and even the support of slavery, to name just a few of the obvious consequences of words that have taken on power over the centuries. This may seem like ancient history to some. But what happens to a child who grows up believing he or she was born flawed and some wonderful perfect person had to suffer a horrible death to keep them from eternal hell because of that flaw? How did it come to be that the man who put his life on the line, in part to teach us we do not need a broker in order to have a relationship with the God within, ended up becoming the only powerbroker for anyone who wanted to be right with God?

The need to be saved or redeemed like a coupon at the store implies we are incapable of having a direct relationship with the great mystery we choose to call God. It also suggests we are always in need of someone else to fix our lives. I believe this would have been repulsive to the Jesus I have come to know over the last 40 years.

What does the 12-year-old think when she hears her parents reciting that they believe in Jesus Christ, the only begotten Son of God? Does that mean my Jewish, Muslim and Hindu friends are wrong? Does that mean only a boy can be a child of God?

Almost any clergy person who has been to a graduate seminary in the last 40 years no longer maintains Christian beliefs based on Constantine's and Athanasius' Fourth century reformation. More accurately, it could be called a hostile takeover. But it seems once they get into churches they tend to fall back to ways of the past and the customary language of the church. The comment I usually hear is there are few resources to explain the Christian story in a different way with new language. I suspect this may be the task for progressive leadership over the next several decades. In the meantime, there are already some very creative, faithful and spiritually inspired people out there who are doing splendid things with new interpretations and fresh language while telling the Jesus story.

The Future of Progressive Christianity

As I travel throughout the country these days, speaking and preaching, doing workshops, and attending conferences, I am frequently asked the same question. "Do you really think this progressive Christian thing is a movement or is it going to be a passing blip on the radar screen sometime in the near future?" On a few occasions the question comes from someone trying to make a point. But most of the time it is a sincere question from an interested person. Either way, I find myself uncertain how to respond.

That might seem like a strange statement coming from the president of this exciting organization. After all, through my writing and speeches I have been sharing the almost unbelievable data about the growth progressive Christianity has been experiencing. This includes the number of new national organizations referring to themselves as progressive Christians. I have written about the newest studies showing that self-identified progressive churches are actually growing and thriving. We have reviewed numerous exciting books that provide progressive Christians with scholarly support and freedom to approach their Christian faith in a new, and I believe, exciting way. So why do I hesitate to call this a sustainable movement?

First, I believe progressive scholars and theologians have created a Christological vacuum in the last three decades which is not being filled with much in the way of substance. We have done a marvelous job of deconstructing Jesus, but have not done a very good job of reconstructing a Jesus upon whom to build a compelling Christology or progressive Christian spirituality. While there have recently been a few bright lights, the focus for many progressives continues to be on knocking the legs out from underneath tired creedal beliefs, debunking apologetic history or simply focusing on the social gospel. Until I see more signs of that changing, I hesitate to make too many lofty projections.

Secondarily, the term progressive Christianity is still relatively new. Further, it is being used so frequently and loosely, we have created a lot of confusion about what we mean by the term. This confusion opens up a great deal of criticism by those Christians who do not want to see any substance to this as a movement. Most individuals and organizations using this term as a self-identifying adjective, have avoided providing any clarity about their theological bias. They also have not wrestled with their Christological beliefs, at least not publicly.

Far and away my biggest concern is that I am seeing little progressive teaching going on in the churches I visit across the country. This often becomes quite evident after I have done a workshop and preached during Sunday services.

Let me share a story. I did an all day workshop hosted by a Progressive Christianity.org affiliate church somewhere in the Midwest. We had a wonderful turnout for the workshop with attendees from several churches in the area. The next day I day I preached at the regular church services. It was a midsize church with about 200 at worship. As always, I had asked the senior pastor weeks earlier if there were any subjects he would like me to avoid. He assured me I could go for it.

That morning I went for it. I talked about how different our lives and our world might be if we let go of the creedal beliefs as history and started focusing on the spiritual teachings of Jesus. I poised these questions: "Why do we have to believe Jesus was God before we can be a follower of his ways? Why do we have to believe Christianity is the only way before we can practice it?" I pointed out that it didn't seem to be necessary for Buddhists or Hindus as a couple of examples. I went on to share a vision of a faith that was not afraid to encounter the mysteries of life, knowing we have been given a path that leads to fulfillment, peace and joy. Best of all it has been tested over the centuries.

In short it was the kind of sermon I have been giving for over two decades. After the service I was engulfed with a small crow. Many of the folks were obviously emotional. One woman had tears streaming down her face when she said; "I have been waiting for over 60 years to hear someone say those things in my church." Although they were not all quite as emotional, most of the people in this group shared similar feelings. I was a little uncomfortable as the senior pastor watched us from a distance.

After services I joined the pastor and his wife for lunch. Before the soup came he wanted to know what the group was saying to me. When I told him he just stared straight ahead for a full minute. Then he quietly said, "If they knew what I really believed they wouldn't say that." If they knew what he really believed, I wondered? Now here comes the punch line. This wonderful, caring, intelligent man has been the senior pastor at this church for over 17 years and they still don't know what he believes.

If this story was an isolated one it would not bother me. But I have heard variations on this same scenario so many times in the last couple of years I have lost count. Many of the involved churches might have a small group that meets and talks about new scholarship, new Christologies but often the pastor does not attend these gatherings. He or she is careful to avoid the hot-button subjects as the teacher, the preacher or the leader.

If a true progressive Christian movement built on a whole new understanding of theology and the Jesus of history is sustainable, it will not happen because of organizations like ours no matter how hard we work and no matter how many more progressive organizations pop up. It is going to happen in the pulpits and the pews of our local churches across our country. It is going to happen when people in the pews know what their trusted spiritual leaders really believe. It is going to happen when clergy become the teachers again. It is going to happen when people in healthy communities get excited because they are learning and can talk openly about their religious questions. It is going to take open spiritual communities and courageous clergy. We can provide the tools. More importantly we can help each of you share those tools with each other.

So, I am afraid it is still too early to predict if this is indeed a movement that will be sustainable or just another blip on the radar screen of religion movements. I will do whatever to help you make it the former.

CHAPTER TWO

What is God?

The God Thing

There were about 200 people in the audience at a lecture I was giving. Part of my talk was devoted to an overview of the scholarship that has knocked the foundation out of a belief in Jesus as the only begotten Son of God and the sacrifice for the sins of the world. The presentation was well received and the questions lively and thoughtful. Most of them were directed to further clarification of what some saw as a demotion of Jesus. Others were more interested in what my perception might be of the future of Christianity. There seemed to be no rancor in the room and plenty of positive feedback. There also seemed to be genuine excitement.

I did notice one gentleman in the back of the room who started to raise his hand a couple of times but never held it up long enough for me to call on him. When I left the podium he headed directly for me. He waited a minute for some of the others to move away and then he came close. In almost a whisper he said, "So what do progressives do about the God thing?"

It was interesting that the entire audience seemed very comfortable redefining Jesus as an enlightened, wisdom teacher as opposed to the traditional role the church officially collared him with 1,600 years ago. But this man felt compelled to ask his question about God in private and then did not feel comfortable to wait around for a meaningful conversation about it.

I suppose I should not be surprised. I remember a woman who was very active in the church I once led. She had come out of the Southern Baptist tradition and was there in large part because of our openness to the LGBT community. Over the years when she was part of the congregation, she was able to make lots of adjustments. She moved along the progressive road with some ease as we deconstructed the traditional Jesus story and redefined his new role. She was also comfortable when we changed the way we did Sunday morning gatherings. We wrote our own liturgies, sang different kinds of music and regularly had great speakers from different faith traditions. Then it hit her one day. I had long ago moved past a being in the sky who answered prayers, guided us personally, and comforted us when we were down. This God also had expectations about how we should act, believe and think and who ultimately required our worship and adoration. When she realized I did not believe in that kind of God, our relationship took a major downturn.

In spite of the increasing number of people who classify themselves as non-religious or spiritual but not religious, close to 90 percent of our population still say they believe in God according to a Pew poll. However, if we put 100 people in a room who said they believed in God and asked them to come up with a statement that defined and described this thing they called God, I would guess there would be close to 100 statements and probably some red knuckles.

Even if a group of progressive Christians gathered I'm afraid they would have a hard time agreeing on what we mean by the term God. I think it would be relatively easy for most progressives to agree upon what we do not mean. We would be clear, for example, that we were not referring to some anthropomorphic being who may or may not respond to our prayers and supplications. We would not mean the supernatural theism that has haunted Western Christianity for over 1,600 years.

Things might get tense when we started trying to decide if we believed in a God as a separate entity or whether we believed in a non-dualistic creation. Some might use terms like pantheism, panentheism and something called creatheism—God is a holy name of Ultimate Reality. However, I doubt if even that select group could agree on characteristics that fit everyone's perspective—or anyone's perspective for that matter.

Why is this so hard? Some might suggest looking in the Bible for some hint. The challenge is we are talking about a supreme Mystery too big for most of us to fathom. Every day, between our space travels, our amazing telescopes—including the Hubble—and the growing understanding of our universe, scientists constantly find new and truly awesome information about our universe. This quite often raises, rather than answers, more questions. What we do know is there are thousands of solar systems in our Galaxy. An average galaxy contains between 100 billion and one trillion stars. Our own Milky Way galaxy seems to contain about 200 billion stars and we're actually about average in the number of stars.

Scientists tell us that if you make a circle with your thumb and finger, about the size of a half dollar, and look through it into the sky, you will be looking at over a billion solar systems, any one of which could support life.

Hold on to that thought and then let's try and move to some description of God. The challenge, of course, is many of us want some sense of a personal God. But when we talk about a personal God, even for those who truly feel they have had an experience of something they may want to call God, we are not describing God. We are describing our experience of a Great Mystery.

None of us can do anything more than describe our experience. To move from our experience to a description of what God is or what God wants is just something we must admit is beyond us. As Dr. Gordon D. Kaufman, concludes in his book, *In Face Of Mystery*, ". . . *In religious myth and symbols, and in theological doctrines and reflection, we are dealing with matters of profound, ultimately unfathomable mystery; the ultimate meaning of human life, the final truth about the world and our place within it, is simply not available to us humans.*"

So what do progressive Christians do with the God thing? Whatever it is, we must admit if anything, it is a mystery beyond our comprehension. We can rename it as the Supreme Mystery, Ultimate Meaning, Unity or any other imprecise term. But it is time to reject the dualistic idea of two realms, the real and the mysterious, the natural and the supernatural. I now experience the Supreme Mystery almost every day of my life in some situation or place, in some conversation, or with someone.

Secondarily it is time, once again, to acknowledge there is no one, nothing outside of myself that needs my praise, my thanks, or even my obedience. I can choose to live in harmony with the operating forces of the universe or I can ignore them. It will not affect what happens to me when I die. However, I also know there are certain practices in my life that will help me see, hear, taste and feel the awesome miracles around me every day, wherever I go. We must learn to be comfortable in the midst of the unknown.

God Talk

At one time in my career, I had the opportunity and privilege to meet with a group of people who were searching for new ways to tell the Christian story. The group had gathered in Chicago to search for ways to communicate and hopefully find new language to communicate the message of Jesus to children. It was made up of clergy, active lay-people and scholars.

More than once, while participating in one of these gatherings, I was overwhelmed with a sense of gratitude. I wondered, "How did I get so lucky to be involved with such bright, informed, caring people who really are dedicated to making a positive change in their lives, in the lives of our children and in the world?"

The conversation moved along pretty smoothly until we got to the topic of God. It was not that we disagreed but rather it was how we talk about something we agreed cannot be talked about.

It was relatively easy, among all these conversations, to agree upon what we did not mean. It was clear for example, that we were not referring to some anthropomorphic being who may or may not respond to our prayers and supplications. We did not mean some supernatural theism that has haunted Western Christianity for over 1600 years. We were not talking about a separate entity and we had interesting conversations about whether there was any dualism in all creation.

Sometimes we tossed around terms like pantheism, panentheism and something called creatheism (God is a holy name of Ultimate Reality). But we did not seem to be getting any closer to finding terms, descriptions or even characteristics that fit everyone's perspective—or anyone's perspective for that matter. It became particularly challenging when we realized we were trying to communicate something about this yet indescribable, mysterious phenomenon to children. How do we teach our children about something that is indescribable?

Flying home from Chicago while pondering all this, I pulled out some of my notes from our meetings. I was reminded that the great theologian Paul Tillich once suggested that we should stop using the word God for a hundred years because it is so loaded with historical and emotional baggage. I suspect his suggestion may have been made in jest but either way it was intended to make a point.

In one of our sessions, a New Testament scholar pointed out that Jesus would have been appalled with what Western Christianity has done with the term God. He pointed out that as a Galilean Jew, Jesus most likely thought and spoke in the Aramaic language. He would have used Alaha where we often see the word God in Christian scripture. According to Aramaic scholars like Neil Douglas-Klotz, the closest translation of Alaha into English would be Sacred Unity, Oneness or Allness. Douglas-Klotz argues with this understanding there could not have been the kind of dualism that is still so pervasive in Western Christian theology.

Although this perspective was helpful, it was still more about what the term God did not mean rather than what it does mean to progressives Christians. This challenge is not new for thinking and aware people. It is much easier to use God to explain that which we do not understand or to support our personal bias.

Rudolf Bultmann, brilliant theologian of the last century, struggled with this same issue. He wrote a about it in an excellent essay called, *The Crisis of Faith*. In it Bultmann points out that we are constantly confronting our fragile world, dealing with finite things with our vulnerability. He suggests there is a power we experience but neither our wishes nor our will can change it or bend it to our needs. He also points out we do not create some of the most beautiful, powerful, lofty moments in our lives. As wonderful as those experiences are, we cannot make them last. Eternity escapes us. Bultmann concludes there is a power controlling the temporal and the eternal. He calls this power, God. He writes, *"This 'mysterious power'—the power which limits man and is master of him, even when he thinks he is his own master—is God."*

In his 1985 book, *A Primer on Radical Christianity*, Gene Marshall points out *"Bultmann was not referring to a supernatural power out there somewhere who invades our natural realm."* He simply says this mysterious power all of us have experienced every day of our lives is what he is refers to as God.

After taking a brief look at some writings of Catholic theologian Hans Kung, Protestant scholar, Schubert Ogden and Rabbi Harold Kushner, Marshall posits it is time to get rid of what he refers to as the Two Story Mind-Block—*"the assumption that there are two realms: the natural and the supernatural."* Marshall calls for a new metaphor for this mysterious reality. He writes, *"The new religious metaphor (which pictures the awe-filled experience of reality opening up in the center of ordinary reality) enables us to open ourselves to reality in both its familiar naturalness and in its awe-producing strangeness. Reality is both known and unknown, ordinary and profoundly mysterious. Only when we accept and honor this mysteriousness in the midst of ordinary life, will we stop trying to wrap life up in neat intellectual boxes."*

I found this helpful but I was still left wondering how we talk about this new metaphor, this mysterious reality. Serendipitously, while I was in the midst of this struggle to find ways to talk about God, I pulled out a *National Geographic* magazine. It focused on the unlikely possibility that we earthlings are alone in the universe. The article featured more of those almost unimaginable pictures of "small" parts of the universe taken from the improved Hubble telescope. In one photo we can see a galaxy 150 million light years away. It dwarfs our own Milky Way phenomenon.

The pictures alone should be enough to shake our common sensibilities. But the article made a good case for the idea that our little, insignificant planet is probably one of many capable of sustaining life. Like so many of the Hubble revelations however, it forces anyone who really wants to take in what is revealed to us about our teeny perspective, that trying to put objective, quantitative qualities onto something we call god is a little silly. I wondered if the early church father, St. Tertullian, knew more than he understood when he wrote over 1800 years ago, *"That which is infinite is known only to itself."*

I was brought back to Marshall's comment that it is time to *"stop trying to wrap life up in neat little intellectual boxes."*

What happens when I open myself, without fear, to this Mysterious Reality in my life? I may not be able to identify it or quantify it, but I can describe what it is like to experience it or experience something I do not understand. I can share the ways I intentionally live and think that cause me to experience it more often as I open myself to both the natural and its awe-producing strangeness. As I engage the awe-producing strangeness more and more often, it does not seem so strange at all. It may also be that I simply grow more comfortable with it. Maybe most importantly, I can happily admit I could be wrong about all of this. Yet like a child, I still get excited with the awesome discoveries I have made and will continue to make on this journey.

After all, no child is a stranger to awe.

God and the New Atheist Movement

I love the witty British scientist and atheist, Richard Dawkins. I've never met the man, but I still love him and I am glad he continues to get the press he seems to generate. The funny thing is I agree with much of what he says. Yes, I realize he has set up a straw man god, and a silly mythical Jesus most people with some minimal theological training would simply dismiss. But the truth is, this straw man god and mythical Jesus are still represented, prayed to, bargained with, called up, blamed or thanked in the vast majority of our churches today.

I attended a conference a few years ago at one of the better known seminaries in the country. At one point, representatives from several of the denominational offices were invited to share their thoughts about the future of the church.

When the conversation shifted to new theologies and a response to the new atheist movement, I heard nothing but confusing and convoluted responses. These denominational leaders seemed to be more defensive than creative, more dogmatic than inspiring. In their attempts to hold onto a tired tradition, they seemed to admit they had given little thought to anything new. They used the word God with such authority you would have assumed we all understood what that word meant. It did not seem to fly with most of the young seminarians in the audience.

For over 30 years, I have been encouraging people in our mainline churches to let go of the ancient theistic God we incorporated into the Greek Christian tradition nearly 2000 years ago. Yet, we cannot to seem to let go. I have had little problem convincing most people we do not need to hold on to the traditional story of the historical Jesus. I suppose I have the *Jesus Seminar* and other good scholars to thank for that. But I have run into a dense wall far too many times when I suggest we need to get rid of the God in the sky who hears our prayers and fixes things for us when we are good children. I do not believe God is an external being, a supernatural power, always prepared to intervene in human history. Nor can I perceive of a God who is a parent or judge and rewards and punishes obedient or disobedient children according to their proper behavior.

While most progressive Christians no longer hold on to this simplistic, even childish concept of God, with rare exceptions we still talk about what

35

God wants from us in our churches and even in our homes. When I travel across the country to progressive churches my teeth are on edge when I listen to readings, prayers, songs, and rituals. They seem to imply God is waiting for our correct action or personally wants us to do something like feed the hungry or take care of the poor. Let's face it, most pledge drives start with God's call upon us to give. We still do petitionary prayers in most congregations as part of the worship service.

With what we now know about the immense universe, black holes, evolution, and our tiny little planet, isn't it time to change the entire paradigm? Do we really think there is some entity, some power that needs to be pleased? At best this seems like an arrogant, superstitious and even an idolatrous assumption. Even the traditionalists tell us God is unfathomable, all powerful. Why would we assume this 'I Am' needs anything from us? Any such idea suggests a theistic and dualistic model we must eventually let go of. Nor have we come very far when we think it's a big deal to call this entity Mother/Father God.

You see, I think we have had it all wrong for a very long time. I do not think Jesus was telling his followers how they were supposed to act or behave in order to please God. I believe he, like other inspired wisdom teachers, was offering his teachings about how to *experience* this thing we so casually call God. What did Jesus mean? We have no way of knowing, but I suspect he meant something very different than what we normally perceive. I believe it is far more likely he told his followers that by living a certain way, by extending themselves on behalf of others, by loving generously, for example, they too could experience Alaha. Neal Douglas-Klotz, an Aramaic scholar, suggests this Alaha term would best be translated as Sacred Unity, All-ness or Oneness.

I do not believe Jesus' teachings were channeled from God so he could tell us what God wants from us. Rather, they were the result of his profound experience of a complete Unity of all life. That peace and sense of completeness eludes mere words. Wisdom teachers tell us this phenomenon cannot be known. It can only be experienced and anyone has the opportunity to have that experience. There are many paths and they are teachable. They can lead ultimately to an experience of the sacred, the Divine, the "I am" so many people are searching for. We could even call this heaven on earth.

So why is it so hard to give up the theistic concept of God? For some, it is because that God has been a comfort for them. In some cases, this model of God has been the only source of true love in their lives. But for the vast majority of people who hold onto that traditional God, the alternative is just too scary. We are talking here about a giant mystery, an unknown.

In Western culture, most of us are extremely uncomfortable with unknowns. That discomfort has led to some pretty amazing scientific discoveries but it is no help on a truly spiritual journey. That is why I find most people are uncomfortable with theologian, Dr. Gordon D. Kaufman, who concludes in his book, *In Face Of Mystery*, ". . . *In religious myth and symbols, and in theological doctrines and reflection, we are dealing with matters of profound, ultimately unfathomable mystery; the ultimate meaning of human life, the final truth about the world and our place within it, is simply not available to us humans.*"

That is why I love Richard Dawkins and the rest of the New Atheist movement. Their sometimes brilliant, and, often penetrating work, is forcing more and more people to rethink what they mean by the Germanic word, God. As they make us aware of the simplistic ways we are still thinking about this god in the sky, we can become more aware of the awesome mystery that lies before us. Then we may begin to learn the real meaning of faith. With the help of a teacher who has experienced the Grand Mystery, we can move toward something that can never be known but only experienced. What an amazing journey that can be.

". . . *what is called knowledge in everyday parlance is only a small island in a vast sea that has not been traveled . . . Hence the existential question for the knower is this: Which does he love more, the small island of his so-called knowledge or the sea of infinite mystery?*" *Foundations of Christian Faith by Karl Rahner,* The Crossroad Publishing Company, 1982

I Wondered Why

I have often wondered why it is so important for some people to keep Jesus as the only way. As president of ProgressiveChristianity.org, I get angry email from concerned Christians on a regular basis. The vast majority of them start off by being pretty polite. "I agree with much of what is on your website but are you saying that perhaps the beliefs a Muslim holds, or a Hindu holds, or a Buddhist holds, is just as true as the beliefs a Christian holds?"

It is not unusual for these same people to quote a familiar passage put into the mouth of Jesus by the writer of John: "No one comes to the Father except through me." (John 14: 6) I used to spend a lot of time trying to explain the historical context of that passage of John. It was probably written over 80 years (two generations) after Jesus' death. It is the least historical document in the Gospels.

It is a reflection of a tumultuous period when the followers of Jesus were being rejected in the synagogues and were no longer considered Jews by their families and friends. It was the beginning of recriminations that tore apart religious leaders, social settings and families at the deepest level.

When this is understood, many of the Christological sayings of the writer of John take on new meaning and make a lot more sense. This includes the unfortunate translation of John's condemnation of the Jews in general. This is a poor translation taken out of context. It should have been translated as only the Jews who rejected us or did not accept Jesus as the messiah. The one fact that all biblical scholars agree on is that Jesus was born a Jew, he lived as a Jew and he died a Jew.

In every case my efforts to try and explain how these passages came to be were met with everything from strong disapproval to outright rage, including a couple of death threats from these concerned Christians.

What is it that makes it so important for Jesus to be the only way, the only one, the initiator of the one true religion? There is so much evidence making this a very illogical conclusion. Is it our competitive human nature? Is it our need to be right in spite of all evidence to the contrary? Is it fear?

Why can't we simply allow Jesus to be a very special human being who had a profound experience (or experiences) of the divine that changed his understanding of reality. My guess is, when people noticed this change, Jesus was asked to spend the rest of his short life trying to teach others how they might have the same experience of the Oneness with God. They wanted to learn how to experience Oneness with all creation, how to live in Sacred Unity.

Is he the only one who has had this experience? Of course not! Books and libraries are full of the stories of others who had such an experience. They were also changed by their new awareness with new eyes to see and ears to hear. You may even know one of these people today. Many of them became teachers like Buddha, Lao Tzu and Mohammed. Their beloved followers also wrote about them years later. If you read carefully and get through the hyperbole, you will see their experiences were very similar and their teachings covered much of the same themes. It all starts with becoming aware of who we really are—part of the divine Oneness. God, or the Divine connection is not out there, but within.

So how do we pick our teacher or teachers? We search for one who speaks to our culture, social situation and willingness to commit. If I wanted to climb Mount Everest for the first time I would find someone who has been there, listen to what they have to teach me about doing it and try my best to follow that path. I want to follow someone I sincerely believe has been there. I want to focus on the teachings, not the teacher. I want to commit to the path, not worship the one who made the path.

How do I know I have the right teacher? Buddha reportedly said, *"Believe nothing, no matter where you read it, or who said it, no matter if I have said it, unless it agrees with your own reason and your own common sense."* Jesus' disciples were concerned about knowing if they were on the right path after he was gone. He soothed their apprehension by telling them, *". . . you will know by the fruit that it bears."* In other words we have been given the tools to assess the truth if we are willing to use them.

New Testament scholar, Robert Funk, once wrote that if Christianity is going to survive, we would need to *"demote Jesus . . . who has been isolated as the divine son of God, coeternal with the Father"* to his true persona as a wisdom teacher. Although I do not disagree with Funk's conclusion, I do not see it as a demotion but rather as a freeing. What an incredible thing it would be if we pulled Jesus off the cross as an icon to be worshipped and let him be free to be the teacher again. What an empowering thing it would be if we actually became disciples of a human being who experienced the Absolute Oneness of all Creation and then said, *"follow me and you too can experience what I experienced."* What would our churches be like if that really happened? Then we might have to take Jesus' egalitarian teachings on compassion, non-judgment, forgiveness, unity, love, and the Divine connection within more seriously. Maybe that's the problem.

CHAPTER THREE

Does the Church
Have a Future?

A Painful Experience

The state of mainline—old-line—churches is not good. The statistics on dwindling church memberships and data on the number of churches that are closing is disheartening. I share this information in workshops and lectures all over the country in the hope people will realize we have to do something different in our faith communities if the church as we know it is going to survive. Let me be clear. When I say "as we know it" I mean as something different than the ultra-conservative, fundamentalist, cultic, fear-based or abundance-promising churches that appear to be surviving if not thriving in our country.

Most of the time, I think people do not believe me. I am frequently asked the source of my information. Other times someone outright challenges my numbers based on their own experience in their respective church. For the record, most of data I use comes from an annual publication produced by the National Council of Churches. The NCC is dependent on numbers from the respective member denominations. Frankly they are probably softened. I have had several conversations with denominational executives who confess, off the record, that the numbers they give to NCC are optimistic. According to other studies, mainline churches are closing on an average of somewhere between seven and ten thousand churches a year.

When I present these statistics to folks who have gathered to have a conversation about the benefits of moving in a more progressive direction, I must admit, I have become a bit desensitized to them. They are just numbers, after all, but frankly they help me make a case for change.

One two day workshop I did felt very different, however. It was painful—very painful, actually. It was a relatively small turnout, maybe a little less than 60 people both days. It turned out there were people from about ten churches represented. The average age of those in attendance was something over 70 years. The first presentation I offered was about the state of the church. At that point, I took a close look at the status of our beloved denominational churches. No one challenged my numbers or even seemed surprised. They were clearly more interested in solutions—solutions that were probably too little, too late for most of them.

During the break for lunch I had planned to take a quiet walk to get centered and a little refreshed. One gentleman asked if he could talk to me for just a minute. It turns out he was really distraught. He wanted to know if I had any ideas about what he could do for his dying church. He told me he had been part of his church for over 50 years. Apparently they were going to have to close their doors after the first of the year. "What do we do?" he asked again clearly in desperation.

I encouraged him to find another church or start a home-based church group with the 10 or 12 people who were still there. He nodded his head like he agreed but his obvious pain hit me. We chatted for another minute or two but I felt helpless.

As I headed off on my planned walk, a woman standing a few feet away came up to me before I could take three steps. She asked if she could speak to me for just a minute. She told be her name was Helen and explained she was from another church destined for closing. She had apparently overheard my previous conversation. The circumstances were a little different. They had a building to sell and hoped to start a faith community in a storefront in the same area. She wanted to know if I thought it would work.

I asked what her little group planned to do that was different from what they had been doing when they had their own building. She looked at me for a long time and then with tears in her eyes she said she didn't know. "We are all pretty old you know," she said wearily.

I was at a total loss for words. Without thinking I put my arms around this loyal, dedicated, faithful old woman and just hugged her. It did not seem right. Here was this woman who we all know had served her church for most of her eight decades. She visited the sick in hospitals; baked cakes for the potlucks; sewed costumes for the children's pageant; raised money for the new building and was probably a consistent tither for her entire life. Now, in the years when the church should have been serving her, her beloved church was dissolving before her eyes.

I was exhausted the next day, as I flew home from the other side of the country. I could not get Helen out of my mind. Frankly I could not get the many Helens across the country I have met in the last fifteen years, out of my mind. That's when it hit me. I sat there stunned. I had tears coming down my cheeks. I realized my statistics were no longer just numbers. They were real, hurting people who have lost their cherished churches during a time in their respective lives when they most needed them.

I was never certain if all these folks had come to the lecture and workshop hoping to find the silver bullet, some miraculous idea that might save their respective churches or if they simply wanted to share their stories and their pain. Either way, I have not been able to get them out of my mind or my heart. I hope someone got something out of our time together. I know I did, but it was a very painful learning experience.

Dandelions in the Cracks of the Sidewalks

Does the Christian church have a future in the Western World? Does a contemporary form of Christianity have a future in the United States? Certainly it would seem so. The vast majority of the population still refers to themselves as Christian. However, things seem to be changing. In 1950, 91 percent of the U.S. population called themselves Christian. According to more recent polls by both Gallup and Harris, less than 75 percent of the nation still claims to be Christian.

In the 1950s roughly 70 percent of the population said they attended church on a weekly basis. Today, that claim is something closer to 48 percent of the population across the country overall. It remains considerably higher in the Southern states and much lower on both the West and East Coasts. It appears even these numbers are suspect according to several trailing surveys. Follow-up interviews have indicated these figures are probably something less than 30 percent nationally with similar regional differences.

In 1948, two percent of Americans interviewed by Gallup volunteered that they had no religion. The number stayed in that range until about 1970. By 1972, Gallup measured five percent with no religion. In 2008 the same poll suggested 12 percent of the population volunteered no religion with an additional three percent refusing to answer the question.

I would suggest the falling membership of mainline denominations is a more reflective statistic of the current situation in the U.S. today than any other measurement. The number of Christians who identify themselves as Protestant, including denominational, non-denominational, evangelical, Charismatic, and other, has fallen from 91 percent to 77 percent. Mainline or old-line denominations lose the most members. According to Gallup reports, roughly half the members of mainline churches are over 50 years old. Other pollsters suggest the number is at least a decade older. Six-in-ten Americans aged 70 and older (62 percent) identify themselves as Protestant. But young adults, ages 18 to 29, are much more likely than those age 70 and older to say they are not affiliated with any particular religion (25 percent vs. eight percent).

You get the idea. Since it is difficult to get accurate current information, I will not quote figures about the number of mainline churches closing across the country every year. But let me point out that more than one denominational executive has told me, off the record, that "we are probably closing dozens of churches every month." Another executive from a large denomination told me that if their denomination was a business, they would immediately close hundreds of churches as non-redeemable.

Any way you look at it, the picture is not pretty for those of us who love the church. So why do we keep doing what we are doing? As they say on the farm, are we beating a dead horse? At this point, I believe, as do all of us at here at ProgressiveChristianity.org, healthy spiritual communities are an important part of a healthy culture and society. We are not ready to give up and we still have hope. More importantly, we are seeing some very interesting and even exciting things happening on the horizon promising new life. However, these are not the churches or faith communities of the past.

Let's be perfectly clear. The Christian church, by design, does not change easily. Unlike science, business, technology, and social practices, the church has built-in brakes designed to withstand change. When the scientific community discovers new information, it is tested, openly discussed and when necessary assumptions and models are changed. However, from a selected group of books written after decades of oral tradition with multiple additions and redactions, the fourth century church deemed just one book, supposedly created by God, was to be considered Sacred. The church declared this Canonized book as Holy and finite. During the first three centuries of the early Christian movements, there were great debates about who and what Jesus was. What was his mission? Many of these debates were politically motivated. All were shaped by a Greek and Roman world view wholly unlike the culture of the man they were supposed to be honoring. These debates were more about power than they were about the experience of the divine. And just to make certain everything was tethered nice and neatly, the church created Creeds so it could officially decide who was correct and who was heretical with punishments that never fit the crime.

So here we are, in a world utterly different than anyone in the first or the fourth or even the 16th century could possibly have imagined. In large part, our churches continue to do things the way we have always done them. All too often it is still about power.

In the last 50 years, we have experienced an explosion of information about the historical Jesus, about the conflicted roots of the early Christian church, about the formation of religions and myth, and about the manipulative formation of what we refer to as the Bible. This new information should have changed not only our thinking about the personhood of Jesus, but certainly should have changed the way we think about doing church. Because it has not happened churches are becoming less and less relevant for our time. This leads to church doors closing on the fingertips of those who have supported their precious communities for most of their lives with finances, hard work and a lot of heart.

Where then is the new life I referred to? I find myself thinking of them as dandelions in the cracks of the institutional concrete.

First, we have seen some wonderful examples of new life in many of our affiliate churches that are intentional. They have publicly positioned themselves as churches endorsing a new way of approaching their Christian tradition. The ones that seem to experience the greatest energy and even growth in this declining market start with a more contemporary theology and Christology. They move from there to an emphasis on values, relationships and spirituality rather than on beliefs and creeds. Some of the qualities we can easily identify in these churches include active pluralism—real connections with communities of other faith traditions, shared space and the use of combined rituals. Another characteristic we have observed is a comfort, acceptance and even affirming relationships with people from the GLTB communities. In all of these vital churches we have studied there is no sexual orientation issue.

While many of these models tend to show up in new start churches, we have seen real change occur in several older mainline denominational churches. This usually happens with a congregation that has decided it wants to re-identify itself as a new kind of church. Most of these churches, generally led by an inspired pastor, went through a process of discovery. Probably the most consistent quality we have seen in these change agents is their ability to articulate a clearly redefined purpose of the church. They are usually spiritually grounded and have a positive vision for the future. It helps if they have some skills in dealing with conflict.

Some of these talented folks have their own creative ideas and are entrepreneurial. Others have used one of the dozen consultants who are now available, some with more success than others. Some are using a whole new operating system in order to view not only the church, but their faith and even their world perspective as well.

Dr. Rev. Tom Thresher, author of a *Reverent Irreverence*, has used his experience with Integral Theory to create new possibilities for the church and Christianity. His book tracks his experience in a church he pastors in Western Washington and offers a vision for change in the future church. He provides a model integrating Eastern wisdom and Western enlightenment. Yet it leaves room for traditional as well as progressive Christians and anyone else who would like to experience what he refers to as Christ consciousness. When those in leadership realize the purpose of the church is to help others experience the Divine at the deepest levels, then the focus of the congregation is on practices and behavior and not on beliefs and creeds. I believe Thresher is onto something very important.

I am hopeful the young people in the Emerging movement will continue to offer something substantial to a new and vital understanding of the

Christian faith. Phil Snider and Emily Bowen, both ordained clergy in the Disciples of Christ church, certainly believe there are plenty of opportunities in the Emergent movement to help the whole church evolve. In 2010 they wrote a book called, *Toward a Hopeful Future: Why the Emergent Church is Good News for the Mainline Congregations*. As co-pastors of a church in Springfield Missouri, they speak and write from experience. Like Thresher, they offer not only a vision but a model. Best of all, they provide tools and many tips garnered from their own experience of trying to accommodate young people from this changing spectrum. They make it very clear that our mainline churches cannot keep doing things the same way and expect these young people to conform to our ways, our theologies and Christologies. Emergents are as uncomfortable with absolute certainty as they are with our typical mainline worship services. But they certainly represent dandelions in the sidewalk cracks of our church institutions.

One of the other places we continue to see new life is in the growing number of people who are forming intentional spiritual groups in their homes and small meeting rooms. Typically, they have no plans to grow into a traditional church. We continue to get requests for educational materials for children and adults, for rituals for small groups and simple music they can use in their gatherings. They meet on a variety of days of the week and frequently share a meal. While some call themselves Christians, the majority seem to feel they do not need to identify with any particular religion. They often create their own blend of rituals borrowing from a variety of traditions. It will be interesting to see how these groups develop over the years but their formation indicates a growing hunger for community and spirituality not being met in our typical churches.

So yes, there are reasons we are still here. I believe we are experiencing a move away from creeds and Christological debates toward a greater focus on values, behavior and spirituality. There will continue to be a more interest in a spiritual path than in dogma. I still see purpose in forming communities to help each other develop a Christ consciousness and to provide the opportunities to experience the Divine. I am certain it will happen at some point, even if it does not happen in our existing churches. The opportunities, the teachers and the models are there and ready to go. The question is, are we?

What are We Teaching?

I was sitting in an almost empty coffee shop one Sunday evening. I was reviewing my notes I was planning to use for a Confirmation class I would be teaching in our nearby church. Suddenly a group of about 12 young people in their late teens and early twenties excitedly barged into the restaurant. They began pushing tables together so they could all sit down, ending up right next to my table. They obviously seemed like nice kids who were smiling and affectionate with each other. This gathering was clearly a regular thing. They knew right where they were going to sit, they knew the waitress and apparently they knew what they were going to order. No one wanted menus.

I had a pretty good idea where they were coming from because they all had their Bibles. Each one was marked with those little color tags so one could quickly find the correct chapter or book. For the most part those Bibles look used and worn. I admit I wondered if they ever carried a new Bible out in public before it looked worn.

I quickly learned I was correct. They had come from a nearby mega church with over 10,000 members at that time. More interesting for many of us, they had vital and expanding youth and young adult programs. These programs and their attendance made the rest of mainline church leaders in the area sadly envious.

One of the young men saw I was looking at them. He smiled and asked me, "Are you a Christian." I hesitated, and then said, "You might say that. I am a pastor of a local church down the street." I did not add my normal qualifier, "I may not be a Christian by your standards."

This young man was very impressed. He immediately told the rest of the group I was a pastor. I did not know that for them a pastor is not someone who necessarily leads worship in a church. It is not about someone who has spent four years of college and four years of graduate school training to do a job. It is not about someone who has a current library of over 400 books. For them a pastor is someone who is a "true and committed believer."

One young woman pushed another chair over to their reconfigured table and invited me to join them. After I got settled, I told them I wanted to know something. "Why do you folks spend your Sunday evenings in church?"

One guy, who seemed to be a leader, explained that when they were together like this "they got closer to the Lord." Another, almost apologetically, admitted she went primarily for the music. But one fellow said he was there because he was learning so much. Excitedly waving his Bible, he went on to say, "Isn't it amazing that the entire Jesus story was the completion of prophecy hundreds of years before Jesus' birth?"

Everyone nodded and then three or four more of them enthusiastically agreed they also went because they were learning so much. One young man explained to me that the Bible was like the manual you get when you buy a new car. "Except the Bible," he explained, as it held it up in the air, "is a manual for life." All of the heads nodded again. "We have classes every week at the church on Sunday evenings and we also get together every Thursday for Bible study at Jeff's house," one person added.

When I asked them if they knew how the Bible came to be written, they were quick to respond. It was written by God they explained. I said does that mean "God had a pen and paper?" Without hesitation one young woman said no, but it was dictated by God through the hands of his devoted believers throughout history. Again the heads all nodded.

My confirmation notes for that evening were about the split between the Northern and Southern Kingdom. So I asked the group if they knew about the Northern Kingdom and the Southern Kingdom that split in the 10th century BCE. "Yes," a couple of them responded. I asked why they thought that happened. I was impressed when one young man responded that it was because Solomon's son wanted the other ten tribes to pay more taxes and the tribal leaders rebelled. With barely contained excitement, he shared why it was wonderful. You see, he explained, this had all been predicted in scripture because the ten tribes "had forsaken God's ways." In Isaiah, he posited, it states that all of the tribes would be united when Jesus Christ reigns in his kingdom and all of the tribes would get along. For the record it does say something like that in Isaiah 11:12-13 but it refers to a Prince of Peace not Jesus.

Everyone in this group looked at him with pride. This young man knew his Bible. And then it hit me. They believed they were getting an education. They thought they were working with a manual not only promising you a good life but life after death. They thought they were learning something about history. They were genuinely excited about what they were learning and how it had changed their lives. They felt they had found a way to maneuver through the difficult challenges life throws at every one of us. They believed they had the answers and the rest of us were wandering in the desert.

They had no clue how the Bible came to be. They had the idea the Bible was always looking backwards trying to explain what happened with myth and metaphor. They had no thoughts about anything in the Bible supporting misogyny, racism, child abuse, murder and sexism just to name a few unpleasant human frailties that seem to be supported by an angry God. In their minds they were getting an education that had been dictated by God. That young man's ability to quote scripture, or something close to scripture, made him a hero.

I believe one of the failures of the mainline churches is not taking religious education seriously for over a century. It is true that today more churches are taking advantage of excellent educational products provided by organizations like Living the Questions, publications and lectures by the Jesus Seminar and Westar, and our own PC.org website and publications. Unfortunately they are probably too little, too late. Since most of these resources tend to focus on the deconstruction of the old Christian story, they are little more than a confirmation of what aging members of our congregations have suspected for decades. This new information may be interesting for them, but their children—and now grandchildren—who have never been committed to a community-do not get it.

And where is the next generation? We chased those away 40 years ago. What they heard as children in our churches did not compute with their later educational experiences. And frankly churches did not seem like a place to experience joy. For far too many of them, churches were more about fights and rules than they were about love and compassion. They were more about judgment and prejudice than inclusiveness. Surveys indicate they did not see churches as models for anything they would want to emulate in their lives. Churches for them certainly did not provide a manual for living or how to experience eternal life.

For me this is sad. I believe there are teachings in the Jesus tradition that can guide one into a more fulfilling, meaningful life. There has always been a path that can lead one into an experience of heaven here on earth; a path that can split the curtain between the eternal and the finite. With some wonderful exceptions we, as the institutional church, have not been teaching it. It has been easier to focus on the oughts rather than the real opportunities to experience new life.

I cannot help but wonder where the Christian churches would be today if we had listened to people like David Friedrich Strauss over 200 years ago. What would we have been teaching in our churches today about myth? What if our church institutions had celebrated the cutting edge work of people like George Gordon, Walter Rauschenbusch and Harry Emerson Fosdick in the 19th and 20th centuries instead of trying to silence them? I suspect we would be in a different place now.

So that brings me to today. What are we teaching in our churches? Are we still teaching mythology like it is history to our children? Are we still telling people they ought to act in a certain way in order to please a theistic God? Are we still insisting the historical Jesus had a unique birth, was sacrificed as part of God's plan for redemption and without a belief in that you are not a Christian or even a follower of Jesus? Or do we just ignore all of that tradition? And if so what have we put in its place?

I believe the survival of a modern Christianity will depend on the way we answer these questions.

CHAPTER FOUR

Evolving Christianity

From Belief to Faith

In the mid-nineties, I was invited to participate in a new organization that was intended to give a more public voice to the "liberal" form of Christianity. Frankly, the energy from this fledgling organization stemmed from a common desire to respond to the growing influence of the religious right on the politics and culture of the time.

We also had a second agenda directed at reviving the obviously declining mainline churches. The underlying assumption by the founders was that if we enlivened our congregations with a new message about the Christian call for a more just world and provided opportunities to live out our call "to do unto the least of these," more people would be interested in finding ways to help create a more just world. Then our congregations would flourish again. At that time in my life, finding ways to grow churches was a primary concern.

The original members of this forming committee were quite impressive. They included two seminary theologians and a couple of university professors, a denominational executive, and four or five ministers who were leading churches with active social justice ministries. It was a stimulating group of people and I was excited to be part of something that held such promise.

As the group discussed different ways we might organize and get our message out to churches and the general public, I had the growing feeling we were avoiding a serious issue. What, I wondered, was the theology and Christology driving our mission? At one point I suggested we go around the room and share our personal perspectives on Jesus and on the term God. I also suggested that we include how these perspectives would impact our understanding of the mission of our group.

When asked for clarification, I responded: "What is driving this mission? Is it because the Bible says we should do these things? Do we believe that Jesus was the Son of God? Is God telling us to do these things? Are we suggesting that people should do good works to get into heaven?"

For a full minute there was dead silence in the room. Then there was a lot of mumbling, twisting and turning. No one was looking at me as they grumbled among themselves. Finally the leader of the discussion, a wonderful, kind and gentle scholar, suggested I write a paper and present it at the next gathering. He suggested we could each take turns doing this. I heard groans.

It will probably come as no surprise that my presentation did not go well. I do remember one thing in particular that seemed to anger more than one participant. I suggested it was time to let the *Trinity* go. Yes, I know there are lots of nice and even clever ways to re-interpret the Trinity. Many of today's Biblical scholars and theologians have gone to great lengths to formulate ways the church can still be Trinitarian as we allow Jesus to become more human. There have been some lovely, even poetic ways of doing just that. But most of the time, these theologians are no longer referring to the Father, The Son, and the Holy Spirit. They are referring in large part to the spiritual components of the number three.

Today we know the whole Trinitarian concept was simply a solution to a dilemma that occurred when the Roman church decided Jesus was God, not just of God or a likeness of God. Constantine wanted to get rid of Arius and his devoted followers. Arius had nearly lost his life in his brilliant attempt to show Jesus as an angelic-like human, God's first creation. But the more politically situated Athanasius won the battle with the phrase, "The Son was fully God, co-equal and co-eternal with the Father."

With Jesus now officially deemed God, the Roman church could now legally condemn non-believers and arrest such trouble makers like Arias, a popular priest and his followers. With this, Constantine and the Roman Church were officially wedded. But there had to be a way to explain this new victory. How would a monotheistic church explain two Gods? It was the term Trinity that came to the rescue, a term borrowed from Tertullian over a century before. In my opinion, this was the sad start to the official church. It is still a bone in the throat to people of other faith perspectives. It is still a stumbling block today for those who search for a more relevant faith tradition.

I will never be certain why this concept was so important to so many members of this group. I do believe it was about power. But it had become clear I was going to be a thorn in the side of their valiant efforts, so I moved on.

My point in sharing this story is that I must admit for some reason, beliefs seemed important in this situation. It made sense to me that if we were going to attempt to counteract a growing group of Christians who had very clear beliefs we needed to speak from our own common beliefs. If we were going to try and publically distinguish ourselves from the religious right in the political arena, we needed to be able to demonstrate that we had an identifiable, legitimate foundation for our actions.

On the other hand, I would argue that all creeds or beliefs deemed Orthodox have been created by people far more concerned with power and influence than about spirituality, equality or even truth. Too often, the proponents of true belief have been more interested in being right than about being true.

That is precisely why *ProgressiveChristianity.org* states right from the onset what we mean when we say we are Progressive Christians. We give a list of what we refer to as the 8 Points. Are these beliefs? Are these creeds? I suppose they could be considered one of those things, but they are simply intended, at least in part, to help people know we are different than Orthodox Christians. As most of you may know, we intentionally review, change or refine these points approximately every five years.

I do think one of the complications is that we so called religious folks often confuse the terms, belief and faith. I have heard these words interchanged by people without hesitation in the same sentence or thought. Of course they have very different meanings.

Belief is something you hold because you presume you have some facts. You believe in them. When I was in college studying chemistry, there was a chart up on the wall with all the components that make up matter. You could count them and some people actually memorized them. Those components were treated as facts. If you wanted to get a good grade you better believe they were facts.

Today we know those particles can possibly be divided and re-divided infinitely. We also know today we were only examining approximately 10 percent of matter. The other 90 percent is still a mystery. Scientists refer to it as dark matter. (To any chemist reading this please note that with good reason, I graduated with a degree in political philosophy, not chemistry.) All beliefs should be tested and when you find out the facts have changed it would seem to me one should then change one's beliefs. Otherwise you are imprisoned.

One of the challenges of living in this marvelous age is that questions seem to be infinite and answers more distant. I once heard a physicist say to his audience that today there really is no such thing as a fact unless we agree upon the operative paradigm. For a lot of people that kind of thinking can be frightening. However it really means living a life of faith. But what is faith?

Faith is not based on facts but rather assumes a mystery. The very word implies an unknown, at least when we are referring to religious or spiritual concepts. I have faith there is a force, a tuning fork if you like, that is part of all creation. I have faith that as I live my life in tune with that force, when I try and stay in harmony with that Infinite Mystery, my life is more fulfilling. It is more alive, exciting and joyful, and yet at the same time it is filled with more contentment and peace. I have faith that there have been teachers throughout history who have learned how to tune into that rhythm and have offered steps or a path so others might have the same or similar experience. I follow one in particular.

My beliefs change with a certain amount of ease as my information changes, and these days new information is coming at us in an increasing rate of speed. So my beliefs change regularly as my information changes. My faith will only change if I find it is no longer producing the "fruit of the tree." My faith will only change if I can no longer see an improvement in my life. My faith will only change if I no longer experience joy or feel connected and content.

Beliefs tend to get in the way and hinder our growth when we refuse to test them. They can keep us from experiencing a more fulfilling life when we are unwilling to change our perspectives even when our information changes. Beliefs become a problem when they are misused as a tool of power over others. And beliefs can hold our growth back when we use them to support our ego, our sense of self-importance or superiority.

Biblical scholar, Greg Jenks published a wonderful book couple years ago called: *Jesus Then and Jesus Now*. In this book he writes: *"For me, neither life nor religion is about gripping the answers. I know very little about Jesus, even less about God, and not much more about myself. Despite those serious gaps in knowledge and understanding life goes on, and I choose to live with the questions rather than fret over a lack of answers. That choice is itself an act of faith. It is my faith. My credo."*

I think that sums it up rather nicely for me and I hope for most of you.

Don't Go There

Over the last couple of decades, I have given several dozen lectures, led even more workshops, and shared literally hundreds of sermons that all focus on one broad subject—the changes occurring in our understanding of the Christian faith. Sometimes I focus on the impact of changes in our world view, sometimes on modern science and religion, and other times on the newest research in biblical scholarship. I usually bring the dialogue back to the impact of these changes on the local church. I know I am frequently asking people to stretch their theological boundaries. I know I am also almost always asking people to change their thinking. This makes for some interesting commentaries and behavior from my audience—sometimes an angry outburst, sometimes a slammed door. Most often there are tearful hugs and/or a quiet thank you.

Therefore, I suppose I should not have been surprised by an incident with a woman who was obviously agitated by something I said during one of my talks. I was leading a workshop on the subject of spirituality in the progressive Christian movement. This was one of several break-out workshops that followed keynote speakers at a four-day conference. The night before, I presented the keynote address on the progressive Christianity movement and spoke about its potential impact on the local church. The excellent turn out for the workshop was a good indication my lecture had been well received. Maybe that's why I was caught a little off guard.

With her anger barely contained, she told me in no uncertain terms that she thought I was trying to rip the heart out of Christianity. "Quite to the contrary," I responded. "I am trying to put the heart back into Christianity by building a faith based on experiences of the heart that are not dependent upon Christian myth, dogma, and creeds." But she would not hear any of it.

"How could you?" she asked. "How could I what?" I asked.

"How could you suggest Jesus was not born of the pure virgin?" she almost shouted.

I suddenly realized she was talking about comments I had made the night before regarding the role of myth in the Christian story. In a general comment about how our understanding of mythology and its role in scripture had changed over the last several decades, In that lecture I suggested that the Virgin birth and Immaculate Conception were convenient myths or midrash that had been borrowed from the Hebrew scriptures to demonstrated that Yeshua was indeed the messiah. I had suggested the concept of the virgin birth was probably the result of a mistranslation of Isaiah and the sexist era in which the Christian scriptures were written.

Frankly, I was surprised by her outburst. It was not so much that she was upset, but because it was the first time after any of my talks someone had been upset by my suggesting this particular Christian myth was the result of a mistake.

Later, the same woman stopped me in the hallway and wanted to explain her outburst. It was a long story about her Catholic background, her spiritual practices, and a whole lot of things that really did not make sense to me, but seemed to make sense to her. However, she did say something that was helpful. She started by telling me she "really appreciated my talk overall," and was in complete agreement with my general thesis. However, as she walked away she said, "If only you hadn't gone *there*."

Suddenly, I was reminded of a similar incident. This time a man who had attended one of my speaking engagements, caught up with me as I was getting ready to leave. We stood outside by our cars in the cold and talked for 20 minutes. He was completely engaged and amicable until I questioned the need for Jesus to be the one and only unique God in our world. This man got red in the face and said, "Don't go there!" and I didn't.

Interestingly, we had talked comfortably about other parts of the Christian story, how they might have come to be and why it was okay to let them go, or simply let them be myth. But for him it was unthinkable to let Jesus only be an enlightened man, a teacher and a prophet. For him, Jesus was God. It was another *don't go there.*

Recently, I was on a conference call with a highly respected seminary president and three other people. As we were discussing the future direction of ProgressiveChristianity.org, he suggested one of the things I might want to consider was moving past being an exclusively Christian organization and shift more towards a Unitarian Universalist perspective. It was as if I had been socked in the stomach and the wind had been knocked out of me. At first, I could not respond. Although I didn't say it out loud, my first thought was *don't go there!* When I was finally able to respond, I mumbled, "But I love Jesus." No one was more surprised by my response than me.

As I thought of these three incidents, I realized if we dig deep enough, most of us seem to have a "don't go there" spot in our beliefs and traditions. It's a place where we lose a little of our otherwise rational thinking. I also suspect our inability to get past those *don't go theres* often holds us back from our personal growth and change.

Certainly education helps. Right now an abundance of educational opportunities are available for anyone who wants to learn. In the last four decades, there has literally been an explosion of information about religion in general and about Christianity in particular. This offers us both the opportunity and the freedom to examine our traditional views about our religion and the things we may not have wanted to look at very closely. If we cannot fully engage a spiritual path, it will never engage us. We will never really find out where it is going to take us.

At some point, we may have to take a hard look at those things we are holding onto and ask ourselves: "Do I really believe this and why? Do my beliefs make my life and my relationships more healthy and whole? Do my beliefs lead me to an opportunity to experience joy and to share joy? Do they help me feel more connected to the rest of creation? Do they lead to me loving myself a little more at the end of each day?"

Ultimately, all religions were and still are intended to bring us closer to God, Krishna, Allah, Primordial Consciousness, Pure Consciousness, Sacred

Unity or your particular vision of Oneness. All religions started as a path for transformation and transformation means change. Change is seldom easy, but it is a necessary component of life. Sometimes the only thing keeping us from experiencing that potentially profound transformation is letting go of our "*don't go theres.*"

Aren't We All Christians?

Frequently, after a lecture or seminar, during the QandA, someone will ask me: "Why do you have to call it Progressive Christianity? Aren't we all Christians?" These were usually people who seemed to be a little on edge, and sometimes even angry. However, their question was sincere and frankly, it is a good one.

I think it is important to note that the term progressive was part of the American Christian dialogue over 100 years ago. Toward the end of the 19th century there was an active group of well-respected clergy who initiated a movement that had a profound impact both short and long term.

In his fascinating book, *The War for Righteousness*, Richard M. Gamble writes: "*The self-described progressives among America's Protestant clergy at the turn of the 20th century were well known in church circles and beyond for their advanced thinking on theology, politics, and foreign affairs. As they faced the prospect of a new century, these ministers and academics thought of themselves as broadminded, humane, and cosmopolitan, in harmony with the very best scientific, political, and theological wisdom of the age. In short, they were among the right thinking leaders of their day. These reformers have since been labeled liberal or modernist by historians, the word progressive suited their character and their times.*"

This group of reformers included such well-known names as Congregational ministers Lyman Abbot, Washington Gladden, George A. Gordon, and William Jewett Tucker, who was also president of Dartmouth College. Harry Emerson Fosdick, Shailer Matthews, and Henry Churchill King often served as highly visible and quotable spokesmen for the group.

Certainly this movement had strong social influence—not all of it good—as Gamble points out in his book in some detail.

One of Gamble's main themes was that this group of men saw the change as inevitable, much like evolution. Most of them seem to feel that God was on their side. Righteousness would prevail with a new understanding of one's faith. Then World War I was fought, so many lives were lost, the country was heading for a depression and the League of Nations ultimately failed. There was still evil in the world and somehow the perspective these fearless men had on Christianity did not seem to fit the situation. It also caused a back-wash called Fundamentalism which we still have with us today.

However, I believe it is important to point out that even back then the movement was first about rethinking theology and attempting to move Christianity into the 20th century. William Jewett Tucker wrote: *"The first effect of the progressive departure in the field of strictly theological inquiry was to bring about a change in the prevailing conception of God . . . the conception of God must be affected by the advance in our understanding of nature."*

Henry Emerson Fosdick once reflected that progressive leaders of those times, *"deliberately, sometimes desperately worked to adapt Christian thought and to harmonize it with the intellectual culture of our time . . . adaption was the only way we could save our faith and its achievement was a matter of life and death."*

Like our predecessors, the leadership of ProgressiveChristianity.org believed our primary purpose was to actively engage in examining what we mean by God, Christ and Jesus. This was based on the abundance of scientific, historical and archeological information we now have available which we did not have even a hundred years ago. Although the progressive Christian movement is considered new by most people today, it has a long history that dates back to some of the first century disciples of Jesus and a few of the early theologians, particularly in the Eastern Church and the contemplative tradition of the faith. It was always a faith that was more interested in behavior rather than beliefs, compassion rather than creeds and the Mystery rather than absolutes.

So how do I answer the person who wants to know why we need the term progressive Christianity? Aren't we all Christians? My short answer is there are three good reasons.

I believe, as individuals, we need terms like progressive Christian to remind us we are on a spiritual journey into the Great Unknown. The idea that we are always progressing helps us not only from becoming complacent about our faith, but hopefully keeps us from assuming we have arrived. Reminding ourselves that we are a progressive Christian can help us stay awake so we might see who we really are at that moment as a divine creature, part of something so large it is beyond our imagination. Being a progressive assumes we are all connected at some ontological level. We are constantly moving with a faith that assumes we are moving toward something good, something holy and something divine.

I believe we need the term progressive Christian so we can talk to others about our faith in ways that are not often heard in typical Christian settings. It is frankly a great way to start a conversation—or end one. It allows us a way to describe ourselves with a new vocabulary and new metaphors. For those who still care about the church, we need to practice our faith, and model it for others rather than telling others what they ought to believe.

Finally I agree with Henry Emerson Fosdick. I believe the church needs progressive Christianity for survival. As he so eloquently said, progressives *"deliberately, sometimes desperately, worked to adapt Christian thought and to harmonize it with the intellectual culture of our time . . . adaption was the only way we could save our faith and its achievement was a matter of life and death."* Yes my friends that was over 100 years ago. Don't you think it's about time?

Creeds & Deeds: Change and the Unfathomable Mystery

It was the Sunday after a two-day regional ProgressiveChristian.org event where I had been the keynote speaker and workshop leader. As I often do, I had offered to preach for the Sunday services and was sitting up in the chancel area with the pastor and worship leader. This was a wonderful, active midsize church of maybe 250 people who had taken their commitment seriously to be a progressive church. After a lovely music opening everyone stood up, and prompted by the worship leader began to recite ProgressiveChristianity .org's 8Points. My heart almost leaped out of my chest. I quickly looked at the program and realized the 8Points had been printed for everyone to follow.

At first I thought this was something special, possibly to acknowledge my presence. Or maybe they were doing this to commemorate what had been a very big weekend for this church. But as I slowly looked around the room, I noticed some people were barely looking at their bulletins as they recited the 8Points in unison. I even noticed a couple of people with their eyes closed as they spoke these familiar words with feeling.

I was very glad there were several other things that had to happen before it was my time to speak. I realized I was having very conflicting feelings about what had just happened. On one hand, I felt very moved that here were some dedicated people who, every Sunday, apparently recited words I had helped craft. This meant a great deal to me.

On the other hand if you have followed my concerns about religious belief systems over the years, you know I am very wary of anything that approaches a creed or an orthodox belief system. I would argue that all creeds, or beliefs deemed Orthodox have been put forth by people far more concerned with power and influence than about spirituality or equality. Too often, they have been more interested in being right than about being true.

The development of the Nicene Creed offers the perfect example. One does not have to read very much about Athanasius' efforts to destroy the Arius movement in the early fourth century church to know Athanasius was not a very nice man. Some people today might posit he did what was necessary to save the church. It was the brutal Constantine who called for the Council of Nicaea. And it was Athanasius who became the chief spokesman for the view that *"the Son was fully God, co-equal and co-eternal with the Father."* This decision, based on the vote of the Bishops, solidified the Roman church's power to decide who was right and who was wrong, who was in and who was out. The consequences were often devastating.

There is little difference today except people now feel free to walk away from churches with creeds and beliefs that no longer make sense to them. I no longer feel these creeds can be explained away as metaphors or a way of connecting to the ancient fathers of the church. They are most often seen as anachronistic at best or misogynist at worst. Modern fundamentalism is just another example of how belief systems can do harm and deny the things we often consider basic rights or freedoms.

Some scholars will argue that if the creeds had not been created in the fourth century the church would have collapsed. We have no way of knowing that of course. I tend to believe it is likely the teachings of Jesus would still have had a lot of positive value for people. Admittedly, I find it strange that some still take these ancient creeds so seriously. They were, after all, written by people who did not know where the sun went at night, what caused rain, or that women were more than incubators for birthing babies.

Having said that I must admit I see another challenge. In a past article I referred to my visits to a couple of events sponsored by people who see themselves as part of what is called the emerging church movement. I found these gatherings fascinating. For one thing, I discovered many of these primarily young people had gone through some significant changes in their understanding of Christianity. I questioned whether these changes were the result of serious study or their social settings. However I did find these changes had little to do with substantive changes in their theology or Christology. And I did not find there to be much interest in discussing these issues.

I was told by two people who were event organizers that my understanding of Jesus as a mystic teacher made them uncomfortable. This may explain why I have been invited and then uninvited to two of these events as a speaker.

I welcome any change away from the fear-based, rules-oriented Christianity so many of these young people were apparently raised in. However, I believe more has to change than that it is okay to drink homemade beer or to welcome gays and lesbians into our communities. If we are going to nurse the Christian remnants back into vital communities, we must address the scholarship that allows us to create a new Christianity for the 21st century.

It is hard for me to imagine gathering a healthy, vital community together as followers of Jesus with widely differing views on who he was. Half the people believe Jesus was a teacher of a way of life. The other half still holds the view that "the Son was fully God, co-equal and co-eternal with the Father." How do you have a conversation with those opposing positions? In other words, if we cannot have dialogue, maybe we need some kind of an Athanasius/Arias debate to see if we can get over that mountain. I am uncertain how that would go based on the experience of the fourth century Nicaea Council.

In his book, *The Fourth Gospel: Tales of a Jewish Mystic*, John Shelby Spong writes that the creedal system *"seems to have locked Jesus into a pre-modern world, to have defined God as an invasive miracle-working deity from outer space, and to have made the work of engaging the world in dialogue not only difficult but almost impossible."*

If creeds and statements of faith turn into prisons for an Infinite Mystery, is there a way to express our current beliefs that does not end dialogue and the ability to change as our information changes? We posed those same questions to some of our website readers and we were astounded by the response. We were virtually overwhelmed with both articles and suggestions for open-ended affirmations and statements of faith. There were so many we could only post a small percentage of them.

This kind of exchange is something we progressive Christians can do. We can have dialogue. We can exchange ideas. We can change and be changed for we accept that it is all part of experiencing an unfathomable Mystery. This is one of the reasons we have changed the 8Points, our guiding principles, three times in the last 15 years and they most likely will be changed again. As Gretta Vosper wrote in the forward for our new Study Guide: *"Progressive Christianity cannot be nailed down to one thing. It lives in flux. It always will because that is its nature. It always will because it must."*

Big Tent . . . Big Surprises

I did not want to go. It took two phone calls from David Felten with the *Living the Questions* organization, before I would reluctantly agree to help promote the event. A third phone call required me to pull off the freeway to argue with this dear friend. He insisted that I come to Phoenix to see what was going to happen when a bunch of young people get together and talk about what it means to be part of the so-called emerging Christianity or Emergent church movement. Please note, none of these labels have clear definitions or clarity in their meaning at this point. They are still in formation. If I am right, that is where they intend to stay—in the process of forming.

The event was called Big Tent Christianity (BTX). It was primarily organized by a group out of the Claremont School of Theology. The Dean of the school, Professor Clayton Phillips and his right hand man, Trip Fuller, provided leadership. Fuller is an ordained minister. He attended the Divinity School of Wake Forest University and is working on his PhD in Philosophy of Religion and Theology at Claremont. I would guess he is also a wannabe rock star. For the record Clayton Phillips refers to young Trip Fuller as his boss.

The movement, if that is what it can be called at this point, appears to be made up mostly of former fundamentalist, conservative and evangelical Christians. They are speaking, blogging, texting, tweeting and Facebooking about what it means to be a follower of Jesus today. Based on my reading of their blogs, dozens of conversations with them and listening to the speakers, a high percentage of them seem to be experiencing a sense of emancipation from former beliefs that felt stifling. Those beliefs no longer fit either their world view or their vision of reality.

Carol Howard Merritt, a keynoter, is a pastor of Western Presbyterian Church, an inner city church in Washington DC. She told a powerful story about her days as a student in Moody Bible Institute where she questioned nothing until the day she was attacked on the city streets. She realized there was no one in the school she could confide in about what happened. It was a great awakening of sorts that lead to a graduate seminary degree and eventually an exciting ministry in a mainline denomination. She told several stories about how some of her young congregants came to the conclusion that the religion of their childhood was no longer working for them and they sought out change.

If most of these young people were asked to articulate a theology or even a Christology, I would guess it would sound similar to what was being taught in mainline seminaries in the 1970s. However it did not seem like many of them had an interest in systematic theology or even in debating Christology. They were far more interested in finding things they hold in common and focusing on ways to live a different kind of lifestyle they perceive is different from mainline America.

In part, because of the growth and vitality of these emerging communities, and even more importantly the average age of the youthful participants, the emerging movement is getting a lot of attention from denominations, religious sociologist, and even funding agencies. Tattoos, rings and grunge clothing were the norm at this event. A few of us grey and white heads in our button-down shirts and khaki pants were sprinkled throughout the crowd. But there were no uniforms, no specific fads I could see. It was just a wonderful mix, some 300 strong, of very interesting people. One way or the other, they seemed to believe Jesus has something important to say about the way we live our lives.

Okay, I admit I was uncomfortable with rows and rows of people sharing tweets while the speakers were talking. Two or three times I started to say something when I realized this was not my world. Yes, there appeared to be a bucket full of arrogance in some of these young people. Because of the attention they are receiving—often from the very institutions they so openly disregard—they have been thrust into the limelight. But hey, they are young and they want to change the world. It takes a certain amount of arrogance to think you can change the world, and God knows we need change.

I must admit there were some big surprises. I was stunned by how many people who attended knew me or at least knew something about Progressive Christianity.org. Predicated on my assumption that most people who attend these events were barely out of the Conservative/Orthodox era in their religious beliefs, I also assumed I would feel uncomfortable introducing myself as president of an organization some people claim is out to destroy Christianity. Instead, no less than 20 people expressed their gratitude to us for co-sponsoring the event and sending out flyers about BTX to our entire mailing list. There were untold others who recognized my name and knew all about our organization. I realized I could no longer write them off as unsophisticated if they were on our mailing list. I also found it interesting that these were not the same people who normally attend our events. They were young, excited folks who were glad they were there and happy to see me.

Another surprise was the quality of the speakers. I had never heard Brian McLaren speak before, although I had read a couple of his books. McLaren, possibly the father of the emerging movement, asked the audience to consider a new model when thinking about Jesus. Using some simple PowerPoint graphs, he shared his own transformation. From a believer who thought that only one's belief in Jesus as personal lord and savior could keep one from suffering eternally in hell, he realized he had been looking at the Christian narrative from the wrong direction. The old model started with an assumption about who and what Jesus was. That particular model, he argued, was not biblical or historical but was rather a Greek interpretation influenced by Plato and Aristotle. The narrative, he argued, needed to be reinterpreted in reverse starting with ancient Jewish lenses. Not only did I learn something from his talk, but I heard something I was not expecting. So much for assuming the room was full of conservative and even Orthodox Christians. I could not say enough about the way McLaren handled this delicate subject in what had to be a theologically mixed crowd. I have become a fan of this gifted man.

The third surprise was to learn how much verbal and written abuse some of these emerging bloggers and speakers must endure. I do know a little about the vile hatred coming from so-called conservative Christians who believe I am attempting to destroy Christianity. They have no hesitancy to let me know what is going to happen to me when I die. I occasionally worry one of them may want to speed up the day that will occur. But when someone goes on our progressive website they know what they are getting. I have been a progressive/liberal Christian since my youth. What I write and speak about is just a continuation of that journey. In contrast, most of the emerging speakers have come out of a conservative tradition. It is apparently shocking to those they have left behind. It is a threat to their world view and I suspect that frightens them. Two different bloggers told me it gets very nasty sometimes. I read some of the feedback on two of the blogs. It must take a certain amount of courage to make that transition public.

The next thing that hit me was the vast majority of people gathered at this event who actually talked about how being a Christian should impact their lives. Not only do they talk about it, they care about it and it appears they do something about it. I could not help but think about the dozens—if not hundreds—of workshops I have done over the years. In large part they have been in old churches with aging congregations. What those folks usually want to know is, "How do we fix our church so it will be like it used to be."

These young people were asking, "How does following Jesus change my life." I am not certain where this will go when they have kids in college and are worried about their 401k. Right now these young people, many of them parents of young children, believe following the Jesus path will lead to a better life, healthier families and possible salvation for mother earth. I could not help but wonder what would happen if those kinds of conversations were going on in all our mainline churches? It might be one of the places where progressive and emerging Christians will find healthy and helpful common ground.

I was touched by what appeared to be the genuine care people had for each other in spite of what must have been some pretty significant differences in their religious beliefs. I overheard an emotional but compassionate conversation among some of the BTX leadership about what would be acceptable behavior. Apparently one attendee had become outspoken about the so-called heresy going on there. This was a big tent but they were not going to condone bullies. I also felt these young people did not have that phony, pasted on smile I have seen in some places when the slightest inconvenience can bring out anger. It sincerely felt like a joyful and exciting place with lots of laughter, fun and some killer homebrewed beer in the evenings.

Finally the biggest surprise was my struggle to sort out why I had been so resistant to going and seeing with my own eyes what was actually happening in the emerging church movement. It was not a pleasant sorting. You see, I realized I had made all kinds of presumptions and judgments about what to expect. At the same time, I sincerely believe Jesus was teaching a spiritual path that can lead to a Sacred Realm here on earth, living an interconnected life without boundaries or borders between us. I have committed my life to trying to follow that path. One of the primary lessons is to avoid making judgments about others and learn to meet them where they are. I painfully realized I had failed to do something I feel very strongly about. I made lots of excuses and managed to maintain a modicum of dignity. However, the more time I spent with some of these young people, the more I realized I had something to learn from them. I even realized that someday, if I really want to save Christianity, I may need to get out of the way. I liked what I saw and I am actually excited about the possibilities.

Fundamentalists Anonymous: Engaging Recovering Christians

Sometime in the late 1980s I got a very strange phone call. I actually thought it was a prank. At the time, I was a very progressive Christian pastor in a very conservative area in Southern California. I had been interviewed in the newspaper a few weeks before and had already received a few crank calls and some pretty nasty mail from some outraged conservative Christians. But this young man sounded very sincere. He wanted to know if we would consider hosting a Fundamentalist Anonymous (FA) chapter in our church. I had never heard of the national group and figured no one in the church had heard of it either. I asked if it would be possible for me to meet with him. I wasn't certain how anonymous this had to be. I assured him that whatever we discussed would remain confidential.

The next day, the young engineer who worked at a nearby aerospace office, stopped by the office. He was nervous at first but seemed to relax as he told a little bit of his story. His family had been missionaries in the U.S. for a fundamentalist Christian church. His father was a very domineering man. He basically disowned his son for going to a liberal university instead of the Bible College supported by their small denomination. The young man had a hard time socially in the university because he did not seem to fit. He had a very difficult time with a Western civilization class he took his freshman year. His discomfort changed to curiosity, however, with the encouragement of a couple of his friends. He then took every class on religion and philosophy he could fit into his required course work. Somewhere along the way he said, "I suddenly felt like I had been lied to all those years."

For the next ten years he went through periods of anger, distrust of people and cold sweat fear. At times he would go back to the church of his youth and end up feeling terrible. Then he was introduced to an FA chapter where he lived in the Midwest and found it very helpful. When he took a job in Orange County, California he began to have anxiety attacks and realized he still needed a support group. That was when he agreed to help start an FA chapter at the United Church of Christ church where I was the pastor.

The group only stayed there for a few months. Too many of the potential participants were uncomfortable meeting in a church, he explained. This was in spite of our being an ultra-liberal one targeted by conservative Christians since its founding. I was sorry they did not stay. I would have liked to stay in touch with this young man. It was the first time I knowingly came across the terrible pain and damage ultra-conservative religion can cause in individuals. It would not be the last.

For the next two decades I counseled uncountable numbers of people who shared their stories of psychological, emotional and even physical abuse in the name of religion. These folks of all ages shared stories of growing up believing they were impure, incapable, worthless, dirty and sinful. It was only through their clinging to the belief that through the sacrifice of Jesus, they could avoid more suffering both here and in the hereafter. Sadly the vast majority of people who shared their stories were either women or gay men.

70

Anitra L. Freeman, a blogger, published a paper on fundamentalism regarding the common traits fundamentalists use to maintain psychological control over members.

- They insist on a rigid hierarchy of authority. The more extreme the group, the more authority is concentrated in one central figure.

- The group, and the authority figure(s) within the group, withhold or bestow love to control behavior. Misbehaving members are cut off from communication.

- They magnify current social and individual evils and dwell on the innate wickedness of man.

- Sexual immorality is often their central cause.

- They promote a truth which is superior to all other truths because it is absolute and unchanging.

- They promote distrust of one's personal judgment, being subject instead to the given truths of the group, the judgment of the church as a body, or the proclamations of a central authority figure.

- They are apocalyptic, foretelling an imminent and horrifying future in which only the faithful will survive. Any disaster in the news is magnified as a sign of the apocalypse.

The emotional and psychic damage occurring when someone becomes involved in these kinds of communities can be extreme. Reading first person stories of people who have gone through these experiences can be very hard. The damage often goes deep. Frequently the damaged person has no place to go. There are no rehab centers for recovering fundamentalists.

In recent years I typically receive somewhere between three to eight books a month from publishers wanting us to write positive reviews to help market their books. I have been surprised by the number of these books written by people who have gone or are going through a difficult transition from an ultraconservative upbringing to a more open understanding of their religion or an outright rejection of it. They write about the challenges of discovering that what they thought was the infallible truth is no longer true for them. Often they believe they are progressive because they no longer believe the Bible is the inerrant word of God, but they retain some very orthodox beliefs. Others reject religion altogether. Some are angry and some are not. The level of rejection and anger appears to have more to do with how long and at what stage they held their religious convictions before something changed their perspective.

In the late 1980s and early 1990s, mainline church growth experts were suggesting the growing ultra conservative, mega church phenomenon might be a good thing for the dying mainline churches. Citing James Fowler's *Stages of Faith*, they assumed these new Christians flocking to the megachurches would mature in their faith. At some point they would ultimately become disenchanted, would leave the mega church and find a local mainline church to continue growing in their stages of faith. It was hoped this would result in a natural growth in our older churches. This has not proven to be the case.

Yes, megachurches tend to have big back doors. They suffer even greater losses, on a percentage basis, than most of our mainline churches in our transient society. However, studies have shown only a small percentage of these ex-mega church evangelical Christians show up in our mainline churches. According to research the vast majority simply stop going to church. They often become part a growing segment of our society self-identifying as spiritual but not religious. This is now one of the fastest growing groups in our country. Some researchers are wondering if progressive Christianity is going to be skipped by others who now identify as spiritual but not religious.

How do we progressive Christians share our perspective so recovering Christians can hear us and actually get excited about the progressive path of Jesus and what our churches have to offer?

The first thing we will have to do is learn how to create more joyful, interactive, and spiritual Sunday celebrations. It will mean making changes that many long-term church members will not want to make. But ultimately, we have to ask ourselves how long can we hang onto the past. We have a lot to learn from these conservative churches about telling our story and for the most part we are not getting it. We have to discover and implement more effective ways to communicate the progressive message in different ways and through different media that fit our contemporary society, particularly if we want to attract young adults.

We will also have to learn to share our powerful message with more clarity and substance. Do we honestly believe that following the teachings of Jesus will really change a life? Has it changed yours? Can we explain why our progressive faith is so compelling and important to us that we think it could be for someone else? Until we know what we represent, we represent nothing.

Are we willing to be patient with recovering Christians who are still struggling with guilt and holding on to beliefs you may feel are archaic? This is where unconditional love and compassion must enter into our practice. Are we more concerned about winning a debate than we are about sharing our positive story? Can we build up someone who does not think like we think or believe what we believe?

Are we willing to take the time to educate ourselves about our faith so when we are asked to have a conversation, we actually know what we are talking about? In other words, do we always have to say, "You need to talk to my pastor?"

We are sharing a message of love with people who have been taught a message of fear. We are referring to a faith in an Infinite Mystery. We are trying to communicate about a great mystery with people who believed only in absolutes and dogmas. We are telling a story of inclusion to people who have been taught only about righteous exclusion. We are trying to demonstrate a boundary free life to some who have believed in the security of separation. We do not have an easy task. But there are a whole lot of searching people these days. They may be ready to let go of the life raft they have been hanging onto but are uncertain about where they can go. It would be nice if we could at least provide a search light that might illuminate another way for them to navigate "the sea of infinite mystery." (Karl Rahner)

Living the Faith vs. Judging

Calvin Mercer is a former fundamentalist Christian who has been born again as a competent theologian and university professor of religion. When he realized what he had been through and how hard it had been to break free, he became fascinated by the fundamentalist mind. At one point his interest was so great he returned to school, got a graduate degree in clinical psychology and was in private practice for over a decade. He wrote a book called *Slaves to Faith* which is a wonderful primer on understanding the fundamentalist perspective on theology, the Bible and Jesus the Christ. In this book, he also offers a psychological profile on the fundamentalist mind with some limited suggestions on how progressive Christians and others might dialogue with them.

I was once reading his book on an airplane. When my seat mate saw the title of the book, he assumed the title referred to the born again Christian's commitment to Christ. In other words he thought we were on the same page. With a smile he said: "Wasn't it great when you finally made that commitment?" Now, whenever something like this has happened in the past, I usually make some remark that assures this person that first, I am more educated than he or she is, and second, we don't agree. This usually works and at least gives me the first punch in what may be an uncomfortable ride at 30,000 feet.

This time I just smiled and asked him what he meant by that question. It took him less than five minutes to articulate how his life had changed when a friend took him to his evangelical church. Within three months he had committed his life to Christ as his lord and savior. His next question was, "When were you born again?"

I had to think about my response since it was a full flight and we still had two and half hours to go. So, I simply said, "I am not certain what you mean by that?" I actually had become interested in how he would respond so I tried to listen with an open mind. I was surprised how easy it was when I made the effort not to judge or critique his comments as he was making them. I did my best to shut down the voice that wanted to make fun of his naïveté and lack of biblical training.

However, I became far more fascinated by how comfortable he was talking about something that was so important to him. It was clear he had done this before on many occasions and he was completely at ease. If I did not evaluate what he was saying, instead of how he was saying it, it was impressive.

74

I think it had a unique impact on me at that moment because I was working on my article for our soon to be published eBulletin. That eBulletin dealt with challenges for progressives to learn how to talk about their progressive Christian faith. Of course it will always be difficult to talk about one's faith. We are talking about great mysteries and a lot of questions that will never be answered because they are dealing with issues and things beyond our comprehension.

Is it too hard to refer to Christianity as a path rather than a belief system—a path guided by compassion, love forgiveness rather than fear? Is it too hard to explain this path is more focused on fulfillment than on atonement? Is it difficult to say you have faith in a God or Divine Spirit or Sacred Unity or whatever you choose to call that energy—an energy that is part of all creation and is in each and every one of us? Is it too difficult to say I don't know how it works because it is beyond my comprehension? I know when I live my life a certain way, including intentional spiritual practices, my life is more abundant, less anxious, more peaceful, less fearful, and at the end of each day, more joyful.

Of course this begs the question. Do we really try and walk the path? Do we have intentional spiritual practices and disciplines? Do we really believe our path is about change and transformation? Do we think our way will actually lead to an experience of the Sacred or the Divine?

I suppose if we really did live this way, we would have a much easier time on airplanes explaining what it means to be a progressive Christian. I suspect if we actually practiced those teaching and had some of those mysterious or mystical experiences, we would have an easier time explaining what it is we actually believe, rather than what we don't believe. I suspect we would be a little more enthusiastic explaining why progressive Christianity can be a wonderful guide to one's life. But then if we were living it, we probably would not have to explain it would we?

For the record, I did explain my faith, what I mean by progressive Christianity and briefly shared what I saw as our differences. He looked at me a little like I was crazy and finally said, "That's cool," and went back to his computer games.

I put my seat back and took a long nap.

Not the Easy Way

Folks often send me emails suggesting I am trying to destroy Christianity. Some tell me I am just ignorant, often suggesting if I would just read the Bible I would get it right. Others believe I am an agent of the devil. Some have even suggested I am the Anti-Christ. I must admit, sometimes my ego gets off on that one. At least it seems that I am important to someone.

Almost all these types of emails suggest the real issue is that we progressives are trying to ignore the hard part of being a committed Christian. That usually includes the accusation that we do not want to believe there are rules we are supposed to live by, given to us by God. The second charge is we ignore the truth that we are sinners. Therefore, they say we believe we have no need for repentance and redemption. Of course, they almost always end with something like, "Ha, ha. You are going to burn in hell." I probably receive two or three of this type of email a week.

I used to respond to most of them but I discovered my responses just seemed to escalate the number of exchanges. Never once have I felt I changed anyone's perspective by responding.

The interesting thing is I really do believe that sin, repentance, and redemption are important elements of a spiritual path. In fact, they play an important role in the human condition. I wish I could find a way to communicate that to these folks. However, I am afraid we have very different perspectives about what these words actually mean and the dynamics they involve on a spiritual journey.

The first hurdle I encountered was my inability to communicate that we need to get rid of the concept of original sin and move to a new model. Many become outraged when I contend Paul was wrong when he suggested we are all born into sin. Although getting rid of a centerpiece of Christian doctrine may be a paradigm shift for most people, many who read this will find they have already made the shift, at least at some operative level. I think it happens to every parent or grandparent once they hold a precious new child in their arms.

The whole idea of original sin has an interesting history. Few people actually know where the concept came from. It was actually Augustine who made the term original sin well known. He appealed to the Pauline-apocalyptic understanding of the forgiveness of sin. But he also introduced the idea that sin is transmitted from generation to generation by the act of procreation. He took this idea from second century theologian, Tertullian, who actually coined the phrase original sin.

All of this theorizing was done by these men after they had already concluded Jesus was the messianic hero whose purpose was to wash the sins of the world away through some act of grace by a judging God. It would take many more pages to go into the lives of some of the characters involved with creating these socially modifying theories. However, based on the historical information we have, I would suggest most of their conclusions were guided less by their deep spiritual disciplines or even by their interpretation of scripture, but more by an apparent overabundance of testosterone.

Origen, (c.185–c.254) probably the most gifted theologian of the early church fathers, had his own share of ideas that would seem strange to contemporary thinkers. But at least he suggested that sin was a sickness and sicknesses can be cured. He broke sin into three different categories, just as he divided the human into three different components. One of them is the soul from which the most serious sin emanates and which requires much more work to cure. Although I am probably oversimplifying here, Origen saw sin as a natural part of being human and an opportunity for both growth—waking up—and an experience of grace.

The ultimate problem for most of the early theologians was their need to identify Jesus as a divine messiah sent by an intervening God to save humanity from humanity's God-given nature. Rather than accepting Jesus as a profound teacher of another way to experience reality (The Kingdom of God), all the emphasis has been on an outside force, (being), going through some horrible heroic act on our poor behalf, and then only if we repent.

This is one of the reasons the term repentance has been so corrupted over the centuries. The term, like so many Christian terms borrowed from other traditions, has been molded to meet the criteria of what became dogma while ignoring the term's powerful history. When we think of the word sin, we often picture a TV evangelist pounding on the pulpit or shaking the Bible and yelling that if we don't repent for our sins, we are going to burn in hell. For many of us, this picture conjures up bad memories and even pain. Over the centuries in the traditional church, repentance came to mean, "Fall on your knees and beg for forgiveness for your sins and ask Christ your Savior for forgiveness."

However, repentance has a long and deep history in early Judaism. So when Jesus called his listeners to repent, the word had a very different connotation. It is not easy to make a direct translation of repent or repentance into modern English. We are dealing with ancient language and symbols that have radically changed over the centuries. Plus, this word which has taken on such power in the Christian tradition is actually formed from a combination of two Greek words: *metamorphoo*, which means to change or transform, *and metanoeo*, which means to think differently afterwards, or to reconsider.

If this is not confusing enough, the definition of the word for Jesus came out of the Hebrew traditions and was originally an outgrowth or derivative of the Hebrew word, *shuwb* (shoob). *Shuwb* is most commonly translated from the Hebrew Scriptures or the Old Testament, as repent. The best direct English translation of *shuwb* is to turn back or away or turn in another direction. Translating ancient languages is further complicated by the fact that most words have many meanings and the meanings are affected by the way they are used in the sentence.

For purposes of this discussion, let me try and offer a workable translation for the word repent: "to reconsider one's actions or thoughts that have caused pain or disharmony, accept responsibility for the damage or harm they may have caused, change the direction or the course of your life, and be transformed in the process."

Please note that a Jew in Jesus' time would not have assumed some outside source was supposed to do the forgiving. This was about the individual taking responsibility for actions or thoughts that have caused harm, seeking forgiveness and making a commitment to change one's ways. The primary responsibility here lies on the individual who committed the infraction, who created the harm or the sin, if I can use that word here. When we do those things, we are assured we will experience peace or redemption.

Using the Book of Thomas as a primary source, Elaine Pagels, in her wonderful book, *The Origin of Satan*, argues that Jesus saw himself as a teacher of a way to experience the Kingdom of God. Referring to the Book of Thomas, often considered a more authentic source of Jesus' teachings than the Four Gospels, she writes, ". . . the Kingdom of God is not an event expected to happen in history, nor is it a place. The author of Thomas seems to ridicule such views."

Jesus said: *"If those who lead you say to you, 'Lord, the kingdom is in the sky,' then the birds of the sky will precede you. If they say to you, 'It is in the sea,' then the fish will precede you."* (NHC II .32.19-24)

However, the Kingdom of God, according to Thomas, is a path of self-discovery.

"Rather the kingdom is inside of you, and it is outside of you. When you come to know yourselves, then you will become known, and you will realize that it is you who are the sons of the living Father. But if you do not know yourselves then you are in poverty, and you are the poverty."

For the author of the Book of Thomas, Jesus was a teacher of self-discovery or self-awareness. This was not some social or psychological process, but a knowing of ourselves at the deepest level. Thomas states, *"When you come to know yourselves,"* (discover the divine within you, then *"you will discover that it is you who are the sons (and daughters) of the living Father."*

For the writer of the Gospel of Thomas, Jesus, like many Jews of his time, saw repentance as part of a process to self-discovery and self-awareness. With that awareness we can experience the Kingdom of God Jesus offered to us. Ultimately the question we must ask ourselves is not "what does God want me to do" or even "what does Jesus want me to do." Rather we must ask ourselves, "What do I need to do in order to experience the Realm of God or the Unity Jesus pointed to."

Thomas, like Jesus, assured us this was not the easy path. That's probably why so many people keep looking for a savior.

Seeking Our Truth

I was a Political Philosophy major at the university I attended a long time ago. I still remember a class from a new professor, Dr. Edwards, in my junior year. The class was something about the development of modern political thinking. It covered what I would call classical conservative and liberal thought. I remember being told that ninety percent of our entire grade would be based on two fairly long papers we would have to write. At one point the professor handed out a long list of controversial issues and our task was to write a paper that would convince others of our particular political position on the subject. He told us he did not care what our position was, but only how well we reasoned and defended that particular position.

This was my cup of tea. This was what I was designed to do. I was passionate, knowledgeable, and opinionated. I picked a subject I felt very strongly about. I was determined to ferret out the truth and make my point. It was a subject I had already given a lot of thought to and had even done some research on it. I never worked so hard on a paper. I wanted to show this guy what I was made of and I knew it was a place where I could score big.

Sure enough. A week later after the paper had been turned in and was graded and returned, I was not disappointed. It was an A+. The professor made long comments about the papers for each student. I was a hit. I scored big and was very proud.

But several weeks later the professor gave us our next assignment. Write the paper again arguing from the opposite perspective of your first paper. I don't think anyone in the class was happy about the assignment but no one was more upset than me. This was not just a philosophical exercise for me. I was passionate about my original position. I knew it was the truth, the whole truth, so help me God.

This was like asking Ron Paul to argue for expanded welfare. This would be like asking Pat Robertson to make a case for the fallibility of the Bible. This was asking Gloria Steinem to argue convincingly that a woman should stay at home to raise the children and care for her husband.

I am actually a little embarrassed to admit I got a pretty good grade on the second paper. What does that say about my convictions? The funny thing is, by the time I got through reading all the material I needed in order to write that paper, I had begun to see the other side of the argument. I learned a lot in that class, especially about truth. It can be ambiguous and pliable and gray. That makes it no less important to seek.

If we are willing to work, to educate ourselves and move past our simplistic biases; if we are willing to be open, truth of any kind can be elusive. But the search can lead to new understandings and new perspectives. Bertrand Russell, one of the great philosophers of modern history, once wrote

"Subjectively, every philosopher appears to himself to be engaged in the pursuit of something which may be called 'truth.' Philosophers may differ as to the definition of truth but at any rate it is something objective, something which, in some sense, everybody ought to accept."

"But," Russell continues, *"every philosopher will agree that many other philosophers have been actuated by bias and have extra-rational reasons, of which they are usually unconscious, for many of their opinions."* In other words, philosophers agree that other philosophers are unconsciously biased and are not always rational in their search for truth.

Plato was one of the first philosophers to argue there was ultimate truth that could be discovered through philosophy. Plato believed the highest goal in life was to become a philosopher. For him a philosopher was one who loves the *"vision of truth."* For Plato, truth meant knowledge of beauty.

Truth for Pythagoras meant finding the *"the harmonic mean"* or *"harmonic progression."* For Pythagoras, as some of you may remember, *"All things were numbers."* Mathematics for him was the way to find external truth. Of course he did not know about new math or quantum physics at that time.

We could spend a whole day talking about how the great philosophers of history defined truth let alone how their conclusions differed and why. Russell points out something we understand better today than we have in the past. All great philosophers throughout history are prisoners to some degree of their time and environment. Although they may deal with ultimate issues and truth they are captives of the force of their culture and society.

When it comes to finding religious truth it can be even more interesting, challenging and dangerously subjective. Dr. Gordon Kaufman in his book, *In Face of Mystery*, points out that a central problem with traditional conceptions of religious truth is they have all come out of authoritarian relationships in which *"the truth . . . was something known to a teacher or prophet or guru, and he or she, then communicated it to others, who received and accepted it."*

Dr. Kaufman continues, *"Religious truth appears to be understood on a model of property: it is a kind of possession owned by one party and thus not directly available to others, a possession which can be passed on . . . if the owner chooses to do so."*

Think for a moment about your own feelings concerning religious truth or experience. Does it seem there is something out there that eludes you?

Isn't it true that most of us want to know the answers and are frankly uncomfortable when we think we may never know the ultimate truth, at least in this lifetime?

You may not be comfortable then with Dr. Kaufman's response when he writes about religious truth. "... *In religious myth and symbols, and in theological doctrines and reflection, we are dealing with matters of profound, ultimately unfathomable mystery; the ultimate meaning of human life, the final truth about the world and our place within it, is simply not available to us humans.*"

And that my friends, I am afraid, is the truth. The final truth is simply not available to us as humans. I know there are people who would like me to tell them I have a graduate degree in theology and there is this book written by God. After nearly forty years of serious study, one might think I could tell you the truth. But I cannot do that.

As students of Jesus it would seem we could turn to his teachings and find some answers. But here again, most of them are pretty elusive when it comes to ultimate truth. The idea of debating ultimate truth would have been foreign or as we now say "Greek" to Jesus. That is one of the reasons you find the word truth so infrequently in his what we believe are the most authentic thoughts of Jesus, a Palestinian Jew, who spoke Aramaic. The Book of John is the exception as it is heavily influenced by Greek thinking and concepts.

Searching for ultimate truth was by and large a product of Greek thinking. For a Galilean Jew who spoke the poetic Aramaic language, this concept would most likely have been unthinkable. I once heard a scholar say the reasons Jesus did not answer Pilot when he asked him "*what is truth?*" is Jesus would have had no idea what Pilot was talking about. We really do not know what Jesus was thinking or if indeed this even occurred. But the point is ultimate truth was not part of Aramaic thinking in those ancient times.

Jesus was far more concerned about right relationships—relationship with others, with community and with God. The closest word in Aramaic that could be translated as truth would be the word sherara. According to Neil Douglas-Klotz, in his book *The Hidden Gospel*, *sherara* would best be translated as "*The sense of a right direction at a particular time that enlivens one's personal purpose and at the same time harmonizes with all.*"

In other words, one is acting in truth when one is moving in a direction or way that enhances one's purpose and harmonizes with others. For Jesus what was in one's heart was far more important than one's reasoning capacity. He would have been far more interested in one's actions when it came to perceiving truth than in their concepts of good and even more interested in their motivations. He would have been more concerned about the right use of the law than in debating the right law.

Jesus may have had some concept of an ultimate Creator or God force. Beyond that it is hard to fathom him having a more definitive truth. Nor would he have believed any human was capable having such a truth. What he repeatedly explained to the best of our information is that we can come to experience God and to know attributes of God. I suspect he would have agreed with Dr. Kaufman who wrote 2000 years later, *"The final truth about the world and our place within it is simply not available to us humans."*

Does that mean we cannot gain any knowledge or understanding of our creation and our Creator? How do we know anything about the right way to live, to love? Is it all relative? Is there no compass on which to base our actions? Can we believe in a concept of religious truth?

First, if we believe Jesus offers us a window into the mystery of God, we have his life and a fairly substantive amount of his teachings to help us. I think the teacher and disciple who wrote the book of John had the right idea when he put these words into Jesus' mouth, *"If you love me you will follow my commandments (or my ways)."* The first century evangelist indirectly describes this relationship when he wrote in the same passage, *"When you are in [Jesus,] [Jesus] is in you . . ."* I am certain that was the experience of this writer when he struggled with some of the same issues of truth in those very difficult times in which he was writing. The wonderful heretic, Arias, suggested Jesus created the footsteps, the path we need only follow, to experience the same intimate relationship with God experienced by Jesus. According to Arias, if we followed the path of Jesus with full commitment, we could be adopted by God as a Son or (daughter).

Secondarily, in all three of the synoptic gospels, Jesus reminds us we can tell if something is good or bad by the fruit it bears. This seems like something that should be obvious. In fact it was sage advice offered by a teacher before Jesus. It is amazing how we can get caught up in an ideology or a perspective on something we may perceive as truth and not realize it is producing bad fruit. That is why some religious "truth" purportedly based on the teachings of compassion can become so utterly abusive and damaging. We can ask: What does this truth, this teaching produce? Is it something good? Is it harmonious with the rest of creation? Does it bring peace?

On a personal basis we can ask these questions: Does this seem to bring about fulfillment? Am I more at peace or contentment? Does it seem to bring me closer to others, to God, to the Ultimate Mystery, or am I more separated? It is my contention that any spiritual path that separates us from the rest of God's creation and creatures is not a healthy path.

Thirdly, in the words of Dr. Kaufman, *"The best image I know for conceiving what religious truth [theology] ought to be is not the exegesis of religious texts or the arcane debates of learned intellectuals . . . but rather free flowing, open and unfettered conversation.* (Pg 66)

The Sacred Unity, Allah, or that force we call God, can ultimately come to be known through practice and experience. But these practices and experiences are conditioned by the cultures and settings out of which they come. They have taken on many forms and manifestations throughout history. Today we must struggle to find our religious truth as has always been the case, in community and in practice *"with free flowing, open and unfettered conversation."* We may never find the ultimate truth but the journey should lead to some fascinating, purposeful and fulfilling places.

The Other Jesus Story

A couple of thousand years ago a baby boy was born in the northern part of Israel, in the area of the Galilean Sea. Some would say he got a bad start in life. As an oppressed Jew in a country run by a tyrant under the auspices of the Roman Empire, he was born into very hard life.

As a Galilean Jew he was a minority of a minority. Under the best of circumstances he would have suffered the worst kinds of oppressive abuse in an already oppressive society. The religious leaders of his time were co-opted as they served two masters, the Romans and their temples. They would have been little help in the struggle of his people to survive.

More than likely he also suffered the consequences of being considered a part of the Mamzer caste—those of unknown fathers or what today we would call illegitimate or bastards. It was considered a low caste within a low class in those days.

But from the beginning this child seemed different. He appeared to have an innate wisdom far beyond his years. This nature was bothersome to many and ignored by others. A few who were attracted to him knew from the beginning he was special, a natural leader. Even as a young boy while he was growing up, people went to him for his advice.

Maybe it was his hard life and his experience with prejudice . . . or maybe it was the deep spiritual practices he incorporated into his daily life . . . or maybe it was the inspiration of his teacher, the one they called the Baptist . . . or maybe it was a path that had already been written into his DNA. Whatever it was, this young man seemed exceptionally sensitive toward others. He was intuitive and interested in others. He seemed concerned about issues beyond survival.

At some point, like all great spiritual teachers throughout the ages, he had a series of peak experiences. One time however, something happened that he had never experienced before. Over the years he would reluctantly try and explain it to others but there were no adequate words. Everything as he had understood it before had melted away and he began to reformulate his reality. Whatever happened, however, was obvious to others.

He began to talk about things differently. He seemed more content in spite of his difficult life. He seemed happier, even merry at times. People were attracted to him for reasons they did not understand. Others realized he exuded sincere love and compassion. Those who were the closest to him recognized he had somehow changed, and they asked him what had happened.

With some hesitancy, he tried to explain he had experienced something like the Kingdom of God or a better translation in Aramaic might be the *Realm* of Sacred Unity.

But this did not satisfy his friends. "The Kingdom or Realm of God . . . where is that? Is it in the Temple?"

"No," he would answer. "It is everywhere. It is above you. It is behind you. It is within you," he explained. "When you make the two One, and when you make the inner as the outer and outer as the inner, and the above as the below, then you will experience the Realm of Sacred Unity."

"But how can that be?" his friends would ask. "Can I see it or feel it or measure it?" they asked very agitated.

He would look at them with compassion and obvious love in his eyes and try and explain to them that you cannot understand it until you find it. But when you do find it, you will want to celebrate.

Most of the time his friends and the curious would wander off confused and frustrated. But now and then one or two would linger and ask him more questions about how to experience this mysterious Realm. Slowly a small group formed who wanted him to teach them how to find this place called the Realm of Sacred Unity.

And so he began to teach the way. First he said you must trust the power of the Spirit that flows through your life. If you do not seek it while you are alive you will die and not know that you are one.

"What else?" he was asked.

"Maybe most important you must learn to be still. Our scriptures tell us we must be still to know or experience God or to experience Sacred Unity."

"But we pray every day," they might have responded. And he would say, "Be still."

"And then what must we do," they asked.

"You must repent. If you have caused harm to yourself or to others, you must accept responsibility for your behavior or thoughts and make a commitment to change your ways, change the course of your life.

And if you want to cleanse your heart and free your head, you must forgive not once, not twice but seventy times seven.

When you have forgiven everyone you can think of so that you are free of the poison in your heart, then judge another no longer.

And when you no longer judge others, you will be free to offer the love and compassion God offers to you. And when you can offer such love without judgment or conditions you will find the doorway into the Realm of Sacred Unity you seek.

But to open that door, you must also be generous with your heart and your possessions, as if you have an abundance of both. For if you live as if you have abundance you will experience abundance. Do not worry about what you have or what you will wear but be conscious about what you can give."

Then he looked at each one of them slowly with an unusually stern look. And he said, "When you have mastered these practices you will be ready for the last two. They can be the most challenging and should not be done unless you have mastered all the others."

When they all grew quiet he said, "Every so often you are presented with the opportunity to help another who is in danger or is suffering. Do not pass by that opportunity even when it may be a risk to your life or your livelihood.

When someone is suffering at the hands of another and we do nothing we have lost our way, our faith and our experience of the Realm. However when you do take that action, without judgment or anger, even when it puts you at risk, you will experience a Oneness and sense of Connectedness to the Presence you have never experienced before."

His new disciples shuddered with trepidation although with some excitement.

Then he smiled and chuckled and said, "And finally, I beseech you, do not take yourself so seriously. Learn how to celebrate and laugh. Celebration and laughter are God's lubricants of life. It will come naturally when you have entered the doorway into the Realm of Sacred Unity. Your laughter will come from the deepest place in your belly and will tickle your heart." Then he sat down.

As time went by some of his new disciples began to practice the path. They began to have powerful, life changing experiences. They began to see why he had taught them the way. They began to understand what he had told them. As they began to become freer and more fulfilled, others noticed and wanted to have the same experience.

The teacher continued to teach but most could not understand this strange behavior. But some did understand as they tried to practice it. These students realized this rabbi was very special. So special, they started telling stories about him. Because of the suffering of their people, they began to think maybe he was the one who was going to lead them out of their perilous lives. Maybe he was the one they had hoped for over 500 years. People began to talk about a new messiah and a new Kingdom.

And so the authorities became afraid he would cause them problems. When they came to question him, his friends and followers wanted him to fight back. He refused but would deny nothing. And he was killed by the authorities for they feared him.

But they could not kill his spirit. They could not kill the love his followers had for him and he had for them. And so his story has been told for two thousand years—sort of.

I share this story today because quite frankly, it is not told often enough. Even sadder, it is seldom lived or modeled. We have buried this simple but powerful story in creedal and tribal divisions. We have disguised its meaning in fancy robes and ecclesiastical symbols of power. We have hidden the truth in eschatological and scriptural debates. We created and used the story as one of fear rather than love. We've done everything in our power to ignore the path because it means letting go—not holding on. It means having a willingness to become vulnerable instead of powerful.

I believe we are living in a new age and a new time when more people are ready, as Eckhart Tolle writes, *"to let go of identification with form, dogma and rigid belief systems in order to discover the original depth that has been hidden in our spiritual tradition. People are hungry for a path that leads them to an experience of the Sacred Unity or of the Holy . . . as some would prefer to call it. And guess what? We have one. It is a path that can take us from theory to practice . . . from practice to being; from want to fulfillment. It only begs for teachers and practitioners."*

Bishop Spong, in his 2008 book *Jesus for the Non-Religious*, writes *"The call of the God experienced in Christ is simply a call to be all that each of us is—a call to offer, through the being of our humanity, the gift of God to all people by building a world in which everyone can live more fully, love more wastefully and have the courage to be all that they can be . . . That is how we live out the presence of God. God is about living, about loving and about being."*

"God is about living, about loving and about being." I believe this last line is the one those of us who call ourselves progressive, open, enlightened, evolutionary Christians need to hear and heed.

To Hell with Hell

I remember a strange encounter I had with a young man in one of the last years of my ministry. He was probably in his late thirties and had been attending our church in Irvine, California for several months by himself. Although he always sat in the very back of the church near an aisle, as if ready to make a quick getaway, he always made certain to take the time to say hello to me before he left.

One day as he went out the door, he asked if he could make an appointment to speak to me privately. I said certainly, and we set up a time. When he arrived he was obviously nervous and he had a hard time getting to the point. I did learn he was a professional in the medical field and he had lived in this country for over 25 years. He had been raised a Muslim but had married an American Christian woman who apparently attended a more conservative church. I suspect he was in our church because we hosted a Muslim congregation for their services. I had also recently been invited by an Imam to speak at the dedication of a new Muslim school. I was honored for my efforts to publicly condemn the growing prejudice against the Islamic community after 9/11. I'm not certain what kind of message his wife was hearing in her church.

We had a very long chat about progressive Christianity and Jesus as a prophet and a teacher. He told me he appreciated the fact that our church had both a Jewish and a Muslim congregation holding weekly services there. He told me he had been listening to my messages very carefully and he liked the idea that Jesus was talking about compassion as a path to an experience of the Holy or Sacred.

Then he got to the point. He said it seemed I did not believe God punishes people or sends them to hell if they are not believers who follow the rules. "Don't you believe in hell?" he asked with a bit of desperation.

"I certainly do not believe in a hell after death where one is tortured forever," I told him. I would have no interest in a God who would do that for any reason. "Quite frankly," I added, "there is very little biblical evidence that Jesus believed or taught such a thing." I told him I think we humans can create our own hell here on earth and unfortunately, we often do. That's what the Jesus story of new life is about—moving from our own hell to new life.

My young friend could only shake his head. Finally, after being quiet for some time, he looked at me with a real sadness. He said, "I don't think I could be a good person if I did not think I would go to hell and be tortured eternally after I die." I was astounded. By this time I knew enough about this young man to know he was a good family man, he was in a helping career, he was generous and he seemed to be extraordinarily honest. Certainly he was with me. All I could do was stammer, "But you are a good person."

I never saw him in the church again although we did have a couple of strained encounters in public places. But I often thought about him and was very sad. Is this still the kind of thing our children are growing up learning in our more conservative churches? Is this what Muslim children are being taught? Do they grow up believing that without the right belief or the correct actions they will go someplace after they die to be tortured and burned forever? Do they grow up thinking that without that threat they cannot be a good person? Or that they cannot be a precious child of the Universe?

The fact is there is no clarity in the Bible about what we now almost casually refer to as hell. First off, there is a big language issue. Three different words in the Bible with different meanings are all now translated as hell in English bibles. In the Hebrew Scriptures *Sheol*, a word now translated as hell, originally most likely referred to a place underground where bodies are buried. The ancient Israelites had no concept of life after death or resurrection. Their immortality was gained through the growth of the tribe, as a people and through their offspring. There was some vague sense of something like a ghostly existence under the earth that remained but it was not considered life.

Of course much had changed by the time Jesus was born. Clearly things had changed when the evangelists wrote the gospels. Israel had been occupied by the powerful and influential Romans for over 100 years by that time. The Greek culture, with its emphasis on mythology, along with the dualistic Mystery Religions of the surrounding areas had a profound impact on the Jewish culture. When you think of dualism, think Plato and Aristotle, think shadow and light, imagine good and evil in a constant struggle. It was here that the concept of the separation of the dead was merged into the thinking of the remnants of Israel and the nucleus of the new Christian movement.

The only word consistently translated as hell in the Christian Scriptures was Gehenna, literally the Valley of the Hinnon. It was better known in its time as the Jerusalem city dump where everything was disposed of, from garbage and sewage to unclaimed bodies. Clearly the people of Jesus' time would have known where that place was and what it was like. It was often smoldering with fire. It made for a powerful metaphor. Jesus' references to Gehenna make more sense as a metaphor than they do as a place where you are actually going to go after you die.

It is far more likely the Jesus of compassion was metaphorically referring to a life that has gone astray when one cannot seem to repent and change, rather than to some place where his loving Creator was going to torture one for eternity. Ironically I believe Jesus saw through the dualism of his time and our time. Frankly unless he was getting trained by Greek scholars, the whole idea of dualistic reality would have been foreign or even unimaginable for Jesus. Once one has had an experience of Perfect Unity, or Oneness the dualistic universe disappears. Scholar John Dominic Crossan refers to this as *radical egalitarianism*.

Why do we have these ideas of eternal punishment being promulgated you might wonder? Why do so many religions have this dichotomy—this need for correct belief or severe punishment, the idea that some are in and some are out? I am afraid it's what it has always been. It's about power. Religions, particularly those considered Religions of the Book, have always been about power rather than about love, compassion and an experience of Sacred Unity. It does seem like we spend a lot of time and energy trying to get out from those shackles in order to find our way to the holy, the sacred, the Unity we all yearn for. Power and fear will do that.

I wish I could have somehow made that clear to my young friend who asked me if I believed in hell. I am afraid he is already experiencing some kind of hell from just worrying about it. How sad.

What Have We Done?

Several years ago when *The DaVinci Code* was so popular, I wrote a short article about the book. It was published on the church website where I was pastor at the time. I was surprised by the number of people who called and asked if I was going to be doing any speaking on the topic. As it turned out, I did end up doing about six presentations for folks in mostly small groups. The vast majority of them did not attend our church. Most of the gatherings were in private homes and one was in a synagogue. Two of the groups were made up of people from two different synagogues. Another one was made up of mostly women from one of the local Catholic churches. It was fascinating to observe the different perspectives these individuals brought into the discussion with their diverse backgrounds.

Most of the people who attended these presentations wanted to know what was *true* and what was not true in Brown's thesis and "scholarship." Was

Jesus married to Mary Magdalene or not? Did Jesus have children or not? Was there really some secret society withholding information about the real facts about Jesus? Was there some historical document that could prove all of this?

I think some folks were a little disappointed when I explained most of Dan Brown's so called scholarship, was poor scholarship at best. As you may recall, Brown's book was based on the premise that Jesus was married and had a family with heirs who are still living. However, I do believe the case can be made that he was most likely married.

I also made it clear that while most of the recent search for the historical Jesus has revealed a tremendous amount of information, it has raised as many questions as it has answered. What we have learned is more about the historical times in which Jesus lived. This has been helpful for scholars to reconstruct the roots of the Christian tradition and has given us a better perspective on what Jesus taught.

In my opinion, the importance of Dan Brown's book is that it has raised the serious issue of how poorly the church has treated women throughout the centuries. Frankly, with some rare exceptions, it still does. Although it was not my main purpose for being there, I tried to give them a perspective on how the male leadership of the Roman Church, and later protestant traditions, manipulated, misinterpreted and ignored Christian scriptures to keep women in a secondary or subservient role.

Most of the participants were surprised when I explained that nothing in the Christian scriptures would even suggest Mary Magdalene was a prostitute. It is far more likely she was an early disciple of Jesus and a woman of means. I told them few characters in the New Testament have been as sorely miscast as Mary Magdalene. Her reputation as a fallen woman originated in a sixth-century sermon by Pope Gregory the Great.

Most of the people were fascinated to learn that the mythology of the virgin birth was likely the result of mistranslation of an Isaiah passage. According to the Isaiah passages that Matthew borrowed to create a prophecy, the expected messiah would be born of a young, unwed girl. It may even have been an intentional addition to the story. Young, untouched women being impregnated by a god to create a hero/savior was a significant part of the mythology of many religions of the day in Egypt as well as other parts of the Middle East. Either way, it supported the bias that a woman who had sex with a man was somehow unclean or spoiled, especially unmarried woman. I never bothered to get into the issue of the Immaculate Conception. This belief suggests that Mother Mary, through divine grace, was preserved as immaculate from all stain of original sin normally passed on from mother to child through sexual impregnation. The belief was and is for many, that Mary's mother was purified at her moment of impregnation.

It was also very interesting to see how different people—especially the women—reacted to our conversations about the early Christian interpretations of the creation stories from Hebrew Scripture. A few wondered if I was taking the information I was sharing out of context. Others were visibly upset and a few became very emotional. When the women from the Jewish synagogues heard me explain how the Christian theologians and church leaders used the creation stories from the Hebrew Scriptures to support their sexist ideas and what they saw as Puritan Christian sexuality, they were obviously disturbed. One woman from a synagogue turned toward her friend and asked, "What have they done?" I believe it is time for progressive Christians to address that question again and again. "What have we done?"

I suppose we would have to go back to Tertullian and certainly Augustine to find the roots of the blatant misogyny. I remember how shocked I was when I learned that Thomas Aquinas continued to skew the information. *"Women,"* he wrote in *Summa Theologica, "are subordinate in nature and in purpose . . . they have not sufficient strength of mind to resist the concupiscence."*

I find it almost laughable these men who apparently had a very hard time controlling their own sex drives, found it so convenient to project those own desires, their rampant cravings on to women.

Of course some of these issues have been addressed by contemporary, mostly female theologians like Rosemary Ruether (*Sexism And God-Talk*, 1983) and Joan Chittister (*Heart of Flesh*, 1998). But we are still a long way from true equality and a healthy, wholesome, spiritual approach to human sexuality. Sadly, we are short on models and examples for real change.

Referring to some of the early Christian theologians Chittister writes: *"Those ideas not only justified the oppression of women; they were also the ideas that by implication, created a spirituality that limited women and anchored men in notions of preeminence as harmful to the men themselves in one way as they were to women in another."*

Ruether, in her classic book, suggests this patriarchal development of Christianity, "has distorted the original equivalence of all human beings and has created instead hierarchical societies of privilege and deprivation, domination and exploitation."

Chittister continues; *"Revolution happened everywhere in the modern world, but little of it happened for women, and for most yet today, much is still to be accomplished around the world."*

More recently, literally dozens of books address the injustices and suffering the distortions and sexual bias of early Christianity have caused and continue to cause women. Some of the more recent books have pointed out that the net result has been terrible damage to the healthy evolutionary and spiritual growth of our society for both men and woman. I do not think very many people believe we have a healthy attitude towards human sexuality in the Western world today, especially in the United States. Twenty minutes of television will generally demonstrate that sad truth.

The great irony of all of this is that many of the causes of this unhealthy sexuality can be traced back to the church. Jesus' teachings, that we can learn to experience all Creation as Divine, including women and men, have been lost in the process. Our continued subtle and not so subtle patriarchal bias has been a road block for us to learn to see and experience all creation as One through a practice of radical egalitarianism. We all lose in the process, especially our children.

Yes there has been some progress. There are a few females in top corporate and government positions, a few female Bishops in the Anglican Church and more women leading protestant churches. I believe we have to look deeper at what we have done to human sexuality by both our ignorance and our refusal to dig deeper. This is not just a private matter. It affects our entire world.

I believe it's time to go back to the question the woman asked her friend at one of my presentations. We as Christians and as a society need to look carefully at our history and the impact this history still has on our society. We need to ask, "What have we done?"

I am beginning to believe that until we educate ourselves, until we confess, until we repent, we really cannot move to a new life and a new perspective. The world needs that today just as much as it did 2000 years ago.

Will Christianity Die or Evolve?

One of the things we have learned from the study of evolution is that species do not necessarily evolve unless threatened by extinction. When 90 percent of our world was covered with water, the early aquatic species of our planet had no need to change. However, as the water began to recede over a period of thousands of years, many of these species, in some unexplainable process, began to grow legs and lungs. Possibly more importantly, they had to give up their gills and fins. I find this both fascinating and telling.

I don't think there were any meetings to discuss or vote on how these species were going to have to change. Nor do I believe there were consultants who offered their expertise about how they could save themselves by doing what they were doing, but to do it better.

As participation in our local churches continues to drop like a rock across the country more churches continue to close. One has to ask if there is a future for the church in particular and for Christianity in general. There are plenty of commentators who are predicting total demise within the next few decades. Quite frankly it is hard to argue with them. The numbers offer no indication there will be a meaningful future for churches, at least as we think of them today.

However, human beings are social animals. We like to create communities. We like to have places where we can talk about deep and important things. I remember hearing a highly respected conference minister in the United Church of Christ say something during his retirement banquet. It has stuck with me for nearly three decades. "I am no longer certain who and what Jesus was, and I have no idea if I believe in God or if life has a purpose. But I do know I want to be around people who are interested in these things."

Many of us still want to be around people who wrestle with the angels, who do care about the deep and often conflicting issues that come up in our lives. Something in these meaningful and challenging topics draws us together in authentic community. By authentic I mean a willingness to share from the heart at the deepest level. I am referring to a level of intimacy not often found at typical social events or even in organizations focusing on social service.

So sociologists and commentators are having some interesting conversations these days about the future of Christianity. Some argue we need to get back to the basics—yes, the fundamentals like Salvation through Christ. That might have some value except the fundamentalist churches are aging faster than the progressive Christian churches. Furthermore the data shows young people with college educations, particularly in the liberal arts, are simply not buying the old Jesus story. Frankly they have little interest in religion at all.

A significant number of scholars and commentators are celebrating the dying of what they believe has been and remains a detrimental institution for our society. They often point to the absence of religion in Europe. They note how those countries have aggressively built public institutions for the support of their citizens in need. In some ways, one could argue they have become more Christian in their public actions than the United States.

So as we often do with these conversations, we come back to the question, "Is there a future for Christianity and what might that look like. Will Christianity die or will it evolve into something new?" After 25 years of visiting hundreds of churches, speaking at large conference gatherings, interviewing groups of students on campuses and corresponding with too many people to count, I must admit I am not necessarily an optimist. However I am beginning to see some interesting developing patterns that could indicate new life. It is far too early to decide if these are signs for the future. I may just be projecting my own bias into what appear to be some interesting sprouts but I think they are worth noting. They may even be a whisper of a future voice.

First, I am aware of some churches making substantive changes throughout the entire life of their congregations. They are not just adding a contemporary service or adding a rock band. They are making changes from the ground up. They include everything from liturgy to seating arrangement, from theology to language. For example, they are eliminating church words that mean nothing except to people who grew up in church. They are also changing the focus from beliefs to behavior and from proclamation to education. The focus in these communities is on the historical Jesus rather than in the creedal Christ.

These changes have not come easily or without pain. But what we are seeing is communities of interested people who are excited about what they are doing. They tend to be proud—joyful even—that they may be forging a new path.

However, there is a major challenge for this shift beyond the inevitable pain of change. Faith communities that form themselves around the wisdom teachings of Jesus will naturally be more interested in how the participants are actually living their lives. I would presume there would be more attention paid to how the participants treat each other and relate to the world. It will assume some accountability that is not normal in our larger church communities. The emphasis here is not on saving souls or church growth. Rather it is on learning together how to follow a path that could change the way we relate to each other and the rest of the world.

The goal, I hope, would be to actually help each other live the teachings, not necessarily debate them or ignore them, but to practice them. The intention would be to become a "people of the Way" community like the earliest Jesus followers but in the world of the 21st century. While I have seen this model work well in small groups, I am not certain if it will attract enough people to support what we have come to think of as church. That model includes real estate, building upkeep and paid staff. Time will tell.

The second phenomenon I am observing is the establishment of churches or faith communities within a church. A few years ago I was asked to give a presentation at a local church on Sunday morning. I knew the church well and was frankly surprised that anyone in this very traditional mainline church would be interested in hearing what I would have to say. I arrived at 8 a.m. and was escorted to a large classroom. I was amazed to see over 40 people already there sharing coffee and sweet rolls. It was a surprise in part because I knew the membership in this church was something under 200. This group seemed to represent an unusually large percentage of the church.

It turned out to be a wonderful 90 minutes. These people were well read, interested, and asked informed questions. They seem to delight in new information and different perspectives. When the time was up, I suddenly wondered if I was expected to join the group to attend their regular worship service. But after the chairs were stacked and the coffee cups were cleared, the majority of these folks, along with me, walked out to the parking lot, got into our cars and went home.

I realized this was their church. I learned that only about half of those folks were official members of the larger congregation but attended this small group meeting weekly. I have now encountered more of these church-within-a-church models and I wonder if these kinds of gatherings will be the nucleus of the future.

In the last couple of years I have come across another phenomenon that fascinates me. I have now been involved with four independent organizations formed in large part to attract and finance progressive speakers, biblical scholars and Christian educators to inform and inspire them. It appears there are more of these organizations in the South. I assume this is because most churches in the area refuse to have anything to do with progressive Christianity. A young man in Birmingham, Alabama recently told me he could not tell his pastor he was attending the event where I was speaking. Sadly he told me he could not even tell his friend and neighbor of 25 years where he was going that night.

These groups may host the better known authors and speakers two or three times a year. They normally gather somewhere between 100 to 300 people for these events. They all seem to have regular email publications and websites. There is usually one volunteer managing the day-to-day activities and a volunteer board. The speakers might be Bishop John Shelby Spong, Marcus Borg, Brandon Scott and other familiar names. However, they are not the typical large conferences with multiple speakers and break-outs.

The fascinating part is that three of the four organizations have developed active small groups. The fourth one is working on starting them. Usually these small groups meet once a week in someone's home. They may study a book together, talk about a recent speaker, or someone will volunteer to lead a discussion on something they want to share. At least a couple of these groups have a potluck meal or pot of soup once a month. I was a speaker at one of these events. I discovered this organization already had seven active small groups and they were talking about starting two more. I wondered, as I traveled home that week, if this could be a small bud trying to pop its head out of the ground? If so, what might the new church look like?

Some scholars believe mainline churches can be revived with a new theology and Christology. Marcus Borg, Bishop Spong, and to some degree John Dominic Crossan, fall into this category. I think their perspective may be influenced by the fact that when these high-profile speakers are invited to speak, they usually encounter large, enthusiastic crowds. I worked the church growth circuit for over 20 years. All too often I felt the pain of the small elderly remnants in declining communities as they struggled to find a way to save their church. I tend to believe if Christianity is going to survive more than another few generations, it will have to find a whole new model.

There are a few new books out on this subject you may find interesting. I highly recommend David Galston's book, *Embracing the Human Jesus.* (Polebridge Press 2012) Galston provides an outline of a new Christology based on the wisdom teachings of the historical Jesus. He also offers a way this new Christology might take form in faith communities. The book is informed by an experimental community Galston has helped form. I have asked Galston to keep us informed about their adventure in Canada. You can follow his blogs on their website: http://www.questcentre.ca/.

I also want to recommend Frances Macnab's book, *Discover a New Faith.* (Spectrum Publication 2012) Macnab, both a scholar and the Executive Minister of a church in Melbourne, Australia, has mapped out a new and unique direction for Christian communities in the 21st century. It might appear to be a bit shocking for many people as he suggests moving past some traditional sacred cows. But as I have suggested, I no longer believe tune-ups and adjustments are going to be enough. We need to find a way to gather as Christians in a way that is relevant to the growing number of people who apparently have less and less interest in church.

So will the church evolve or die? That just may be up to the courageous clergy and their dedicated communities. Maybe together we can build a new future.

What Kind of Music do we Use?

In all of my years as a pastor, my favorite service was the late evening candlelight service on Christmas Eve. It somehow combined all the best things about church for me. The sermon was short and the evening was always festive, moving and deeply spiritual. But over the years I realized there was one thing about that service besides the candles that was special. It was the music.

Admittedly the music did not match the grandiose music performance of our amazing choir, guest soloist and visiting orchestra during Easter services. It may not have been quite as exhilarating as the music of the combined choirs and instruments during the Thanksgiving service we held with the

Synagogue that shared our space for nearly 15 years. But a minor disaster that occurred one Christmas Eve made me realize what had made the music so important.

We had never used a hymnal for this particular service. But one year, shortly after purchasing the new UCC hymnal, we decided to use them for the service. The worship committee printed out the first and second verses of over a dozen familiar Christmas carols. Frankly none of us looked closely at the words or noticed they had been altered in the denomination's attempt to make the hymnal gender neutral. From a philosophical standpoint I have always appreciated these efforts. But in this case it did not work out well.

It started at that magical moment when we turn down the overhead lights, light our individual candles and begin to joyfully sing the carols together. It was not long before grumbling could be heard. There were not many changes to the words but enough to throw people off. Some were using words from memory and others were following the hand-out. The singing began to sound like any congregation trying to sing new hymns—nothing short of awful. Fortunately most of the people in the pews only needed the music for the second verse for most carols. When I finally realized what was going on, I suggested that everyone put the paper sheets down and sing from memory.

A week or so later when our planning committee was reviewing our experience we all agreed to go back to the slides we had used for years for those few visitors who had not memorized the carols. I was surprised, however, how upset some people continued to feel about the loss.

A few years later, while I was doing research on the growing mega-church phenomenon, I began to grasp what really happened that night. Over time, I have become clearer why so many people felt such a loss that night.

I believe any truly spiritual path must understand its main function is to provide the opportunity to experience genuine Unity, or Oneness with all Creation. There are many ways to say the same thing but every church, religious, or spiritual gathering is trying to help the attendee experience that Oneness. I am convinced one of the places we can do this is with music.

The mega-churches, in large part, figured this out decades ago. But go into a typical church today with 60 members and listen to them try and experience Oneness or a sense of connectedness as they stumble through a difficult hymn. At some point most people are just hoping for the hymn to be over.

I do not care if you are a fundamentalist, a conservative, or an evangelical megachurch, the music should be designed to offer an opportunity to experience that connectedness with the Divine and each other.

I get tired of hearing my colleagues and scholarly friends make fun of the so-called praise music common in so many of the mega churches and even in smaller evangelical churches today. We may hold our noses up in distain but those churches continue to attract young people. I have attended many of those services over the years and watched the faces and expressions of those participating attendees. They are experiencing something few people do in our intellectually sophisticated mainline services. The words they use are simple and repetitive as is the music. Most of the time after going through one verse most people no longer need for written music. In many ways these simple repetitive songs are like ancient chants.

Forget the fact that most of our mainline churches are singing songs with music that no longer fits our Christology. The music does nothing for most people. Simply changing the words and correcting the theology is not necessarily going to make it any more palatable or experiential.

This is why most growing churches from all perspectives now include music with drums and with simple lyrics that can easily be memorized. This kind of music allows you to feel the beat. It does not have to be rock music but still something you can feel. Some churches encourage dancing in the aisles. People in general and young people in particular want to feel some connection to the sacred, the divine through participatory music.

When I say participatory I don't necessarily mean everyone has to sing or dance, although these can be positive spiritual activities. What I do mean is the music touches the soul at some deeper level. It can be an action that helps someone recognize they are connected to something greater than themselves. For some it might mean sensing deep connection with other participants. For others it might truly be a path to the experience of the Ultimate Divine. For a few it might be all of that.

A few years ago I attended a Compline service at Saint Mark's Cathedral in downtown Seattle. The Cathedral started this service in the 1950s and it is still going strong. The service is held every Sunday night at 9:30 p.m. and is attended in large part by people between the ages of 15 and 40 years old. The time I attended, there were several hundred people nearly filling the large sanctuary. I was told attendance ranges from 200 to over 600 hundred depending on the time of the year.

The Compline service comes out of the monastic tradition and is primarily made up of chants and meditative music sung by a small choir. The attendees can sit, lie down or walk around anywhere they feel comfortable in the Cathedral.

I interviewed some of the young students I met in a nearby coffee shop after the half hour service. I discovered few of them attend church nor did they think of themselves as religious. But they seldom missed a Sunday night. The common expression I got from them was that it helped them feel connected and they liked the way it made them feel. A couple of them were able to articulate a sense of belonging to something greater than themselves. But not one of those I talked to had a theology or Christology they were willing to share with me or the group. They generally agreed that they love the experience and miss it when they do not attend.

I have sat at the edge of drumming circles for an hour or more on many occasions. I admit I never interviewed the participants but I do know most of them gather at least once a week. I believe they would have echoed much of the same comments the young folks expressed who attend the Compline services. It helps them feel connected and part of something larger than themselves. Others have found that same connectedness by attending Taizé services on a regular basis. Most of who attend do not necessarily see themselves as religious. I suspect many of them might be uncomfortable with the actually language of the chants if they were translated but I doubt if that would stop them.

Like the young people who attend the Compline services, they are not concerned with the words or worried about the religious implications. They are doing something together and experiencing Oneness or connectedness seldom experienced in our disconnected, competitive and sometimes downright callous world. Few of them, I am sorry to say, would find this connectedness on Sunday mornings in most of our mainline church services.

For over 20 years in my former church, we sang the same closing song. It was the word alleluia sung over and over, often with lovely harmony. We changed a lot of things over the years in that church, including buildings, bulletins and music. But I think I would have put my career and possibly my life in jeopardy if I had insisted on changing that one thing. It was rare when I did not notice tears of sadness, tears of release and tears of joy during that very short time in the service. No theology, no Christology, no sermon could have done more than those couple of hundred people holding hands, often with eyes closed, going someplace into themselves yet connected to something much larger.

So I go back to the question. What is the place of music in the progressive church or gathering? I suggest starting with a clear understanding of what our goal or purpose is for our progressive churches. From my perspective that means using and creating music, chants and meditations that bring everyone together. We want to create an opportunity for our participants to have an experience of Union or Oneness. That means a union with others in the room, with the creation and all sentient beings and with the Ultimate Mystery we call God.

We need to give consideration to things like: Is it inviting, simple, does it have a beat, is familiar and/or joyful? If it is difficult to learn, to sing, to play or understand, I suggest we leave it to the professional or volunteer musicians for their special performances. It seems to me we should be looking for an experience that deeply connects us rather than concerning ourselves about echoing the sermon or the theology of the day. Maybe then we can sing or chant our way into the Infinite Mystery.

CHAPTER FIVE

The Spiritual Journey

Always a Seeker

I have always been a seeker. Even as a young child, in my Sunday school classes, I asked a lot of questions. I took church attendance very seriously, seldom missing a Sunday and participated in all the special events. I sang in the children's choir and eventually in the adult choir every Sunday. I assumed leadership positions when asked and even attended regional and national events as a youth representative for our Presbytery. But more than once, I was told I asked too many questions, suggesting I did not have enough faith. One of my favorite Sunday school teachers even set up a meeting with our rather strict minister once so he could deal with all of my questions. He was certainly nice enough, but in a rather patronizing way he suggested my questions would someday seem rather childish when my faith matured. Little did either of us know then that they would never end.

I don't think my experience was unique for those of us who were growing up in small communities in the 1950s. Some people just shut down and quit thinking about those ultimate questions. Others simply quit going to church. A few people like me kept looking for answers. The answers we found seemed to lead to other questions. That is probably why I ended up taking so many philosophy classes in college. That is why I drove all night to hear a talk by the radical Bishop Pike in the 1960s. And that is why I have sought out every opportunity to expand my understanding of the meaning of life and how to live it ever since. In the late '60s, I studied the works of G.I. Gurdjieff. Years later I met regularly with a group of followers of P.D. Ouspensky, a student of Gurdjieff. I studied various Eastern and eso-teric teachers for three decades.

The strange thing was that although I never felt like I had found the answer or the correct way, it never seemed like I had been wasting my time or going down the wrong path. Quite to the contrary, the more I learned, the more interested I was in going further. I also have met a whole lot of very interesting people during these years who were on a similar journey. Some of them became life-long friends.

It is unfortunate that some large conservative churches have labeled a *seeker* as someone who has just not quite got it or found it yet. They often have special services for those whom they deem to be seekers as opposed, I presume, to believers. I have had a rich and rewarding life as a seeker and I do not expect that to change. We are referring to something that is ulti-mately unfathomable at best. That is what faith is all about.

The teachers I encountered over the years, from books as well as in per-son, came from very different worlds, backgrounds and social settings. How-ever, without exception, at some point in their lives, all of them had some extraordinary mystical experience that changed the way they viewed reality and themselves in that reality. They suddenly had eyes to see and ears to hear something significant they had not experienced before. Though they used different languages, metaphors and teaching styles to explain what they had experienced, it was clear to see, with a minimal amount of study, they had more in common than not.

As a result of the incredible abundance of biblical scholarship done in the later part of the 20th century which continues to this day, many of us welcomed the opportunity to re-engage Jesus as a great spiritual teacher. I found myself drawn to the man who clearly had a life changing mystical experience that not only changed him but changed the people around him. I was no longer trying to ignore things that made no sense to me, even as a young boy. I began to see Jesus as one among other teachers who had a com-mon message about who and what we are as humans and our relationship with all Creation.

None of that would have been so exciting or as meaningful if I had not immersed myself over the years in other great teachers, both traditional and esoteric. Certainly the most influential and helpful reading I did over the years was in the various Buddhist traditions. I am most familiar with the Tibetan perspective. On the surface there are significant differences from the teachings of Jesus and the Buddha. It also seems important to note that the historical Jesus had only four to six years to formulate and articulate his teachings. The Buddha's teachings evolved over several decades. Certainly these two great teachers were coming out of very different cultures and social settings. However, it was the in-depth Buddhist teachings on compassion and kindness that helped me begin to understand the teachings of Jesus as a path that could enable others to have a similar experience of the Divine.

It was my study of Buddhism that began to open up a new meaning to Jesus' teachings on the Kingdom or Realm of God on earth. It seemed clear to me that the Four Immeasurables or Four Limitless Qualities of the rich Tibetan tradition were very similar to the most fundamental and dynamic teachings of Jesus. As I read about the role of the warrior-bodhisattva who comes down from the mountain in order to alleviate suffering, I gained another perspective on the life story of Jesus. Interestingly, it was the Buddhist tradition that brought me back to Jesus but it was a very different Jesus than the one I learned about in my Sunday school class more than 60 years earlier.

I am glad I was a seeker and I am glad I continue to be a seeker into the mysteries we cannot possibly fathom or even imagine. I am glad there are other seekers who continue to grow and change and are willing to live with a tender heart for this world.

Practice, Practice, Practice

When I was about 13, my parents decided to find me a new piano teacher who might inspire me to go to the next level of competence. I had been taking lessons for four or five years at that point and both my former teachers told my parents I had a talent that should be nurtured. So every Wednesday afternoon, immediately after school, my Mom would drive me over 20 miles each way so I could have the benefit of a teacher who had shaped the music careers of more than a few professional pianists.

From the very beginning he was not certain about my commitment, probably for good reason. I loved all sports, I loved riding my bike in the hills that surrounded our home and I was discovering girls. Practicing the piano was no higher than fourth or fifth on a long list of things I wanted to do with my non-school time. After nearly a year of wrestling with the teacher over my commitment, with my parents over my priorities and with my own guilt, I knew things were not going well. One day, while I was playing my assigned music with my teacher sitting next to me on the piano bench, he began banging his hands on the keys. "Practice! Practice! Practice! If you do not practice you will never know what it means to be a musician," he yelled. And then as he stood up, with a purple face, he said, "What a waste!" And I was suddenly no longer his student.

Over the last five decades, as I have searched for a meaningful spiritual path that might bring purpose, fulfillment and peace to my life, I have often reflected on that experience with both mirth and awe. It must have been a funny scene, fit for a Woody Allen movie. The truth is, I know that teacher was right. He touched upon a truth that goes beyond piano lessons. We will never discover what it means to become something meaningful unless we practice until it goes from our thinking to our being. This is especially true if you want to become something that requires unique skills whether it is surgeon, teacher, electrician or yes, a musician.

I often wonder as I look out over the religious landscape in our world today, how many people who call themselves Christian actually practice being one. I don't mean by going to church every Sunday, or memorizing the Bible or wearing an obvious cross around your neck. It does not mean honing an air tight argument about what one has to believe about Jesus to be a Christian or blindly reciting creeds. I mean when someone gets up in the morning, they start the day by actually practicing being a Christian based on the teachings of Jesus.

You do not have to have a Master's degree in Divinity or a perfect attendance record in your local church to know what that means. You don't have to create a long list of things you are not supposed to do or live in fear of eternal damnation. You simply need to practice living the teachings. It is the music score Jesus gave us for this dance of life in which we are all participating. It is the path to an experience of the Realm of God. These teachings really are not that difficult to discern and I believe there is little debate about their authenticity. We may miss a couple of them and we might not be able to do all of them all of the time. But what is important is our willingness to practice, practice, practice! Here are seven teachings that certainly will give you a good start:

1. Practice compassion
2. Practice trust
3. Practice forgiveness
4. Practice non-judgment
5. Practice generosity
6. Practice thankfulness
7. Practice joy.

As simple as they are to list, we all know they are often difficult to do, just as a piece of classical music is hard to play unless we have practiced and practiced. It is a big step to go from talking about these teachings, to practicing them. It is an even bigger step to go from having to think about them while we do them, to just *being* them.

I often wonder, with some sadness, if Jesus the Teacher returned to earth today and looked at the religious landscape if he would have the same frustration my former piano teacher had. Would he want to yell, "Practice! Practice! Practice! If you want to know what it means to *be* a Christian then you have to practice it until you become it?"

I suspect he observed the way a lot of pious people lived out their understanding of Christianity, he would be like my former teacher and would shake his head and mumble, "What a waste!"

Love or Fear

I know it is not accurate or maybe even helpful to create simple dichotomies. But as I look back over my life and think of all the wonderful, unique and interesting people I have come to know, I am beginning to wonder if we can put people into two basic categories-those who live their lives motivated primarily by love and those primarily guided by fear. This statement, of course, requires some qualifiers. When I refer to love, I am not thinking of romantic or addictive love here, but rather a love for life which probably includes a love for self as well as for others. Likewise, when I refer to someone primarily driven by fear, I am not referring to someone who is necessarily paralyzed by fear or for that matter lives constantly in fear. Rather I refer here to someone ponders all of the things that could go wrong before making a decision or taking an action—if indeed they ever take action or make that decision.

I also do not mean to suggest that people who are primarily motivated by fear do not experience love or people primarily motivated by love do not experience fear. I have come to wonder if these are just two different perspectives or lenses through which we humans view our reality. We see either something very scary or something very interesting, exciting or even wonderful.

I was a guest lecturer in a college class on religion one year. During my first presentation, I asked the students, ages 18 to 20, with a few older adults who were as old as fifty-five, if they saw themselves in a world full of dark forces and obstacles they had no power over. I asked them if they lived their lives and made decisions based primarily on avoiding these forces, obstacles or what some might refer to as a failure.

Or, I asked, did they view life as something exciting full of adventure, opportunities and unique experiences. This would include those who believe whatever obstacles they encounter, mistakes they make, or failures they might endure, they would view them as opportunities to grow and learn.

I tried very hard to disguise my own bias, but was surprised to learn the class was actually split approximately in half. Age seemed to have very little to do with their relative perspective. I wondered what kind of religious expression one would lean toward if they saw the world as full of dark forces. What kind of spiritual or religious expression would someone who saw life as a journey full of opportunities be attracted to? I have my own suspicions but no scientific evidence beyond anecdotal evidence to support them. I did learn that about half the class considered themselves to be either a conservative or evangelical Christian and the other half considered themselves to be either non-religious or liberal Christian.

Fear is a powerful energy and a tremendous influence on lives. It creates isolation, separation, anger, judgment, and disease. It is the one thing that most consistently stops us from enjoying life. Fear gives you something to be against. Fear gives one an identity. It is always easier to be against something than it is to be open to the unknown. Yet no matter

110

how careful, how secluded or religious we become, life is full of unknowns including our own death.

So what is our greatest fear? I believe it is discovering who we really are, at the deepest level. Maybe it means slowly taking off all the different masks we have created to protect our frightened egos. If we really took the opportunity to look into the mirror of God without fear, we might actually see that we are precious, beautiful and perfect just the way we are—without the mask, without the makeup, without the costumes. It we had the courage to dissolve all of those things our frightened egos have created to help us look better, stronger, more important and influential, we might see the real self. We might truly discover who we are.

Marianne Williamson once wrote: "Our deepest fear is not that we are inadequate. Our deepest fear is that we are powerful beyond measure. It is our light, not our darkness that most frightens us. We ask ourselves, who am I to be brilliant, gorgeous, talented, and fabulous? Actually who are you *not* to be? You are a child of God. You're playing small does not serve the world. There is nothing enlightened about shrinking so that other people won't feel insecure around you. We are all meant to shine, as children do. We were born to make manifest the glory of God that is within us. It's not just in some of us; it's in everyone. And as we let our own light shine, we unconsciously give other people permission to do the same. As we are liberated from our own fear, our presence automatically liberates others." Why not let your light shine brightly and fearlessly, even during the dark months of winter?

So what is the mirror of God? It is a metaphor for the true, divine you devoid of fear and self-doubt. It is the quiet voice always trying to overcome the noisy chatter of your ego as it tries to convince you that you are unworthy, incapable, or a failure. It is the still, quiet voice trying to let you know that you are love and that you are loved. It is your divine self that knows you are part of something wonderful and profound. It is the "you" you may discover when you let go of the protective shield you created because you believe you must have it to survive in this world.

Letting that shield go is not easy, especially if it has been there for a long time. It feels comfortable, necessary even. But let's admit it. It is there because we live in fear. Is that the life we want?

My Struggle with Prayer

I have struggled with the idea of prayer since I was a young boy. A few years after the Second World War, I was very impressionable. During this time the general public began to hear more details about the horrible atrocities in Nazi concentration camps. My grandparents lived in a Jewish area of West Los Angeles while I was growing up in the '40s and '50s.

I spent a lot of time at their home. I knew many of their neighbors were Jewish because much of the local storefront signage was written in Hebrew. I also noticed that several of the boys wore caps on Friday evenings and Saturdays. My grandmother explained they were called yarmulkes. When I asked her why they wore them, she said it was their custom. She did not know specifically why they wore them. However, she noted the men and boys wore them when they went to their house of prayer.

I made play friends with a couple of those boys who wore yarmulkes to their house of prayer on Saturdays. Although no one took the time to explain to me what was happening, I gradually began to hear that many of my friends' relatives were being killed in prison camps in Germany. One time in the movie theater I do remember seeing photos of these tortured people, no more than skin and bones, being released from their prisons. I was horrified.

Somewhere along the way I started wondering why so many of my friends' relatives were being tortured or starved to death in Europe. They had houses of prayer. They prayed to God. I had been told by my parents God answered prayers. I wondered why God could not or would not have saved them. At the time I was thinking it might have been a lot of people. It would have been unfathomable for me to believe there were actually millions of people who were tortured and murdered because the men wore caps to their houses of prayer.

By the time I was in my late teens I had already concluded there was no anthropomorphic God up there who granted wishes or requests to some people and not to others, whether they wore caps on Saturdays or not. In fact, I had pretty much given up on the idea that there was any God who was some separate entity from the rest of the universe. I still held onto the idea that there was some connecting energy or force that was part of all of us and I was willing to call that energy God. But I had no idea what that really meant. I did know I no longer expected my prayers or anyone's prayers to be answered by a faraway God in the heavens, even if they were the most devoted, religious people in the world.

After a couple of life changing experiences that encouraged me to turn my life more inward, I found myself, at 40 years old, in seminary. I wondered if I might get a better idea there of what spiritual people thought about prayer. I was already practicing meditation at least 30 minutes a day. But I did not think of that as prayer. I was simply trying to learn to be still. By that time, when I became really still, clearing the chatter from my head, I had discovered I could experience a certain kind of connectedness, or oneness that gave me a sense of peace and contentment.

Toward the end of my first full year of studies, our school encountered a serious conflict. It involved the layoffs of two staff people. A large group of students felt it had something to do with the fact that they were African American. Others, especially those of us who had done some research, knew there was more involved.

However, the campus was about to explode. There had already been a protest when a group of students occupied the President's office. There was talk about bringing in some outside civil rights demonstrators to expand the protest. As a result, a large group of us, black, white and other, gathered one evening to see if we could gain some clarity on the issues. My real hope was that we could at least modulate some of the tension and hostility. The business manager agreed to come to our meeting to explain what had occurred and respond to questions.

It was a tense evening and fuses were short. We tossed around words like love, forgiveness, and non-judgment but as our agreed upon time was running out, it was pretty clear there was still some lingering suspicion and residual anger in the room.

Suddenly, I got a brainstorm. I suggested to the group of about 40 people that we all stand and hold hands or touch someone nearby. And then we could pray. There was a moment of grumbling as people stood up and slowly and awkwardly started reaching for hands. Suddenly the room became totally quiet, heads were bowed and people waited. But no one offered to lead us in prayer. I finally looked over at a senior who was across the room. I had heard him preach at our chapel services and speak in class. He always seemed very confident. *"Dave, why don't you lead us?"* I asked. There was a long pregnant pause and I realized he was clearly flustered. He finally stammered, *"I haven't had that class yet."*

I knew then I would not have the class on prayer in seminary. Years later I realized if there had been a course on prayer in our school, someone would have had to explain to whom or to what we were praying. They even might have had to answer the question, *"Why don't people who go to a house of prayer and wear Yarmulkes get their prayers answered."* That was not going to happen in a scholarly seminary environment.

For the first five years as clergy, I relied heavily on some of the materials provided by our liberal denomination for our services. I called upon God to bless our gathering; we praised God for creating such a beautiful world; we thanked God for answering our prayers; and we asked God to forgive our trespasses, knowing of course that he/she would. For most people these petitions, our thanks and our praise were routine. I am quite certain for many, this may have been comforting. But in small groups, classes and in individual counseling sessions, the conversations often got much more complex. Although I had intentionally helped create a faith community with participants who felt free to question, to doubt and even reject religious dogma, I still had a hard time explaining why we pray to God in our services. One of my favorite church leaders once asked me with some frustration in his voice, *"If you can't explain who or what God is, why do we keep asking 'whatever it is' for anything?"*

As I had more conversations with people who were looking for answers or at least some logical explanations, I realized I really needed to be able to explain where I stood. If nothing else, it had become clear to me there is something that gives life to that which would otherwise be dead, inert, and/or inanimate. Long before that, I had concluded there had to be a Life Source—infinite, constant and readily available to us. It is within us, around us and outside of us. It is that which gives us life and we have the capacity to maximize or increase its impact and influence in our lives. Although I am much clearer about all of this today, 20 years ago I realized all of the great spiritual teachers, including Jesus, were trying to teach us how to access and maximize that life force in our daily lives.

Somewhere in that time period one of my parishioners became terribly ill with cancer. They had already done surgery but the cancer came back. She was hospitalized several times and then they tried a new, much stronger chemotherapy that pushed her to the edge of death. It made her horribly sick. Over the years I had come to love this woman like a sister and considered her more than a dear friend. I would have done anything to help her. As I stood next to her bed in the hospital I was frustrated that I could not do more. At one point she opened her eyes, smiled and quietly whispered, *"Hi Pastor Fred. Will you pray for me?"*

I felt like my friend from seminary. I wanted to say something like, *"I'm sorry but I haven't had that class yet."* But this was my friend and I was her pastor. She needed something from me and it had to be authentic. I gently laid my hands on her chest just below her neck. I closed my eyes. I tried to find that place I experienced when I was meditating. I tried, with all of my being, to be still and to open myself to that energy of life. I imagined the top of my head opening up and white light pouring through my body into my hands. I simply tried to be a conduit, a pipeline and open myself as wide as I could. The only words I spoke, mostly to myself, were, *"let me be a servant of your healing."* I didn't try to analyze my words or to whom I was directing them.

At one point after about five minutes, my friend opened her eyes and thanked me. As it turned out she recovered from this bout. And although we will never know if it was the new drugs, her strong willpower or the Holy Spirit, she lived a good life for another 15 years. It was several years before we talked about that hospital experience. When I laid my hands on her, she told me she first noticed how warm they were. Then she said she felt that same warmth moving all through her body and she knew something had changed.

I want to be perfectly clear. I do not consider myself a healer. However, over the years I have learned that everything in the universe is made of the same shared atoms, molecules, subatomic particles and is actually some form of vibrant energy. I am obviously not a scientist but I have come to understand that our universe is one interconnected and interdependent creation. Maybe someday we will figure out what Dark Matter is but I am certain it will have something to do with some other vibrant form of energy.

I have come to assume there is some spirit or life force that pulses through all things. Therefore I believe we all have that life force within us and we are surrounded by it. It is in all creation and all creatures. We all have the choice to open ourselves more fully to this life force or we can shut it off as well.

Eventually we can starve ourselves to a spiritual death without it. Obviously it does not matter what path I use to access this constant Life Force nor if I even want to try and change my ways to experience it more fully. The only real judge is us.

For me prayer has become finding ways to open all possible portals to that Life Force. When I am asked to pray for someone's healing now I try and redirect Life Force or Life spirit toward the one who desires healing. But I make it clear that the person needs to open themselves to that same Life Force if it is going to be helpful.

When I am asked to bless the food at a gathering, I ask everyone to close their eyes and I focus my words on all of the sweat, tears and hard work that went into making the meal possible. I always want to mention the ones who tilled the land, the ones who worked with bent backs all day and picked it. I like to remind people about the ones who loaded crates and delivered it, the ones who purchased and prepared it. Then I ask them to consider all of the Life Force that is now held in this prepared food and to give thanks. I then ask everyone to consider as we partake of it that we might be filled with that same Spirit energy or Life Force. More importantly I like to suggest we are now bonded with all of those who have made this meal possible. We are in that sense brothers and sisters.

At weddings I ask the family and the guests to close their eyes in a moment of silence and to surround the bride and groom with light and love. Shower them with so much love they will never forget this day or this love, in good and bad times.

Well you get the idea. I do not think for one moment I have it figured out. The infinite mystery is too big for me to grasp. However, I do know what we have done for centuries is not working in our more progressive and learned lives. And I also know that people have thanked me repeatedly over the years because of the way I have approached the use of prayers in community. I have grown completely bored with any debates about whether God should be addressed with male or female pronouns. The issue for most educated people is much bigger and I believe a lot more exciting.

Just think, if we presume God is a life force that is part of all things, then we actually have the opportunity to experience God within us and in others. Just maybe that is what this is all about.

On Remaining Hopeful

Just a year or so after I graduated from college, I learned that one of my favorite high school teachers had cancer and was very sick. I had very fond memories of this particular teacher. She was one of those you never forget. She was a demanding task master but managed to be fun and funny at the same time. She could make grammar not only seem important but actually make it seem interesting. She would write long responses on our returned papers that had as much to do with how we might live our lives as it did with the content of the paper. Most of all, no matter where you were as a student, you knew she cared about you.

She always seemed to have an upbeat attitude, even when she gave you a bad grade. She just believed you were going to do better next time and we usually did. She had a huge impact on students, not only from what we learned from the assigned books and our essays, but what we learned from her attitude about life. In my early years when I thought I was heading for teaching as a profession, she was the teacher I wanted to be.

When I found out the cancer was in an advanced stage, I realized I needed to visit her. I was not certain what I was going to find but I knew I wanted to tell her what a positive impact she had had on my life.

My first visit was the hardest and I was a little shocked when I saw her depleted body. She quickly put me at ease by saying: "It doesn't look good, Freddy, but don't worry, I still have hope."

I assumed she knew something I did not know and she was going to get better. I saw her a few more times over the next couple of months. Each time she would say the same thing when I would arrive. When I was getting ready to leave, she would often chuckle and say, "Don't give up on me now, Freddy."

However, it became progressively more difficult to remain hopeful. The last time I visited it was very clear to me she was not going to make it much longer. Still she had the same smile, the same sweet words. When she saw how distraught I was, she said, "Don't worry, Freddy, I still have hope there is a better place when I leave here."

We had never talked about religion, nor did we this time. But it seemed like a rather childish comment to me at that time. I was in a post-college, quasi-nihilist, and anti-religious period of my life. I thought Albert Camus was brilliant. I left there angry and disillusioned. I equated hope as wishful thinking, something we employ when all else fails. I thought of afterlife as a token promise to soothe the pain of the oppressed masses.

As time went on however, I began to question if it was her wonder-filled life that allowed her the delusion to have hope in the most negative circumstances. Or was it her hope that helped create and shape her wonder-filled life? And, I might add, it was a life that shaped a lot of other wonder-filled lives at the same time. Even in her fight against cancer, her hope had made her life a better thing.

Over the years, I began to realize my teacher friend knew something I had not grasped in my youth. Her willingness to live in a state of hope was a life decision and a lifestyle. Even though she died a painful death from cancer, she would have been the first to tell you she had lived a wonderful life.

Today, it is very clear to me that hope is not wishful thinking for the weak. It is a positive action that will affect the course of our lives. It is for the strong who are willing to take risks and embrace change. Hope is a doorway to positive creative transformation.

Ernst Bloch, a 20th century philosopher, wrote in an anthology called *The Future of Hope*, that there is something called the structure of hope. To understand that structure we must realize *"what is usually called reality is surrounded by a gigantic ocean of objectively real possibility."* This possibility is partial conditionality. That is, what already exists does not fully determine what will be. Some of those possibilities are merely wishful thinking, or hocus pocus. Others, he posits, have that kind of relation to the world "which makes them effective in the transformation of your life and of the world."

Teilhard de Chardin states that the loss of hope would ultimately destroy the zest for life without which, he suggests, human life cannot exist. He writes, "Ultimately it is this zest for life and that alone which underlies and supports the whole complex of bio-physical energies whose operations, acting experimentally, conditions anthropogenesis."

In other words, without hope or this zest for life, the whole human system collapses—not just your life but the human race—according to Teilhard de Chardin. What an interesting thought that is. Without hope, not only do we lose life, but also we contribute to the cosmic loss of life in the human race.

John Cobb, eminent theologian and father of Process Theology, writes in his book *Christ in a Pluralistic Age*, *"The loss of hope cuts Christ (which he calls Creative Transformation) out from effectiveness in human affairs."* He continues, *"Whenever hope is present in history, Creative Transformation, or Christ is present in the world."*

In the same book, Cobb posits that the primary message in the Christ story is there is always hope for positive transformation in our lives and in the world. *"Christ is the image of hope!"* John Cobb states without reservation.

Quantum physicists today not only tell us we are faced every second with an infinite number of possibilities but our thoughts are a form of energy that affects the outcome of our reality on a moment to moment basis, and therefore, affects the universe. You may not have realized how much power you have.

I suspect, at some level my teacher friend understood this. For her, hope was not wishful thinking as much as it was the guiding light for her life. In part, because of her, I came to realize hope is the doorway to new possibilities, to the God within working in our lives and in history. Hope is an action and an attitude at the same time. It is a form of meditation and a way to mediate one's life. Hope is an indication that God's creative transformation is at work in us.

We are faced with some significant challenges in our world and in our lives today. Just think. If we remain hopeful, we can add to the cosmic positive energy in the universe and create positive transformation in the world and in our lives. Now that is power.

The Path of Kenosis

I had no idea, over 30 years ago, what I was getting into when I accepted an invitation by a good friend to attend something called an Enlightenment Intensive. At the time I was getting ready to move with my wife and three-year old daughter to Berkeley, California to attend Pacific School of Religion. Admittedly I was put off a bit by the rather pretentious title of the retreat. However, if my wise friend thought it might be a good experience for me, I decided it was good enough for me. It turned out to be a life changing experience.

The intensive was three days long. We started Friday morning with some education about the process and what to expect. The leaders assured us that while we might face some difficult moments, they would be there to educate, support and encourage us, both as individuals and as a group. We were given some operating rules designed to bring about the best results. We were told to choose one question out of a list of three to work on for the entire retreat. They suggested that as this was *our* Intensive retreat, we should work on the question, "Who are you?" I know of no one who used another question.

So each day we would do 10 or 12 sessions for 40 minutes each with a different partner we chose at the beginning of each session. One partner would ask the other their chosen question, "Who are you?" and would then listen intently without any physical or verbal response. This monologue continued for five minutes. At the sound of a chime, the talking partner changed roles with the listening partner for five minutes. That process was repeated for 40 minutes, back and forth 8 times until there was a short break. After the break we would find a new partner and start the process over again.

We also had longer breaks that included twenty minutes of meditation and some teaching that helped us understand what was going on. By the beginning of the second day we learned that most of us would go through several steps as our awareness of who we really are, or who we are not, began to become more clear.

Now if you have never done anything like this before, you probably cannot imagine what it feels like to try and tell someone who is really listening to you who you are for five minutes straight. Understand it is a monologue. No dialogue or comments filled the spaces. And that meant no jokes, which was for me the most difficult thing in the begining. We repeated this process 30 times in three days. Yes, I mean 30 sessions, each 40 minutes, responding to the same question.

After I got through the obvious things like, "I am a man, I am a husband, I am a father, a windsurfer, a life-time student, a lover of art, a sexual being . . ." I realized I had barely used up two minutes. At some point, I knew I was looking for things to say that were true but might make me sound a little more interesting. I wanted the listener to be impressed. As a man in his early forties at the time, I wanted the listener to know I was a former jock, was still tough—even heroic—and was the man my father wanted me to be. But all of that started sounding really stupid by the end of the first round and I knew I had at least 29 more to go. By the end of the second or third round I could think of nothing to say about myself that did not sound dim-witted, irrelevant or silly. It all started to sound meaningless. I knew I had to dig deeper.

Like Alice in Wonderland I found myself going down the rabbit hole as I continued to ponder, "Who am I really." Somewhere along the way I became aware of two things. First, I was afraid to go too deep. I did not want to let go of all my accomplishments, all my achievements, all my ego needs. I was afraid to let go of those things that had given me a separate identity from the masses. And secondly, I realized none of those things I was holding onto had anything to do with who I really was. In fact holding on to them, for whatever reason, was keeping me from discovering who I really was and am.

It was a fascinating journey that helped shape not only my seminary experience but the rest of my life. Over the years I have come to realize that during those three days, I was rapidly moving through a spiritual path of *kenosis*—the process of self-emptying. At the time I did not know what was happening but I felt like I was peeling away phony or meaningless ways I identified myself, one layer at a time. It was both scary and freeing. If someone is willing to work the path or engage the process, they just may come to the realization that *I am* is not only enough, but it can be exhilarating to discover you are part of the Ultimate I AM.

Over the years I have discovered the kenosis path is central to almost every meaningful spiritual tradition including Christianity. Cynthia Bourgeault posits that this path was introduced to the West by Jesus (*The Wisdom Jesus: Transforming Mind and Heart*, Shambhala Press, 2008). I agree and have published a couple of articles on this subject.

I share this experience because it focuses on the incredible opportunity we all have to turn the aging process into a spiritual path. Whether we like it or not, as we move toward our elder years, we slowly lose those things we assumed were part of who we are. Our titles, our prowess, our accomplishments, our competitiveness slowly fade. It may not happen in a three-day intensive and we don't always give it much thought, but it happens. We can hang on, get angry or we can engage the process. It is really up to us.

I was doing a workshop a few years ago and referred to the story of the rich man. In that story the rich man had tried to do all the right things—all

121

the things the Scriptures or the Law had required of him. However, he told Jesus he wanted to experience the Realm of God Jesus kept referring to. Jesus told him he must give away his riches. Sadly the man could not do that. Why? Because he would have lost his identity. He would no longer be the respected rich man.

In this workshop I explained that sometimes, when we hold on to these titles and cling to labels, we separate ourselves from others, including the Ultimate Mystery we call God. One of the men attending the workshop just did not get it. He wanted the story to be about the necessity of giving one's wealth to the poor. He happened to be retired clergy who had passed the requirements for a Doctor of Ministry degree and insisted that everyone address him as Reverend Doctor. His wife dutifully referred to him as Doctor. I asked him what he would do if Jesus suggested he give up his titles? He looked at me as if I had slapped him and did not speak to me for the rest of the workshop. I felt badly but several people told me later that it had helped make the point for them.

A few weeks after I retired from a wonderful church I served for 20 years as the pastor, I was sitting at a bar in Hood River, Oregon. It was an annual trip I made for over two decades for some of the best windsurfing opportunities in the world. At one point after a long conversation about windsurfing, life and relationships with a group of other sailors, a young man across from me asked, "What did you say you did again?" I looked at him and I tried to speak. I suddenly realized I had not given any thought to this simple question we all use in social settings. It was like someone had socked me in the stomach. I got so emotional I could not answer him. I had to get up, apologize and leave. It was the beginning of another journey and I now knew, I had no road map.

We are not what we do or what we achieve. We are so much more and unfortunately too many of us miss the opportunity to discover that. Being aware of the aging process can offer us that opportunity as we willingly self-empty, as we give up, as we let go and in the process begin a different kind of adventure. As Lewis Richmond notes in his wonderful book, *Aging as a Spiritual Practice*, "Aging is beyond our control . . . Are you going to just slide or are you going to steer?"

Richmond's book is one of several excelleny books on the subject that offer a benefit to people of all ages. Richmond, a Zen Buddhist, touches on all the right issues to guide us in this journey with humor and insight along with meditations in every chapter. John C. Robinson, a retired therapist and an excellent writer, offers a trilogy of books that can help us ferret out the blocks that keep us from experiencing a new spiritual awareness as we age and transform our lives.

Another wonderful surprise is a book written by one of my dear friends, Joan Chittister. Her book *The Gift of Years* is typical of her writing. It is prophetic, challenging, full of insight, and at times just plain delightful. Finally another new author is Carol Orsborn whose book *Fierce with Age: Chasing God and Squirrels in Brooklyn* received rave reviews. You may want to check out her website, www.fiercewithage.com.

All these books are not only helpful for those of us who admit we are elders or seniors, but they can be wonderful resources for people of any age who are searching for meaningful ways to live their lives in harmony with their friends, their families, their environment, their world and the Infinite Mystery we choose to call God.

The Transformative Power of Myths

I am not certain when it hit me. I think it was after I read Joseph Campbell's book, *The Power of Myth*. I know I was working on a sermon very early one morning and was re-reading the Genesis stories. I had considered these stories to be myth for decades but had given little consideration to how or why they had come to be. Among other things, Campbell describes myth as stories that explain important things that do not otherwise have an explanation. He writes that lasting myth is more transformative and truer than history.

Myths are imaginative traditions about nature, history, destiny, gods and humankind. They often provide explanations for things that would not have been understandable at a time. Like humans, myths were an attempt to explain the ultimate questions that still are with us. "Why are we here?" "Is there a purpose to my life?" "Why do we have to suffer?" "Is there a god or gods?" "Who or what am I?"

Today it is impossible for us to fathom the world view of the ancients who created these stories or even to guess how far back they go. We really cannot grasp what it was like to look up into a sky full of mysterious stars, to watch the days get shorter with no obvious reason, to deal with the seasons or watch babies be born without an understanding of basic biology and science. They lived in a world without airplanes, space ships, Hubble telescopes, physicists, or calendars let alone computers and GPS devices. These were people, after all, who believed the earth was flat and covered with a dome with holes in it. For them, the stars were god's or the gods' light shining through those holes.

Unfortunately when we are trying to analyze or understand the mythology of our biblical stories we often do not understand their perspective. For example the serpent or snake in the Genesis book was a symbol of eternal life. The ancient people would watch a snake lose its entire skin and would seemingly be born again. Therefore when they asked the question, "Why would God make the creature crawl on the ground with no legs, they would wonder what terrible things this creatures must of done to lose their legs.

You might find it interesting to know that the East was always considered a place of rebirth because the sun dies every day in the west. But the sun is reborn in the east over and over. There must be something very special happening over there on the other side of the earth. Were Adam and Eve punished when they were banished to the east or were they given another chance?

I sat there that morning, pondering these ancient stories that have been analyzed, dissected and repeatedly analyzed for maybe three thousand years. My mind flashed even further back in time, maybe four or even five thousand years back. I saw a nomadic tribe sitting around their fire pit cooking their meal and talking quietly, much like the Bedouin tribes I observed when I traveled to Israel.

There was an old woman talking quietly to a little girl, maybe five years old, tucked into her side for warmth and comfort. "Savta," the little girl almost whispers, "why did Alaha make my Ima cry and scream so much when my little brother came out? Did she do something wrong?"

The old lady took a deep breath, looked off into the distance and said, "My Precious One, that is a long and strange story. It all started when our very first great ancestors disobeyed Alaha. You see they lived in a perfect garden and Alaha provided everything they needed. They could play like children without worry about food, or illness or death. But Alaha told them never to eat a certain fruit that would make them aware of themselves. It came from a tree called the tree of knowledge. But the first couple could not resist the temptation to have knowledge only Alaha should have, so they ate of it. Alaha was very upset and told the woman that she and all women would suffer when they had children."

The little girl looked at her grandmother and said, "But why doesn't Abba-leh have to suffer and cry like Sabba?"

Once again the old lady took a deep breath. She was considered the Wise One and she needed to make sense to the little one. She said, "Well my Precious One, your Abba has lost the perfect garden and he like the other Abbas must toil in the fields every day because our first ancestor disobeyed Alaha also."

"Savta," the little girl said looking at her grandmother with so much love. "Is that why Sabba had to die? Is it because our first ancestor disobeyed Alaha?"

"Yes my Precious One. That is why we all have to die sometime. But Alaha gave the first ancestor many years to live before he had to die. It may be Her wish that you will have many, many years before you have to concern yourself with death."

This is the way it could have happened. The wise grandmother wanted to explain to this precious little girl things that did not make sense to her based on the information she had. And so she told a story that helped the little girl hear certain things she might not have been able to grasp without the story. When we try and have the power and knowledge of God, we will fail. Birth is painful and life is not always fair.

The little girl grew up and told the story to her children as did others who had heard the Wise Savta tell the story when they were young. The story became part of the culture, was told maybe millions of times around campfires, in community gatherings and eventually ended up in written form.

Joseph Campbell writes, "*Read myths. They teach you that you can turn inward, and you begin to get the message of the symbols. Read other people's myths, not those of your own religion, because you tend to interpret your own religion in terms of facts—but if you read the other ones, you begin to get the message.*"

These stories will mean nothing unless we try and get into the world of the storyteller. We have to remember, these are the same people who thought the earth was flat and there was a dome covering the earth. They believed there were holes in the dome to let the rain through and the stars were actually the light from a god's eyes that shone through the rain holes.

Myth was and still is common in every culture. Many of the mythological stories of the ancients were very similar in different parts of the world because they were dealing with many of the same unknowns. The responses are both a reflection of their ignorance and their wisdom of the day. They help us learn about the ways of a people and their important concerns. They help us understand how a culture can evolve and change as time goes by and more information is available to them.

But we need to be careful when we try and find answers and divine direction from these stories. They are stories, after all, from people who thought the snake lived forever and if you ate the forbidden fruit you might have to live in the East where the sun is born again. According to the Book of Thomas, Jesus suggested we all have the answers within.

However the myth in the Bible can be helpful since these stories were created by a society and a culture that was committed to having an intentional relationship with that power, that energy we call God. While they did had very different names for that force, it serves as a useful documentary of a foundational time in an important faith tradition. It not only gives us insight into the deepest yearnings of our ancient ancestors, but it provides many of the deepest questions that will always be part of the human condition.

I have often wondered what would happen if Progressive Christians started reading myth from other traditions instead of just ignoring them. Maybe we would begin to see more of the beauty in our own traditions and keep them in the right perspective at the same time. What if we asked ourselves what the original author of a particular myth was trying to explain in their own time? What was the question they were trying to address? Is it a lasting myth and does it still have power? What does it tell us that is still true and transformative?

In his book, *The Pagan Christ*, Tom Harpur suggests we do ourselves, as Christians, a great disservice by missing the powerful and repetitive myth in the entire Jesus story. Referring to such eminent scholars as Godfrey Higgins, Gerald Massey, and Alvin Boyd Kuhn, Harpur posits that all three scholars *"demonstrate that both the Jewish and Christian religions owe most of their origins* to Egyptian roots . . . *We share common myth.*" Harpur demonstrates this in his excellent book.

Burton Mack suggests in his book. *The Christian Myth*, it is the responsibility of contemporary Christians to create new myth, new metaphors once we understand the intended dynamics and purpose of the ancient myth. Tom Hapur addresses this challenge. In *The Pagan Christ* he provides interesting and stimulating questions at the end of each chapter. You do not have to agree with some of Harpur's conclusions about the historical Jesus to benefit from such a reading. What he does show us is that scriptures come alive when we start asking, "*What is the message here that is still true? Where is the transformative power in this myth?*" "*And what is our current cultural myth that will cause future generations to think we were pretty silly?*"

I suspect it is only when we do these things, we can hope to experience the true power of the transformational myth in our own traditions.

CHAPTER SIX

The Blessing of Compassion

A Vacation in Provence, France

When my wife and I made plans to visit Provence, France along with two dear friends one spring, I anticipated a true vacation of rest and relaxation. I looked forward to good conversation, good food and lots of great wine, all away from emails and phone calls. I did not plan to even think about Progressive Christianity or any Christianity for that matter. I should have known my life does not work that way. Three different and conflicting experiences changed my plans. Admittedly, I was a little ignorant of the rich and deep Christian history in the Provence region of France.

The husband of our traveling friends is a history buff. With a little help from the Rick Steves' travel guide, he was happy to create a new adventure each day and we were happy to follow. It would take years to visit all the fascinating little villages, often carved into the rock hills surrounding the fertile soil that has made Provence famous and wealthy at different times in history. Many of these little villages, some over a thousand years old, have been gentrified by artists, musicians, quaint restaurants, wine bars and interesting shops. I could have happily filled my time visiting a different village each day and testing the wines of the area. But my friend and volunteer guide insisted that we visit the Palais des Papes (Palace of the Pope) in Avignon, only a 45-minute drive from our apartment.

It was an amazing site. Unlike the quaint little villages, this was a truly mammoth fortress. Surrounded by walls, it was a small ancient city within a city. I had forgotten that the Papacy had been moved to France in the 14th century and I had no idea seven Popes made their residence in Avignon from 1305–1378. Two more Popes stayed in the area because of the continued unrest in Rome and the Palace was eventually abandoned in 1403.

The tour of the palace was both striking and disturbing for me. I had been reading about the history of the area and the tremendous hardships and conditions the local peasants and laborers lived under. These amazing stone buildings were the result of the labor of the poor and often resulted in broken bodies and early deaths. Neither OSHA nor compassion protected them. Yet the opulence of these buildings was beyond imagination.

I took the time to listen to the tapes giving the history of each of the Popes. With only a couple of exceptions, I was struck by the extreme ego-driven nature of these men. They expected to be treated as royalty and everything about their lives seemed to support that expectation. Most of these popes were involved in territorial disputes and prided themselves on how much influence they had with the kings of Europe. With only two exceptions, each succeeding Pope wanted a larger palace befitting their position.

For example, Benedict XII (1334–1342), a former Cistercian monk, decided the original palace wasn't up to his standards. He had it torn down and a new one was built in its place designed by the architect, Pierre Poisson. This was a huge, powerful fortress in the severe style of the Cistercian monks.

Then Clement VI (1342–1352) didn't think this same palace was up to his standards. He hired another famous architect to design and build a more ostentatious palace to attach to the old one. This roughly doubled the overall size of the castle. The kitchens were enormous and the demands of the big banquets and the visiting dignitaries must have required a huge staff and back-breaking work.

I have spent the last 40 plus years trying to figure out what Jesus was really trying to teach us. It has become increasingly clear that his primary message was that the Realm of God or Oneness with Divinity is available in the here and now. He offered a path so those who choose to follow it can experience this Realm as he did. It is not magic or a one-time thing but rather a way of living and seeing a different reality imbued with divinity. It is about becoming awake or aware of what is real. The path or practice was and is about learning to break down barriers that separate us or divides us from all sentient beings. This can only be achieved through a process of letting go of our fears, our hatreds and our ego needs. This means, in part, letting go of our need to have social power, influence and status. It is letting go of those things that we feel we need to be somebody. It is ultimately about self-emptying, or kenosis.

When I thought about those pompous men who were supposed to represent the highest and best qualities of the one they claimed to follow, I got angry. This is a rare feeling for me these days. But the more I thought about it over the next few days, the more my anger dissolved into sadness. I could not feel anything but remorse as I pondered how far these men had insulted the one who suffered trying to show us of a new life and a new way of living. I wondered if anything has really changed. No wonder the message has been buried so deep. I also knew my playful trip to Provence had changed.

Ironically my second jolt came the day we traveled to what turned out to be one of our favorite villages. This one was far up on a hill, on three levels, with stone stairs and pathways connecting the village. It was near a rock quarry which was the source of the reddish stone from which most of the buildings in the village were constructed. It was a fun place with lots of activity from the local artisans and merchants. We had a wonderful lunch and, naturally, a bottle of wine, and we wandered around the village.

When it started to rain I slipped into a simple little church at the center of this three-level community. It was still functioning after 900 years. I sat down in an old pew in the back of the church and tried to imagine what had been going on in the hearts and heads of the literally thousands of bodies that must have sat on that same old pew over nine centuries. I wanted to feel their spirits, their needs and maybe their pain as they walked into the church. When my eyes adjusted to the light I realized there was a trough worn into the stone down the center aisle. This rounded groove went from the back of the church all the way up to the altar. I got down on my knees and felt it with my hand. It was about eight inches wide. At its lowest point in the center, it must have been over an inch deep.

I pondered how it got there. Suddenly I realized that over the centuries, it had been worn down by people walking up to the altar to receive communion and a blessing. I also realized most of the feet that made this groove in the stone had either been bare or in soft sandals. I was stunned. I could not stop thinking about the number of people who had walked down that narrow aisle after toiling in the fields, breaking rocks in the quarry or building stone structures with no power equipment. How many sore and tired bodies made the 50-foot journey down that aisle for a ritual? The vast majority of these folks must have labored beyond most of our imaginations. It was a hard life but each week they came for their blessing and an assurance that something better was coming. I sat there and thought about how important that blessing must have been for them. Was it the promise of eternal life in a better place where their lives might not be so difficult? Or was it just the moment when they might have experienced a sense of God's love through the touch of the local priest?

I could not shake it out of my mind as we headed back to our apartment that day. How many hard-working peasants in the little village placed their hopes in a future life? They wore a groove in the stone floor in order to receive that hope, that blessing.

I realized I have been working for nearly 40 years to deconstruct the Christian myth of substitutionary sacrifice. I couldn't help wondering what blessing we offer the hopeless, the forlorn and the lost? Will people wear grooves in future church floors to receive a blessing from a new Christianity? What is that blessing, I wondered?

As I laid awake that night thinking about these two experiences, it occurred to me that while Progressive Christianity is built on excellent scholarship, it is after all a product of primarily privileged people. Maybe we do not have a message for the struggling underclass, the laborers who toil in the fields all over the world. It is hard to be a mystic when you are working 12 hours a day, seven days a week, bent over in a rice paddy or a tomato field or in a diamond mine.

My third jolt came with a visit to the little village of Thor near our apartment. We went there for their weekly village market. Every village has one. We also planned to visit the Notre Dame du Lac recommended by Rick Steves in his travel guide. This church was built in the 12th century and was restored in the 18th. It is now a historical landmark. Ironically for me, in the 14th century, the entire village became a fief, divided between those same Popes of Avignon and several other families.

Although it is filled with history and fascinating artifacts, it is still a functioning Catholic church. This became obvious to me as I watched with interest the priest sitting in the back of the church talking quietly to a man I presumed was in his late 50s. It appeared this man was suffering from some kind of deep grief. The priest had his arm around the man's shoulder as they talked. There must have been some kind of sacrament or confession as the priest was wearing a stole around his neck. As he held the man, they whispered and prayed together.

Later, I watched the man get ready to leave. As he approached the front door he looked up at the painting of Mary and Jesus on the wall. With tears in his eyes and a visible shudder, he took a deep breath and genuflected. Then he turned to leave the church. I believe he was feeling a little better.

The same priest had removed his vestments when he encountered a woman who had been praying with her Bible in her hands. They got into a conversation that appeared to be about something that had upset her. The priest slipped in behind her in the next pew and they carried on a quiet conversation while she occasionally pointed to something in her Bible.

At one point the priest laid his hand on her shoulder, said something and for the first time she smiled. As the priest stood up to leave it was clear, even with my language barrier, he had encouraged her to come back and talk some more.

What hit me was that this old, decrepit church was doing real ministry for people in need. It was obvious this priest cared about and even loved his people. These folks were experiencing healing and wholeness and maybe a sense of new life because of this caring. Many priests must have offered this same compassion over the centuries. These things happened in spite of the ego silliness going on a few dozen kilometers away in Avignon.

Maybe the blessing is not about the story, the theology or even the Christology. Maybe the blessing we can offer is the blessing of compassion. I suspect a lot of those grooves in the floors were made by people simply wanting and hoping to experience compassion from the priest waiting for them to come forward.

I still cannot stop thinking about these things, now several years later. Maybe next time I visit France, I will visit the monks and meditate with them. It is possible, if I spent more time with the contemplatives in our tradition, I might not be so critical. Maybe I will experience that compassion.

Christian Laauve (Love)

A few years ago I was at a conference when I overheard a Hindu scholar laughingly ask a group of Christian theologians, "You know what the problem with Christianity is? After a pregnant pause, he answered his own question, "Christian laauve." Everyone, of course, laughed heartily.

The truth is Christian love is a problem for a lot of people, including a many of us Christians. It is a problem in part because of language. Love is the word an adoring husband might whisper to his beloved wife on a 25th wedding anniversary. It is the same word a child might whisper to her puppy. Love is used on the streets for hello, goodbye and in common endearments like "Luv ya man." You can't help but wonder if the word has lost its meaning by abuse and overuse?

Another challenge is the word commandment. The commandments to love your God and to love your neighbor are often considered the foundation of modern Christianity. Yet most people today have a hard time understanding how one can command another person to love someone no matter how good or disciplined one might want to be. As the saying goes, you may be able to get a horse to water but you can't force him to drink. It becomes progressively more difficult when you realize Christians are instructed not only to love our neighbors, but our enemies as well. For a lot of people including Christians, this just does not make sense.

How many of us choose to practice that kind of unconditional love? The truth is, far too many of us live out our own brand of the television program, *Survivor*. We spend a lot of time trying to figure out who is on our side, how we going to improve our situation, our status or power. We might even rejoice at times in the fall of another whom we believe was against us.

Of course the true meaning of the love passages may be lost in translation. The Greek language, for example, has at least four root words for love; philos, etheleo, agapao and eros. If and when Jesus spoke these words, he may have been speaking in Hebrew but more than likely he was speaking and thinking in Aramaic. Unfortunately we are usually working off texts originally spoken in ancient Hebrew or Aramaic, translated into Greek, and then translated into English. Western languages have a very different construct than ancient Hebrew or Aramaic. There seems to be consensus among scholars today, that when Jesus was speaking of something referred to as love in our modern text, in most cases, a better translation would have been compassion.

Marcus Borg, referring to the love commandments, writes in his book *Meeting Jesus Again*, that in Hebrew as well as Aramaic, the word love would normally be translated as compassion. He continues, ". . . compassion is the plural of a noun that in its singular form means womb. In the Hebrew Bible compassion is both a feeling and a way of being that flows out of that feeling."

Neil Douglas-Klotz writes of the so called *Great Commandment*. "The Aramaic word translated here as love is rehem, meaning a love or compassion that can pour from the depths of oneself, as from an inner womb."

Likewise, Matthew Fox suggests the appropriate translation of love in most cases should be compassion. He poetically writes, "Compassion is not about pity or feeling sorry for the other. It is born of a shared interdependence, an intuition of a sense of awe for the wondrous fact that we all live and swim in one primordial divine womb; we live in fetal waters of cosmic grace."

What a beautiful concept! "We all live in one primordial divine womb." We are all manifestations of one Creative Force, sharing the plasma, the cells and the energy of the Creator, Creation and each other.

Today scientists explain we are formed from the same stuff as the stars. We are a piece of, not separate, from this grand, entangled cosmos. We share cells and genes from a smaller gene pool than anyone could have imagined a few years ago. Over the last couple of decades we have learned all humans come from a single, very small group of ancestors. As disturbing as this might be for some people, it gives a whole new meaning to the idea that we are all brothers and sisters.

The point here is they are us. When we actually fathom and even experience this kind of interconnectedness, it is like waking up and discovering, as the descendants of Thomas Jefferson did, that your family is bigger than you ever imagined. We really are "living and swimming in one primordial divine womb." It is not too difficult to imagine this existential awareness is related to the Realm of God Jesus described to his followers with so many positive metaphors. It is not only discovering the interconnectedness of all life that is so exciting, but it is seeing and hearing from a whole new perspective. This can fundamentally change our understanding of reality.

Every spiritual path is designed to help us get past our myopic and ego-centric perspectives, to help us discover our false perceptions about self and others. They also help us shed debilitating fears of living and dying. Most spiritual paths lead to an experience of oneness or dare I use the word *womb-ness* here? It is ultimately about getting in touch with the deepest places in our hearts and souls as we discover who and what we are.

For followers of Jesus' path, the goal is not to talk about the word love or compassion. It is about being more compassionate. The reason for this is not because the Bible tells us we should. Rather it is the way to an extraordinary experience of a different reality—a reality of belonging, of connectedness, of wholeness. It is something we should want to do.

It is about such simple things to take the time to look at the cashier at the market into her eyes and feel love and appreciation. It is about challenging ourselves to treat every person we come in contact with as a loved brother or sister. It is even learning how to understand and even love not only those who disagree with us but who may want to do harm to us. This is the real path and it is about learning to live in the state of compassion.

Christian *laauve* is not the sweet or syrupy thing we refer to on Valentine's Day. It is both a challenge and an opportunity to experience something every person has the chance to experience but apparently few do so fully. But when they discover it, they want to run and tell their friends; they want to share it with their enemies; they want to treat it like a treasure. The nice thing is we do not have to go buy something to get it or send flowers to share it. We begin by just living and being it, every day, not just on Valentine's Day.

Just Being There

It was late one evening when I received the call. The stepdaughter of one our members had been in a terrible car accident. She was in intensive care on a ventilator and in a coma. He asked me if I would come by the hospital and pray with him and his wife. I was there in ten minutes and rushed up to the ICU area using my business card to get through the red tape. Their lovely 19-year-old daughter looked terrible. She had broken bones that could not be put in a cast yet because of the swelling. Her face was badly bruised and swollen. They had no idea how serious the damage was to her brain and other internal parts at that point. Things did not look good.

The young woman attended another church where she had been active in a youth group for a number of years. Her Episcopalian priest was making regular calls to the hospital during the week so I restricted my calls to once each night to get an update. I assured the family we were praying with them continually. We all believed every day she stayed alive, her chances of making it were increased. The following Thursday evening I received a call from the family asking if I could meet them at the hospital. They told me the doctor had run some more tests and they would like me to be there with them when he came to the hospital. I joined them in ICU and went immediately to the girl's side.

I was struck by how much better she looked. The swelling had gone down in her face and the bruises were almost non-detectable. Her color was good and the broken arm was in a cast, already signed by her little sister. I had forgotten how pretty she was and how much she reminded me of our youngest daughter who was just a couple of years younger. As we stood around her bed, I took her warm hand in my own and we all held hands. I began to pray fervently. I do believe that sometimes we all have the ability to become a conduit for a healing energy. If I ever wanted it to happen, this was the moment. I am not sure how long we three stood there around her bed praying but suddenly I realized there was someone else in the room. It had not occurred to me until that moment that there had been no medical staff in that little space the whole time.

The family doctor was quietly waiting for us to end our prayer. After introductions, he looked at me and said that he was glad I was there. Then he said, "I am sorry to inform you that the tests were conclusive. There is no longer any brain activity. Your daughter is clinically dead. I am very sorry."

The parents had known this might be the outcome of the tests and were somewhat prepared, though no parent is ever fully prepared for that kind of news. But I was completely taken by surprise. As the parents quietly wept, I looked at the doctor and said, "No, No, NO!" Suddenly I realized I was nearly shouting and knew I had to leave. I pushed the doors open just as an elderly priest was coming through. He mistook me for a family member and got this sad smile on his face and said, "It will be fine. She is with God now."

I was crying at that point and I shoved him out of the way and said something like, "don't give me your pious crap right now." I was trying to get outside but was confused about how to get out. As I made my way down the hall crying, mumbling and cursing, I noticed people were getting out of my way is if I were a crazy man. When I got outside the building I was out of control. I went to the end of the entryway near the parking lot and screamed profanities at God. I was enraged and must have gone on for several minutes. I finally ended up in a heap on the ground, completely spent. It was only when I got up and turned back toward the building that I realized what a ruckus I had made. I have no idea how long I was in the position but when I looked up I realized people were looking out of the hospital windows from all over that side of the large, four story building.

I was emotionally spent. I just stood there wondering if I could move. It suddenly occurred to me what I had done. I had really let the family down. I had blown it. What kind of a pastor am I, I wondered? I slowly worked my way back to the waiting room and found them with other family members who had gathered. I apologized and told them that I needed to go. They both hugged me and wept but said nothing. On my way home and for the rest of the night, I considered leaving the ministry. "What kind of consoling could I do?" I asked myself. "What kind of strength was I able to offer?" I wondered. "What kind of faith did I represent?"

Two days later I received a note from the girl's mother. I wish I had kept that note so I could accurately reproduce her poetic words but it said something like, "You will never know how much your visit and support meant to us. You were the most honest person in our whole group and you did just what we wished we could have done. You are truly a spiritual person. We cannot thank you enough for being there for us."

I was with the family two days later when they pulled the plug on the life support systems. We prayed quietly and I had a sense there was an angelic presence in the room. There was a peace and a presence around us that could have no other explanation.

We sometimes need to remember that Easter started when the women gathered at the foot of the cross, just being there. Maybe even those faithful women cried out in anger at God as they watched the one they loved so much suffer.

Easter is about celebrating the power of the presence of God's healing ways, even when we do not understand them. It is about our experiences of death and of being lifted up and made new when we ourselves do not have the power to do so. It is about manifesting God's Spirit in strange and unusual ways when we are simply being there for the others, even when we think we may have blown it.

Time to Break for Lunch

A conference I attended a few years ago was devoted to exploring the virtues of interfaith dialogue. I looked forward to that event because I was the senior minister in a midsize church in Southern California at that time. We had shared space with a growing synagogue for nearly 15 years. Actually we shared more than space; we shared pulpits, worship services and interfaith weddings. The Rabbi was a good friend and my closest colleague. I taught classes to his confirmation students every year and he did the same with our confirmation classes. When major Jewish holidays fell on Sunday, our nearly 350-member church became a synagogue during the hours of our normal services. There were usually just as many people there from our church as there were from the Jewish congregation and we always felt honored.

Prior to the conference we had invited a small Muslim community to begin sharing space with us on Fridays and special holidays. Very quickly we began running into some serious communication problems with the Imam. I was also receiving threatening mail from angry Christians in the area and there were a few critical letters in the newspapers. I thought maybe I would learn something from the conference.

The four keynote speakers were made up of a conservative Jewish scholar, a well-respected Muslim scholar, a Buddhist author and a traditionalist Christian. There were workshops on everything from the Wicca tradition to Gnosticism. All and all, it was an interesting gathering.

On the final day, the four keynoters formed a panel and the moderator opened it up to questions from the large audience. For the most part, the questions were polite and generally were about some little interesting fact about a particular tradition. Do you have any dietary restrictions? How many times a day do you pray or meditate? Can you marry someone from another faith tradition?

Finally with some frustration, I stood up, moved to the microphone and asked a question that had been burning in my heart for a long time. After letting all four contributors know how much I appreciated their comments, I asked: "If the four of you all went out to lunch today and sat together breaking bread, would you be able to look at the person next to you or across from you, in to their eyes, without thinking somewhere in the back of your mind, 'this poor soul has really got it wrong . . . or is confused . . . or needs help or is just plain brainwashed?' Can you really look at each other as equal children of God?"

There were over 600 people in the room and there was virtually dead silence, except for an occasional nervous cough. The moderator kept looking for someone to provide a comment and only the Buddhist made eye contact with him with an elfish smile. The moderator finally asked directly if anyone from the panel wanted to answer the question. Two looked away and another shook his head. Then the smiling Buddhist said: "You know that is a good question." Another very uncomfortable minute or two passed and the moderator finally said: "I guess it's time to break for lunch."

Later, I realized how ironic it was, as we ambled off to our respective lunch gatherings. So much of what we have reconstructed about Jesus was about the shared table as a way of practicing radical egalitarianism. I tried to imagine the Jesus of my faith, having lunch with the unique kind people who seemed to gather around him. Did he worry about their religious affiliations? Did he care if they had it right? Did he believe his religion was the only way to connect with the Ultimate Reality?

When he said, "Do not judge another" did he mean except about their religion? Or did he look directly into the hearts and souls of others without religious, tribal, ethnic, or gender concerns or thoughts? Was he able to transcend all those things that tend to separate us into divisive groups and so often turn into violent differences?

We live in a violent world and it seems to be getting more so every day. Frankly it is time to admit that religion offers more opportunities than any other reason for one group or individual to inflict bloodshed upon another. It has been that way throughout history and it seems to still be that way. Although we would like to blame it on the fundamentalists, especially the Muslim fundamentalists today, one need only read some of the angry email

I receive from Christians to know rage and violence still reigns in many of our churches.

It is truly a sad irony that Jesus was killed in part because he taught a radical egalitarianism. He invited so many of those who had been shamed in their society simply for being different, to a banquet of compassion. We will never really know what was going on in the minds and hearts of those people or even in Jesus'. I suspect the lines that had caused conflict in the past disappeared as his tablemates realized they were no longer being judged or condemned. I am certain some of them even experienced the Realm of God in those encounters. Maybe it's time for us to break for lunch.

CHAPTER SEVEN

The World & Christianity Intersecting with Social Justice Issues & the Environment

Imagining a Different World

On the day when most of us wondered if we actually were going to start bombing Syria, someone sent me a link to a video. It features a young teen singer who was competing on the X *Factor* television program in Australia. Few people can watch this video without becoming pretty emotional. You see, this 17-year-old boy is one of two brothers from Iraq who were adopted when they were babies by an Australian couple. Both were missing part, or all of their arms and parts of their legs, with severe wounds all over their bodies. As tragic as this may sound, both of them virtually glowed with smiles that would light up a building. You could have said the same for their adoptive mother.

When Emanuel Kelly started to sing *Imagine*, by John Lennon, the audience went crazy. He indeed has a beautiful voice. How strange it seemed to hear this gorgeous voice coming out of an otherwise broken and tortured body. I do not know how they were wounded as babies, but there is a pretty good chance it was caused by bombs our military dropped. This was paid for by our taxes. Even more likely, it went on our national credit card as we have still not paid for that so-called war.

Over the last couple of years, I have watched this video at least six times. I have never been able to get through it without a few tears. But on this day, as I waited to hear how Congress was going to vote on the limited bombing of Syria, as I pondered what President Obama was really going to do, I literally broke down. How could we do this again? Did we not learn from Vietnam? Did we not learn from Iraq? Are we not learning from Afghanistan?

Just a few days earlier I was in a coffee shop trying to catch up on some email. I overheard two men talking, one rather loudly. He was making the case that we won the war in Iraq. I would guess both of these men were in their early 40s. Although I could not tell if either of them had served in the war, they clearly did not agree. I could not help but wonder how anyone could believe we won anything but a lot of heartache and debt.

Apparently their differences reflect those of the rest of our nation. As we all watch Iraq devolve into more and more of a police state, an increasing number of people are openly questioning if we improved anything with the trillions of dollars we invested. The majority of the country has felt this war was wrong from the beginning. Now, as we look at the wreckage of lives and the economy because of our country's hegemony, the number of people who are dissatisfied continues to grow.

But it does not end there. *According to a Pew Research Center poll*, less than one-third of Americans who participated in combat there, believe the reasons for going to war justified the loss in blood and treasure. We lost nearly 4,500 young lives in Iraq alone and that does not begin to count the physically and mentally wounded young people who will never have the opportunity to lead a normal life.

Admittedly, in the past, I have been able to live with this because I could tell myself these young people volunteered. I would try and convince myself these soldiers were like the nearly 1,500 contractors who lost their lives. They volunteered to go to Iraq and Afghanistan because of the financial gains they could make. It was their decision.

I know this was too simplistic and in some ways unfair. Some of these young soldiers did not have a choice if they wanted to eat and/or support their families. It should also be noted that the same Pew study reported that 74 percent of the vets feel their military experience helped them get ahead when they returned to civilian life. Further, 96 percent said their service had helped them mature and be better citizens.

As I looked at the statistics, I realized the numbers we like to ignore have to do with what we so casually refer to as collateral damage. This is where Emanuel Kelly and his brother come into the often untold story. These beautiful babies, now with damaged bodies, are just two of what was likely hundreds of thousands children wounded and orphaned in both Iraq and Afghanistan. Only because of a beautiful woman from Australia with a huge heart, could these two be considered the lucky ones. There are still tens of thousands of young people with torn bodies lying in dirty beds in most parts of Iraq.

According to the UN, somewhere around 870,000 Iraqis lost their lives during the invasion and ensuing war. It is difficult to accurately count the number of orphans in Iraq now, but in 2007 the UN reported there were over 40,000 children in orphanages. Roughly 40 percent of them were physically wounded. Like Emanuel and his brother, many of these children were severely wounded and unwanted by their extended families.

The following quote is from a presentation given in the Dialogue sessions of the Kuala Lumpur War Crimes Tribunal, in May of 2012. It was reported by Chris Floyd: ". . . *Line up the bodies of the children, the thousands of children—the infants, the toddlers, the school kids—whose bodies were torn to pieces, burned alive or riddled with bullets during the American invasion and occupation of Iraq. Line them up in the desert sand, walk past them, mile after mile, all those twisted corpses, those scraps of torn flesh and seeping viscera, those blank faces, those staring eyes fixed forever on nothingness. This is the reality of what happened in Iraq; there is no other reality. . . .*"

We call this collateral damage when it is not our child, our mother, our wife or husband. But we call it a catastrophe and evil if it is our loved ones, like in New York. This is what I cried about on the eve of a potential attack on Syria as I listened to Emanuel sing, *Imagine.*

I do not believe there is such a thing as a just war anymore, if there ever was one. Our weapons are too destructive and wars are seldom about territory or borders. They cannot be decisively won. Today wars are mostly about ideology and religion. They are about culture. Certainly we have not been winners in the last three wars which we have initiated and participated in.

There are far more meaningful and sophisticated ways to deal with conflict today. We could do better if we developed different attitudes and skills at conflict resolution. It would also help if our leaders knew a little more about the history and cultures of the areas in which we get involved.

But first we have to admit war is big business. It makes some very powerful people in our beloved country a lot of money. Former Republican President, Dwight Eisenhower, warned us of the threat of the military-industrial complex in his final speech as President in 1961. His message has become more powerful and relevant than ever. We also must deal with the policies allowing members of Congress, generals and even the vice president, to influence bills that shift billions of dollars to companies benefiting from war. We must also remove their right to join those companies offering extravagant salaries and stock incentives.

I cannot help but think we would be in a lot better position today if we had used the trillions of dollars we wasted on the last three wars differently. What if we had rebuilt our schools and universities, modernized our infrastructure, invested in research and development and trained new scientists? Think how much we could have done helping other countries rebuild and redirect their economies. Just imagine what it would be like to be part of a country with a reputation for making peace rather than war. Imagine what a different world we would live in. Maybe that is what Emanuel Kelly was thinking when he sang the John Lennon song so beautifully.

Just Imagine . . .

We Live In a Violent World

It seems to me we live in a violent culture in a violent world that appears to become more violent with time. I admit I grew up in what was an ideal era under ideal circumstances. I was a Caucasian boy living in a small community with two stable, loving parents. I did watch a few war movies made during WWII that had some pretty violent battlefield scenes. But this happened once a month if I was lucky and was virtually over long before junior high school. As a young child I did listen to some scary radio shows like *The Shadow*. But I think the most violent thing I heard on the radio in those early days was the terrible crash every week when Fibber McGee opened the hall closet door and everything came crashing down.

I do not mean the world was without violence in the '40s and '50s. I never had to deal with the issues war torn Europe was dealing with. I was not part of a minority struggling for basic civil rights, living in fear. I was not a Jew trying to find a safe place to migrate. I was not watching my family slowly die from radiation poisoning in occupied Japan. I have never been part of a country while it was going through a violent revolution. But I do not see these things as part of the culture. Rather I understand them to be events or periods that most people assumed would someday be better or different.

How many murders, dead bodies, stabbings and shootings do our children see on television every day? How many scenes of violence do they encounter on their computers on a regular basis? How many alien bad guys do they kill, blow up, and maim with their computer games every week? Have the "playful" games had any influence on the mass killings in our theaters, our schools and shopping centers?

What about us? Have we become numb to the violence of our everyday television programs? What in the world keeps us from strengthening our gun laws? Are we not mimicking this so called entertainment violence?

We have created a violent culture. Anyone who does not see this must have their eyes closed. Maybe it goes back to violent beginnings in our own bloody revolution with the French and the British. Or maybe our culture is still influenced by the remnants of the Civil War. I have often wondered if the Southern demand for unlimited gun rights is founded on the fear the Union soldiers might return someday. I remember once asking a young man in Alabama why he needed the arsenal in his house he had shown me with obvious pride. He said, "just in case they try and take them away." But our violent culture is not confined to the South by any measure nor is it confined to the issue of guns.

I did an experiment recently that admittedly was not very scientific. I drew two columns on a sheet of paper marked Violent and Non-violent. I turned on the television just after 9 p.m. and started turning the channels, one by one. When I came across something violent—murder, fighting, yelling, anger, torture or desecrated bodies—I checked the Violent column and moved to the next channel. If it seemed like a gentle, fun program, I checked another column. Of the 30 channels I observed in less than an hour, 22 of them, including a couple of cartoons, had something I would consider extremely violent.

Let's face it. Even our spectator sports which are supposed to be play, have become more violent than anyone could ever have imagined. Just improving the helmets is not going to solve the problem. Forty years ago cage fighting, two men, and now two women, in a cage beating each other senseless using both their feet and fists would have been banned as a sport. It would have been unimaginable that this brutal sport could develop into a major television market. Today it is considered the fastest growing spectator sport in the nation. Its largest organizer, Ultimate Fighting Championship (UFC), recently entered into a seven-year contract with Fox Network for $90 million per year for broadcasting these fights.

I find this all of this very sad and strange. Why strange? You see, we often hear people refer to our country as a Christian nation. I don't agree with that assessment nor do I think it is an appropriate goal. However, the vast majority of people in this country still consider themselves or identify themselves as Christians. Yet, when you read the Jesus story, when you listen to some of the finest Christian theologians and ethicists, it is impossible for me to understand how one can fail to see that Jesus was teaching and promoting a non-violent life.

I find this seeming incongruity particularly difficult to understand. Every January, we celebrate the life of Martin Luther King, Jr. who truly tested the ideals and limits of a non-violent life. He did this with the integrity of one who sincerely believed he was following the path of Jesus. Early on in the movement he said; *"Please be peaceful. We believe in law and order. We are not advocating violence, I want you to love your enemies . . . for what we are doing is right, what we are doing is just and God is with us."*

I resist citing biblical passages out of context to prove a point, but there is an abundance of evidence that non-violence was and is a central tenet of Jesus' teachings. History has many heroes who lived and often died following the non-violent path of their Christ. In more modern times we can look to Mahatma Gandhi, a Hindu, as an example. He probably understood Jesus on this point better than most Christians in our country. More than once he gave Jesus credit for his own understanding that *"non-violence and truth are inseparable and presuppose one another."* He did not think of this as something we do in our temples, churches or synagogues or something we do only in the spiritual part of our lives. For Gandhi nonviolence was a way of life.

"Nonviolence is not a garment to be put on and off at will. It's seat is in the heart, and it must be an inseparable part of our being."

I began to understand the depth this commitment could take over 30 years ago when I took a class on Christian ethics. One subject was the writings and life of Stanley Hauerwas, the Gilbert T. Rowe Professor of Theological Ethics at Duke Divinity School. In 2001, Hauerwas was honored by *Time* magazine as being America's Best Theologian. He once said non-violence is the most important teaching Christianity offers the world.

In this particular class we were reading Hauerwas' book, A *Community of Character* (1981) about living in community with a life devoted to the teachings of Jesus. In this book he wrote that if a gunman pointed his gun at your child, the true follower of Jesus could only place himself between the gunman and the child. At that time my youngest daughter was five-years-old. We were required to write a paper about this statement. I tried everything in my intellectual power to come up with a paper based on Jesus' teachings that would refute this claim and I could not. I was much younger then but I knew what I would do if anyone threatened my children and it was not pretty. However, the challenge to love my enemies has never gone away.

Hauerwas has not backed down. In 2010 he addressed a group of Indiana Wesleyan University students. *"Christians are called to be nonviolent, not because we believe our nonviolence is a strategy to rid the world of war, but [because] in a world of war, as faithful followers of Christ, we cannot imagine being anything other than nonviolent,"* he told them.

We must remember that non-violence for Jesus was not about cage fighting, war or guns. It was about how we relate to the world and all living beings. What if we treated every sentient being as if they were part of God? It is not only our physical actions, not only the way we converse with others but even the way we think. Thinking is just another form of energy and we all know when we think angry thoughts, we put out angry energy. Do you want to take the path seriously? Then observe your thinking, your thoughts, and even your deepest emotions. Then forgive yourself, love yourself and move on with love—even love for your enemies.

As modern Christians, we sometimes struggle to find relevance and purpose in the Christian story today. What if we really took this part of our faith seriously, both as a path to our own healing and as part of the healing our world desperately needs today? I suspect many of us would learn a lot more about what it means to be a follower of Jesus and a lot more about ourselves in the process. And in the midst of these revelations we might actually make a difference toward a better, more peaceful world.

"At the center of non-violence stands the principle of love."—Martin Luther King, Jr.

These Times They Are a Changing

Bob Dylan, in his song "These times are a Changing" reflected what a lot of us were thinking in the 1960s. We young people were leading a revolution for a better world. Many of us sincerely believed, possibly in our naiveté, that we were heading toward a more compassionate and egalitarian world. It was after all, less than 20 years after the end of World War II. We as a country had realized our success had been, in part, a result of an entire country coming together, making common sacrifices and recognizing the absolute necessity of every single person who participated. For a moment we realized no one had been more important in our success, whether they were a five-star general or Rosie the Riveter. We had all been dependent on each other to overcome a serious threat.

We honored the soldiers who came home. We helped educate them, helped them buy homes, and created jobs where a working father could live a comfortable middle class life with a pension and still have money left to send his kids to college.

By the 1960s things had started to change and we were faced with another war. Apparently we had not learned our lesson in the costly stalemate in Korea. Young people were starting to understand we lived in an interdependent world that was getting more and more divided by the haves and the have-nots. Idealistic as it may sound, many of us sincerely believed wars no longer served a purpose and especially a war that did not threaten our population.

We believed President Eisenhower was right when he said one of our biggest threats was the undue influence of the military industrial complex. Many of us had friends and school mates who were coming home in coffins. The growing hostilities in Vietnam provided the coalescing opportunity to protest the direction our country was going and it brought together many diverse people.

With youthful, national leaders like Bobby Kennedy and Martin Luther King Jr., the protests morphed into some of the larger social issues; equality for African Americans, gender justice, and more opportunities for the poor and under-privileged. Thanks to people like Martin Luther King Jr, many of us actually began to see the connections in all of these issues.

Those heady times in the sixties, when some of us viewed ourselves as young prophets of a new world, may be seen by historians as simply a narcissistic blip in the crumbling of an empire. Or perhaps they will be seen as the beginning of something much bigger and much more important. I do believe we helped make some important changes in our country and the world, but today I think too many of us got too comfortable and too lazy, too soon. I wonder if the Occupiers will say the same thing in 40 years.

What we do know is that today the world is changing faster than we could possibly have imagined 40 years ago. Some of those changes are driven by scientific discoveries that are a quantum leap from the age of enlightenment. Some change is the result of technological developments turning the word outdated into something occurring in months, not decades. Could anyone have imagined in 1968, other than a rare few, what impact the computer, and its cousin, the social network, would have on the world?

Some change is driven by a growing awareness of the interdependency of our world. We continue to get the lesson that what happens over there ultimately affects what happens here. Now we can see not only occasional photos of the suffering and the downtrodden. We can see them live, in high definition color. We can hear the sobs from the distraught mothers with dying children in their arms and the anguished cries of the helpless fathers as they pledge revenge.

We are also living in a time allowing us to see, if we choose to do so, that the way we are treating our beautiful Mother Earth is no longer sustainable. We are already seeing the growing starvation all over the world. It does not take a scientist to realize shortages of healthy food could be coming our way. We are running out of clean water, already affecting the majority of the population of the earth. If we continue to abuse our waterways with our poisons, we will be affected sooner than most people believe.

Governments are failing and faltering all over the world because people are trying to hold on to old ways of thinking and old ways of dividing. It is clear people in leadership positions are still operating with a tribal mentality. Real consensus is collapsing everywhere. In the process the rich get richer and poor get poorer. There has been no time in modern history when this has happened more rapidly. For many people it has taken a bunch of frustrated young adults to bring it to our attention.

It appears very few of those protesting in our cities are representative of any faith tradition. Yet they suffer, in barely tolerable conditions, to protest one of the foundational issues in the biblical faith, economic justice.

So the question I ask is, in this rapidly changing world, where has the church been and where will it be in the future? We do know that in the sixties, some clergy were in the streets, marching for civil rights, but it was a small percentage. Many of them lost their churches as a result. More clergy preached about what they thought Jesus would want us to do about the Vietnam War. These actions may have caused one of the largest exoduses in church history. Clergy learned there were consequences in taking a conscientious stand. For the past couple of decades they are being forced to learn that lesson again when taking a stand for full inclusion for gays and lesbians in the life of the church. Based on my limited survey, most of them are tip toeing around the Occupier protests. Denominations are once again being split by righteousness.

The truth of the matter is, with some wonderful exceptions, Christian churches have seldom been leaders on tough, social justice issues: not on slavery; not on civil rights for people of color; for woman's rights or on economic injustice. Nor, I would argue, have they been leaders in a more compassionate world, outspoken in their condemnation of war. Many of my aging friends would argue that religion has been one of the greatest obstacles to creating a more just and compassionate world. However, I tend to agree with the great theologian, Lloyd Geering, who suggested recently that we have a better world because of the teachings of Jesus. But is that enough and do those teachings still have meaning when religion is seen as the problem with so many young people today?

Most futurists believe Bob Dylan was right in 1964. The world is changing and it is changing faster than anyone could possibly have imagined. There is a lot of hope among young and some old that we are moving into a cosmic shift. Some have argued we are in a birth process and what we are going through today is the result of birthing pains. Most of those who suggest this are totally unaware that St. Paul used the same language, nearly 2000 years ago in his hope for a new world order. Others suggest we are going through an epic evolutionary shift that is necessary for human survival.

It appears to me that humans, like other animals, only evolve when the survival of the species is in danger of extinction. Maybe it will happen but if so it will require an incredible growth in our awareness that is not in evidence today. At the very least there will have to be a full acceptance that, as a species, we are truly connected and interdependent, not only with each other but with our Mother Earth.

Now there is a something our churches could be teaching if we want to become leaders in this incredible transition.

Occupy Wall Street

Occupy Wall Street captured the attention of the nation in mid-September, 2011. It continued well into the winter. During those months, I received an email asking me why our organization had "ignored the important Occupy movement." According to this writer, our absence as progressive Christians of some "direct statement of support was unthinkable and disappointing."

The fact is we did not ignore OWS. Several of the articles we published mentioned the movement in very favorable terms. It is true we did not come out with a strong statement as I assume this reader feels we should have done. Our hesitancy to offer such a thing has been based upon two things.

Progressive Christianity has always been focused on theology and spirituality. We do believe, if one was to take the teachings of Jesus seriously, it is likely the follower would at some point end up taking significant risks to bring about a more just world or situation. However, we are always working to distinguish ourselves from those traditional and evangelical Christians who refer to themselves as progressive but only focus on social justice issues. Generally speaking, these folks reflect their belief that Christ, as the Son of God, instructed his followers that God is pleased when we work for social justice. In this understanding, this biblical Jesus was instructing Christians to do good works as the voice of the biblical God.

For people like Jim Wallis, who now often refers to himself as a progressive Christian, the term progressive simply refers to his belief that being a Christian demands that one work for a more just society. It is a call, by the way, that we applaud and support.

However, Wallis and many others who refer to themselves as progressive Christians are not progressive in their theology and Christology. The above referenced email suggests this difference has confused a lot of folks out there.

Secondarily, I refrained from making a statement suggesting I judged those inner city churches across the country struggling with the difficult issue of letting the occupiers continue to use the church facilities as a place of encampment and headquarters. In some cases, the occupiers had been on the property for several weeks, and used the outside for camping. The complications, legally, financially and politically had become very difficult for clergy and church leadership, many of whom are colleagues and friends of mine. It has often been a test of will and righteousness. It has also been a test that can tear a church apart. We did not feel it was appropriate to take sides in the demands that were being made on independent churches and their leadership. Many struggle with their own financial and political issues.

However, a couple of things happened that brought my thoughts back to the reader who challenged our organization to make a statement. One was the letter written by Katharine Jefferts Schori, Presiding Bishop of the Episcopal Church, in response to the ongoing conflict between members of the Occupy Wall Street movement and Trinity Episcopal Church, Wall Street. The OWS protestors hoped to continue its occupation there after being evicted from Zuccotti Park in the late fall.

Please understand, I have the upmost respect for Bishop Jefferts Schori. I believe she has been a breath of fresh air for the Episcopalian Church. But for many, both in and out of the Trinity Episcopal Church, the letter seemed to challenge prophetic witness and the core values of their Christian faith. However, she is also the CEO of an institutional church. Her success as a Bishop will be measured in part by her success in holding together the Episcopal Church in these turbulent times.

Most of the people in Trinity Church, Wall Street, feel they have done their fair share. The church has provided the occupiers the use of their historic facility for restrooms, meeting rooms, places to eat and rest. Apparently the church was split over whether it should provide an encampment area in the church's park next to the church. This was just going too far with too many risks.

Therein lays the issue for all of us. When we are both students and proclaimed followers of the radical Jesus, how far is too far? We know his path of compassion led him to the ultimate sacrifice. The truth is the Christian church is not designed to be radical or even a change agent. Churches, by design, with their creeds, liturgies, traditions, and ownership of properties, are often more about politics than they are about spirituality. I have done church renewal workshops over 20 years in literally hundreds of churches. I have seldom seen radical discipleship as one of the underlying motivators.

Apparently, for some in this church, providing the use of the park was understandably going too far. For the Bishop, suggesting they had done enough might hold the church together. Few of us sitting in our comfortable churches, studies, living rooms or classrooms have had to face such difficult decisions with such challenging political fallout. Someone once said mainline denominations are made up of armchair Christians. We send our checks, our missionaries, and sometimes our pastors while we watch the news in our recliners.

At the time, I thought a lot about those primarily young people who camped in tents, cardboard boxes and sleeping bags for months in all kinds of terrible weather. They desperately tried to bring our attention to the horrendous inequities we have created in our own country. And apparently it worked. They got our attention. A report released by the Pew Research Center found that about two-thirds of Americans perceived a strong conflict between the rich and poor in this country. That was up 19 percentage points from 2009.

I wondered if my faith could have ever called me to such radical behavior. I did not wonder why our denominations did not show greater support for those committed, and in many ways extremely faithful, young people who believed through non-violence they could change the system. I wondered if my faith would ever give me such courage and fortitude.

Something else brought this issue to my attention. It was the result of some research I was doing for another article. I was rereading, *Bandits, Prophets and Messiahs*, by the excellent scholar, Richard Horsley. It had been over a decade since I read this book but it has always stuck in my mind. As I was reading it, I became more and more aware of the similarities between the resistant movements of the first century Jews and the young occupiers. While there were many groups that came and went over nearly 70 years, Horsley states they were all united in their resistance to the Romans and the Jewish ruling groups' treatment of the peasantry. Horsley points out that ". . . in this respect, Jesus shared the same basic concern as the (other) popular leaders and movements."

By the time Jesus appeared on the scene, according to Horsley, it appears somewhere around 90 percent of the Jewish citizenry was barely surviving. In other words, 10 percent of the Roman and Jewish elite owned 90 percent of the wealth. The brutal control and taxation by the Romans had at least the acquiescence of the Jewish leadership. The priest were living like kings. A very high percentage of the population had lost their family farms and the vast majority of Jews were functioning as tenant farmers on land they once owned.

The thing that really caught my attention was how these movements coalesced during the Passover holidays. The great celebration of Passover, when Jews commemorate their freedom from slavery in Egypt, had become an annual reminder of the severe injustice they were still experiencing. It represented another slap in the face, reminding them they had gone from one form of slavery into another. Year after year, Jews would migrate to Jerusalem by the tens of thousands and occupy the city. It was clearly more than a religious holiday. It was a protest of resistance about the completely unfair distribution of economic resources. These protests took on many forms over the decades but they were grounded in one common social issue—the incredible injustice that impacted the lives of 90 percent of the Jewish population. There were different types of protest, some more violent than others. But the vast majority of the people were simply there to make a statement. "We are not going to let you get away with this."

Every year the Roman leadership, with the support of the Jewish elite, would bring in extra troops and arrest and hang protestors by the thousands. Where did they hang them? They hung them on crosses of course, in front of the five gates into Jerusalem. This cruel punishment was meant to discourage further uprisings. But even this did not work for these courageous, radical folks. They believed God was on their side. They did not ask how far is too far. Horsley and others suggest that the story of Jesus' protest in the Temple probably had roots in one of those Passover events.

In my mind, it is virtually impossible to read whatever historicity we have left in these bible stories, and still have doubts where Jesus was on these issues 2000 years ago. Frankly it is also likely he would be involved today, if not on Wall Street, then maybe in Detroit. So the question is not what would Jesus do? Rather it is how committed are you to following the radical path? Or how far is too far?

K.C. Hanson and Douglas E. Oakman, in their book, *Palestine in the Time of Jesus*, write, ". . . in many ways the society in which Jesus lived was struc- turally dysfunctional, since it gave inordinate power and privilege to a very few." Does that sound familiar?

History has repeatedly demonstrated that when any society gives an in- ordinate amount of power and privilege to a few, something is ultimately going to break. These valiant occupiers provided us with not only a model, but possibly salvation from a far worse scenario, a real revolution. From a historical perspective, it appears to me if we are truly followers of Jesus, there seems to be no doubt what our response would have to be: join the move- ment; if not financially support them; if not applaud them; or for heavens' sake at the very least we should be thanking these young people who truly are trying to change the world.

How Far Are We Willing to Go?

I had just walked out the gates of a Gay Pride festival when I saw the protes- tors. It was in the late 1980s and I had been invited to give a short address and to be honored by the GLTB community of Orange County California. Working with the City of Irvine, I had helped create protective laws for Gays and Lesbians in the work place and in housing.

It had been a cantankerous struggle in conservative Orange County. In large part this was because of the muscle the conservative churches had been able to orchestrate in the political arena. I had already suffered some of their venom as pastor of the UCC Church. We were the first church in the area to take a congregation through the Open and Affirming process. The church vote made the front page of the *Orange County Register*. This resulted in protestors, bomb threats, death threats on my life and my family and some pretty crude graffiti on the building. Admittedly, these things seemed unreal and in large part unlikely to actually cause me harm.

But this group of conservative Christian protestors, mostly large men, looked very real. At that point they were headed my way. This group of about 12 to 15 men was blocking my way to the parking lot so I decided to just keep walking. I knew things were going to get serious when one of the men yelled, "that's him!"

Within seconds I was surrounded by these angry, aggressive men screaming that I was a fraud, a heretic and that I was no Christian. Somehow the heretic thing stuck and they all started to chant, "Heretic, heretic, heretic . . ."

The circle kept getting tighter and tighter, keeping me from any hope of a safe escape. One hefty man, well over six feet and 200 pounds, was carrying a large flag on a pole with a picture of Jesus on it. I remember thinking Jesus seemed to be looking down at this sad ruckus. This guy kept pushing up against me, shoving the pole into my body and yelling, his saliva hitting me in the face. I don't think it occurred to me that I was going to die, but I was likely to get hurt very badly.

Suddenly there was a body stepping in between me and this threatening man. Then there was another, and another. I finally realized, in the midst of my confusion, a group of gay men was surrounding me within the circle of aggressors. Once I was completely protected, the inner circle started moving, with me in the center. When we were 30 yards away from the yelling crowd we had a clear path to my car. Hardly a word was spoken but I was shaken. When they walked me to the car, I thanked them and told them how amazingly well they had handled it. One fellow said, "Oh, we are used to it." And then they quietly walked away.

As I sat in the car for half an hour, too shaken to drive, the words of the gentle, young escort kept going through my head and my heart. "Oh, we are used to it." I suddenly realized this is what it feels like to be gay. This is what they have had to get used to their whole lives. I remember crying out through my tears "my God, my God . . . this is not right."

My life changed with that event. I went from being a social activist to a zealot. Never again was I willing to look the other way. I had a renewed sense of what it meant to be a follower of Jesus, to be willing to take a risk on behalf of another. This was not just about some abstract social justice issue. This was about real people, with real lives and loves. This was about people with a constant fear they might have to confront some kind of mistreatment simply because of who they were.

Right then, I realized that the Jesus path is not just about social justice issues. It is about people—people who suffer as victims of power, prejudice, class, color or culture. I saw people at the table of Jesus very differently after that.

But something else happened. I stayed close to some of those men who came to my rescue, for now we had shared a common experience. Over the years we shared our story many times, even learning to laugh about it. Of course we shared new common stories along the way. The lines between us had somehow melted. They were no longer my gay acquaintances but my dear friends. They were no longer they. We had become we.

I have had other experiences like that, going from thinking I was the savior to being the one saved. Them transformed into us; going from the helper to the helped, going from the teacher to the student. As I continued to have those experiences, I realized this is the real value of the Jesus path. It is with our willingness to reach out with the compassion of a mother for her child to the marginalized, the outcast, the enemy, the hurting, the other, that we can experience the dissolving of all lines of demarcation that separate us. And it is here, I believe, that we can discover the Oneness in all life—the Unity in all things.

These opportunities can show up in our workplace, our schools, our churches and on the side of the road. They happen when we start seeing every living being as part of one creation, interconnected and interdependent. They happen when we begin to hear the cries of another as a cry from God.

I believe this very important aspect of the Christian tradition has been ignored by too many of us who claim to be Christian. As a result, we miss profound opportunities to experience the Realm of God, or Sacred Unity, Jesus referred to with such passion. Maybe the real question is how far are we willing to go to experience that place, a state of mind so special that once we experience it, we will go out and sell everything we have to buy it? How far are you willing to go for something so special?

The Spirituality of Mother Earth

There are a lot of reasons why I'm glad my wife and I moved to the Pacific Northwest. They are too numerous to list. We both love the outdoors and the beauty here. We will not live long enough to take advantage of all the natural treasures within a short drive from our home, let alone our island. If you want to hike, ski, kayak, water ski, or sit quietly in the rain forest, it is all here. We are surrounded by a body of water called the Puget Sound. The Cascade Mountains are on one side and the Olympic Mountains on the other. If one has the eyes to see, the scenery is glorious and is a constantly changing panorama of visual delights. "If one has the eyes to see" is the operative phrase. We have discovered some people just do not see or hear the same things we see and hear. Although it sometimes surprises us, we have learned to accept this.

The Pacific Northwest is not for everyone. It rains a lot and during the dead of the winter, and one can go days without seeing the sun. One February it rained for 27 days straight and we were disappointed because we missed a record by two days. The winter nights are long with a sunrise as late as 8 a.m. and sunset as early as 4 p.m. We have watched more than one friend pack up and leave the area because they could not take the weather. On the other hand we love it, even when we sometimes do not like it.

You see, the real reason I love it here is I have become reconnected to nature and the earth. It took me a couple of years to figure out what was going on and what was happening to me. But when I finally figured it out, I was a little surprised. While I have always had an affinity for the outdoors and especially outdoor activities, I realized I have treated nature as an object, something for my enjoyment. What had changed was my growing awareness that I am dependent, connected and part of nature, part of the earth. I am much more aware in ways I have never understood before, that we are related.

The area we live in is still pretty much a complete, dynamic ecosystem. Plants die and then they are reborn. Leaves actually fall come September and October and it gets cold in the winter. The evergreens seem to be eternal, especially the proud 120-foot giants surrounding our home. We do not import water from another state. Our water comes from a deep community well fed by a glacier on Mountain Rainer 50 miles away.

It would be easy to live on food from the local farmers year-round. (Okay, I would miss my avocados and citrus fruit.) Things just seem to grow whether you want them to or not. Every spring, more than a hundred little trees start growing somewhere on our property. We live on a little more than an acre and a third. We have no sprinkler system, no lawn and use no fertilizer except for our own compost. Yet we have a lovely garden we share with our neighbors. It produces most of our vegetables for the summer and what we don't produce, our good friends who also live on the island fill in. We are surrounded by an abundance of huge trees, evergreen plants and a vast variety of natural ground cover.

The wildlife is challenging at times but is another reminder that we are all interconnected. Admittedly, we have netting over our vegetables since the deer seem to like the young sprouts. But we found ways to co-exist and we enjoy their regular visits. We sometimes think we live in a giant aviary. We have become attached to the hundreds of birds that hang out around our home, serenading us in the spring from morning to nightfall. I hope I never get so used to them and no longer hear them. We have developed a particular fondness for the beautiful Bald Eagle that seems to fly over our deck just about the time one of us mentions we have not seen him for a while.

And then there is the air. I am amazed by the people who have lived here all their lives and do not realize what a gift the clean, pure oxygen-filled air really is. Of course the smells of the pine needles, the Madrona leaves, the flowers, and the often wet soil, add a certain distinct flavor. But now when I travel somewhere that does not have clean, fresh air, I grieve for it. It is sad to think this is the way the entire earth was at one time, filled with trees, clean air and clean water.

The winter nights are long and cold. However, most people are aware of the day of the week when the Winter Solstice will occur in any given year. We celebrate it like some people celebrate Easter. I now understand experientially why the Solstice was turned into a religious holiday. I have a new perspective on why most ancient religions, including Christianity, borrowed from earlier religious celebrations centered on the seasons of the earth.

I have come to realize it would be impossible for me to have a holistic spirituality that is not somehow connected and grounded in an awesome appreciation of our Mother Earth. Thomas Berry, a Catholic priest who died in June of 2009, was considered by many to be the father of evolutionary spirituality. He would not have called it that because for him deep spirituality always resulted from the awareness of our interconnectedness and the interdependency of all creation. That's what spirituality was for him. This is a quote from an article he wrote in 1990 called, *"The Spirituality of the Earth."*

"We need a spirituality that emerges out of a reality deeper than ourselves, even deeper than life, a spirituality that is as deep as the earth process itself, a spirituality born out of the solar system and even out of the heavens beyond the solar system. There in the stars is where the primordial elements take shape in both their physical and psychic aspects. There is a certain triviality in any spiritual discipline that does not experience itself as supported by the spiritual as well as the physical dynamics of the entire cosmic-earth process. A spirituality is a mode of being in which not only the divine and the human commune with each other, but we discover ourselves in the universe and the universe discovers itself in us."

Over the last few years, I have developed a greater appreciation for one of Berry's main ideas—that the earth is our mother and not separate from us. We are of the earth and the earth is of us.

Berry spent the last half of his long life pointing out that Christians, in large part, have failed to acknowledge the spirituality of the earth and our dependency on her as Mother. The traditional Christian idea is that the earth was created by an outside source as a convenient gift to support humans for the limited time we each spend here. This could not be any more myopic and self-centered. This has led to crassness in our relationship with the earth, our solar system and the cosmos in general. It has also led to some pretty shallow forms of spirituality.

The idea that the Universe was created by a theistic God outside of us, for our needs has perpetuated the duality myth that no longer fits our understanding of reality or the cosmos. It allows us to produce Christian spiritualties that function in a certain isolated context without regard for the larger society or the very earth that sustains us.

We do know every action creates a reaction. Whatever we do to the earth, there is a reaction. The earth is certainly reacting. Someday we will have to try and figure out how this spiritual attitude allowed humans to attack the earth with such savagery. It is becoming more clear that whatever the cause, we are headed for a major change. Some call it evolutionary change. Others are not so positive.

I realize it is not possible for everyone to move to the forest and smell the naturally sweet perfume of damp earth and fresh leaves. It is not possible for everyone to float in a kayak on a clear lake in the Olympic Mountains, meditate and give thanks for the truly awesome surroundings. It is not possible for most people to see four Bald Eagles in a day as they dip a wing to acknowledge our obvious adoration of their beauty and dignity. It is not possible for everyone to breathe in fresh, clean air with every breath and drink clean water out of a well. But you can know this is still possible and this is what Mother wants for each of us.

In the meantime we can keep Thomas Berry's words in mind: *"We need a spirituality that emerges out of a reality deeper than ourselves, even deeper than life, a spirituality that is as deep as the earth process itself, a spirituality born out of the solar system and even out of the heavens beyond the solar system."*

Trees and Things that Live

I am one of those rare individuals who was lucky enough to spend most of my childhood in Southern California's San Gabriel Valley when it was still in large part agrarian. Our home was surrounded by acres of farmland, orange and walnut orchards. A ten-minute bike ride would get a strong rider to rolling hills that had cattle and horses grazing. If you were a little sneaky you could climb through the barbed wire fence and go skinny dipping with your buddies in a green, somewhat slimy reservoir. That was until my parents actually went to look at the cause of the slime and the strange smell I often came home with in the summer heat. There were several stands of trees with low limbs that were easy to climb and made perfect foundations for building forts. I loved the outdoors and the adventures my friends and I created in those hills with the help of our vivid imaginations.

I also remember fondly my family's regular trips up into the San Gabriel Mountains. Only an hour away from our home, we went for day picnics and weekend stays in a cabin with a wood burning stove. Almost every summer my parents and aunts and uncles rented a large cabin with my grandparents. The five families took turns sharing the space often overlapping with each other. The kids, including my cousins and occasional friends, usually ended up sleeping on the porch surrounded by the thick pine tree forest.

I developed an appreciation for those trees in part because they were a challenge to climb. Sometimes, when we were playing in the middle of them, I felt protected, like I was in a cave. And of course, I appreciated the pine needles we often used to soften the ground under our sleeping bags. Over 50 years later the unique, gently whispering sound pines trees emit as the winds blows through their needles is still imprinted in my soul.

The term tree hugger has been around for a good part of my adult life. It was usually intended to be derogatory applying to a silly person out of touch with reality. There were also political implications. Initially this might have implied one of those harebrained hippy types or even a leftist, out of touch with the real world. I would never have referred to myself as a tree hugger in those early years, even though I secretly appreciated them. However, I readily admit that I saw trees as something that were simply there for my enjoyment and comfort, to do whatever I wanted. Today, I find myself in a very different mindset.

For nearly ten years now my wife and I have lived in the forest on a small island in the Pacific Northwest. Our builder cleared only the trees that were absolutely required to create a space large enough to build our home and a long driveway. He proudly pointed out that he had been careful to leave every other tree undamaged. We were not around when the trees were cleared but I don't think it would have meant much to me at the time. They were lovely trees but they were just trees after all. There were nearly a hundred of them on our property alone. With our neighbors' contiguous property we experience a continuous expanse of huge trees.

Over time we have come to love each one of our mature trees, many of them over 150 feet tall. The smaller trees may never mature because of the lack of sun, but they still wait in the wings for an opportunity to fill any gaps caused by windstorms, fires or disease of their parents. We appreciate them hanging in there for the cause. We have our favorites and we have named many of them. There is Queen, a lush hemlock. She is the most elegant. I have told my children I would like to have my ashes spread under her large, soft, caressing limbs. There is the King, of course. Close to 30-inches at its base, it goes straight up over a 140 feet. He stands alone in his obvious power and strength. There are the Three Sisters out our back window. They sway back and forth in the wind together as if choreographed by a dance instructor.

Then there is the Secret. At one point her limbs barely touching the ground made a small tent. It was the place where my wife and granddaughter had secret gatherings with tea parties, snacks and little people. The tree experts have told us several times that Secret is too close to the house. They warned she would cause serious problems for us in the future. They recommended her removal five years ago. I have had my roaring chain saw against her bark on three occasions but she still stands. With limbs now six feet off the ground and a granddaughter now too old to play make believe, she is no longer a secret hiding place. But she is still a sweet memory for we grandparents.

Last year our neighbors expressed some concern about three of our largest trees on the side of a small hill. A large part of their roots were exposed. Towering over their small home, these trees seemed to be leaning a little more each year in their direction. We knew we had to do something. We reluctantly signed a contract with one of the local tree service companies to come and take them down. The trees were marked on a Friday for demolition on the following Monday. Clearly this was the logical, proper, safe and necessary thing to do. We were sad but we knew we would get on with our lives.

On Sunday evening Charron and I walked outside to say goodbye to these mighty trees. She had written a beautiful poem to honor them. One of the trees was an inspiration for me. I called her Determined. She had obviously been severely harmed as a young tree. There was a three foot curve a few feet out of the ground before she gained the strength to continue her growth straight up. In the place where the curve had formed, there was such a strong bond the professional chain saws would barely cut through it. It was nearly four-feet thick at that point. Even with the bend, the base could still handle the tons of weight of the rest of the 150 feet of tree. It was an amazing example of how one can overcome even the most serious difficulties, and do it with beauty.

After Charron read her poem in honor of the three trees, I went over to each one of them. At this point, crying openly, I put my arms around each one of them, as far as I could reach. Yes, I hugged them. I swear I could feel life flowing through each one of them, especially Determined. Seldom does a day pass when I do not stop at the remaining stump and give thanks for her sacrifice and inspiration.

Our trees, however, are just one way my life has opened up to the reality that we are truly connected and frankly dependent on all forms of life. Once you start watching, it becomes apparent the forest is a living organism. In large part it is in balance. The standing dead trees become habitats for bugs, worms and all kinds of critters. These bring the birds by the hundreds. We have Woody Woodpeckers nearly two feet tall. They can peck a perfectly round, two-inch hole in dead trees. When they are done eating the bugs they are searching for, beautiful little birds make nests in those cozy round holes. I have made friends with squirrels who chatter away and deer who just stare at me while they quietly graze on our plants.

The idea that we humans have been given dominion over the animals, the trees and the waters is just wrong. At some point we are going to have to admit we have been blind to what we have done and are continuing to do. If we do not begin to function in harmony with all Creation, I am afraid Homo sapiens will have a short history on this earth. Even more tragic, we humans will have missed an opportunity to experience an amazing awareness that could have led to a profound, life changing spiritual experience and a very different worldly experience.

Living in a more natural world has changed the way I see everything. When you open your eyes to what happens every day in such perfect symmetry, it becomes more obvious how out of touch our slash and burn mentality has taken us. We have nearly destroyed what was once perfect. Why has it taken us so long to realize that we humans are the cause of the sickness we are now experiencing in our precious world? We may even discover we are the cancer spreading over this beautiful planet.

I think Thomas Berry had it right. We are too busy talking to ourselves and not listening to who and what we should be listening to. We are stuck in the wrong paradigm. Frankly, Christian Scriptures are of little help here. Thomas Berry is correct, I believe, when he suggests we should put them on a shelf for a while until we learn to listen to our real teachers. This includes not only the forest but our sea world, our pets and yes, our horses. In the last ten years I have learned more from the forest, the wild animals and family pets than any books, articles or demonstrations I have encountered. I have come to view Thomas Berry as a true prophet.

Here are a few quotes from the Priest and Prophet Thomas Berry. All of these quotes are from his book *The Great Work*, 1999.

"We are talking only to ourselves. We are not talking to the rivers; we are not listening to the wind and stars. We have broken the great conversation. By breaking that conversation we have shattered the universe. All the disasters that are happening now are a consequence of that spiritual 'autism.'"

"The natural world itself is our primary language as it is our primary scripture, our primary awakening to the mysteries of existence. We might well put all our written scriptures on the shelf for twenty years until we learn what we are being told by unmediated experience of the world about us."

"In our totality we are born of the Earth. Our spirituality itself is earth-derived . . . If there is no spirituality in the earth, then there is no spirituality in ourselves."

Is it too late to make the changes we must make for human survival? Is it too late for a completely new consciousness? Can we help bring about the Axial Shift so many people have been counting on? For my grandchildren at least, I hope so.

Just call me Fred Plumer, Tree Hugger. I would be honored.

CHAPTER EIGHT

Educating our Youth

I Learned a Lot at My New Church

I had been a pastor at fledging church I helped found for a little less than six years when I was shaken to my toes. The wife of one of the original families who helped start the church informed me that their family would be leaving and joining a much more conservative church down the street. I was stunned. Not only were these folks looked upon as pillars of the church, but I considered them friends. With tears in her eyes she explained that their teenage son who had been having some difficulties in school wanted to go to the other church's youth program and Sunday school. She went on to say that she felt it was important to support their son and for the entire family to attend the same church. I was hurt and saddened but I could not argue with her logic or reasoning.

It was nearly a year later however, before I got the second half of this painful lesson. I ran into the young son at a local football game. I had known this kid since he was six or seven years old and now he was almost as tall as me. I gave him a hug and we went through an awkward exchange. For some reason he felt compelled to tell me that he missed me and missed "lot of the things at my old church." Then he went on to say that he thought that he was learning a lot more things at his new church. When I asked him like what, he responded; "They teach who Jesus was, how to read the Bible and I learned about God."

I responded, "That's great, I am glad you like it there and stay in touch." I think I smiled but inside I was torn up. I went home exhausted that night but slept very little. The next couple of days, I plowed through my sermons; I looked at our children's curriculum and the outline I had created for the nine-month Confirmation class. I defensively kept screaming in my head, "What do you mean you are learning more? We pride ourselves on being a questioning, teaching church! You are not learning. You are memorizing!"

I huffed and I puffed and told myself that we should be proud. We had Jesus Seminar scholars come to our church before they were "On the Road." We had professors from the local universities speak to us about the early Christian roots. Our Sunday schools were designed so the children could develop open minds so when they were mature enough, they could make their own decisions. A New Testament scholar at one local university said our Confirmation curriculum was more advanced than some of his own classes. Why the hell was this kid saying he was learning more?

After a couple of weeks of this thrashing, I finally calmed down enough to begin to ask myself what I could learn from this young man. What was missing in our approach to Christian teaching? What were we really teaching our children? What did this young man want that he did not find at our progressive church? What was the pedagogical model we had created, or more importantly what model did we need to create?

This started a 14-year project that was never completed, but we learned a lot. Although we made a valiant effort, it is very difficult for one mid-size church to create a full curriculum with limited staff and volunteers. We brought in outside consultants, read books and tried lots of different things. Some things worked and some did not, but we looked back on the ones that did not work as important lessons. Over the years some principles about our children's education began to become clearer. I have observed some of these things in churches I have visited all over the country.

1. Children want to learn from people who believe in what they are teaching.
2. Models of behavior are far better teachers than dogmatic rules or threats of suffering.
3. As they mature, children want to know the reason why they need to be there on Sunday mornings, other than you are supposed to be there.

4. Children crave community and the support that can come from it and a foundation of common understanding.
5. It is much easier to teach children to listen to their inner voice when they are young than it is if we wait until we think they are old enough.
6. Children want some specific teachings and guidelines that help them find peace, joy and balance in their lives. We believed that Jesus had provided those teachings.
7. Children want a curriculum that is experiential, that provides experiences of inspiration.
8. Children, like most humans, ultimately seek a spiritual connection to something bigger than themselves. It is OK to call that connection God.
9. Children (of all ages) like to have fun.

Even with these helpful guidelines, we found it a major challenge to create a curriculum reflecting them and it is not always easy to find teachers who are comfortable teaching them. The positive experiences we had in those years far outweighed the negatives, however. As we developed the ProgressiveChristianity.org Children's Curriculum, we used some of those same guidelines with many of the same goals.

We wanted to foster our children's concern for the whole human family and share the ideal that every human being is entitled to rights and freedoms simply because they are part of Creation. We wanted them to feel included and be inclusive with those of every class, ethnic persuasion, every sexual orientation, every religion and age. We wanted them to have examples and materials that would encourage them to take a stand against the injustices that confront every one of us each day. We wanted them to grow up experiencing the Oneness in life and to become abundantly aware of all Creation of which they are an important part.

It is our sincere hope that our faith communities know this curriculum is now available on our website and on several other partner organizations and we want you to know we believe that we have met these objectives. We would love to see it being used by every church or small group that wants to teach their children a path of spiritual experience.

Maybe then when a child tells a friend (or former pastor) about their progressive Christian church, they will be able to say: "I learned a lot of things at my church. I learned about Jesus' and a way to experience God and the Oneness of All Life together. I learned how important it is love and forgive. I learned how I can help create a better world for everyone. "

A Changing Organization in a Changing World

You may think this article is a promotion for our children's curriculum, *Joyful Path, Year One and Two*, and you may be right. Each one of our children's curriculum was the result of over seven years of hard work and a budget of nearly $100,000 for each one. Yes, we hope and expect more churches and individuals will discover what so many folks have already discovered. This curriculum is an amazing tool for the spiritual growth for children and adults. We are very proud of the results of this huge undertaking.

But I would like our readers to understand that this is more than an advertisement. It represents the extraordinary changes our organization has gone through over the last eight years. More importantly, it may be an indication of the changes we foresee for the future.

Back in 2001, I asked a good friend who owned a midsize marketing company, if he would help us analyze the mission and marketing strategy for our organization. After spending some significant time studying our situation, his team told us we faced three challenges. First, there appeared to be no clear place for us, as an organization, to advertise our service or products. The social network advertising options like Facebook and Google were not an option then. It does seem a little ironic that today, with our extremely active website, message boards, our Facebook page, and our two weekly and monthly publications, we may now be the place we were looking for fourteen years ago. Second, they pointed out there was still very little clarity in the meaning of the term Progressive Christian. This is in spite of having created eight identifying principles and use of the term in our name, articles and publications since 1994. Third, their research showed attendance in mainline Christian churches was in a rapid decline. They identified it as a declining market.

It slowly became clear that our original mission to create a forum for the exchange of information with churches trying to evolve into something new for the 21st century was not going to provide a sustainable business plan. While we still believe posting on our website provides a marketing value for churches wanting to declare themselves as progressive, it was apparent this was not going to be enough to build a sustainable organization. In some ways Google had replaced that purpose.

In 2007 we received a grant to do an intensive one-year study that would result in a strategic plan for the future. Rather than asking the question, "Where are we today?" this new organization asked, "Where do you want to be in five years?"

Prior to working with us, these consultants had no particular interest in religion or the church. They would have had little interest in the future of the church had they not noticed in their research what they identified as a major—even epic—shift in attitudes about religion in the Western hemisphere. They developed a growing fascination with this phenomenon. The team interviewed scholars, seminary presidents, pastors, lay leaders and executive directors from other progressive Christian organizations.

Among other things, their study showed that if mainline Christian churches had any hope for the future they would need new materials and resources for every element of congregational life. They needed liturgical materials, new forms for congregational worship gatherings and teaching curriculum for all ages. In particular, one need was consistent with everyone they interviewed. There was a demand for a children's curriculum free from the creedal restraints that hampered churches trying to be more progressive. They told us almost everyone they interviewed identified this need as the most critical. One seminary professor observed that we may not be able to change our old churches. However, if we can teach the children a spiritual path based on the teachings of Jesus, those children may very well be the ones who form their own faith communities as adults rather than trying to conform to something that no longer makes sense to them.

As a result, we made a shift. We became publishers creating our first full-year children's curriculum. It is now being used in nearly 800 churches and by 200 small faith communities and families. Raising the kind of money it took to pay writers, artists, editors, printers, and videographers in addition to the intense management requirements for such an undertaking was daunting. Now we know this was one of the most important things we could have done. More importantly we realized our children would be losing something important if they did not have the opportunity to learn about the compassionate and inclusive message of Jesus within a loving community. It was our children who would suffer without having a viable path leading to a more compassionate life and quite possibly, a more compassionate world.

It was never our intent to become a publishing company. Frankly, we recognize that the market base for courageous churches willing to make substantive changes is a relatively small one. There are nearly 300,000 Protestant churches in the United States today. Currently, we have our curriculum in a little less than 900 of them. In spite of the overwhelming excitement and appreciation these churches all share, we do not see that number growing radically in the near future. We do find it interesting that a growing number of people who order our curriculum are from small faith communities meeting in homes as well as young families who are home schooling. This may very well be a substantial part of our market of the future.

Our efforts to create curriculum is not limited to our children. The Study Guide for the 8Points is now in its fifth printing. In two years we have nearly doubled the liturgical materials now available for free on our website. You will also find we have improved both the search options as well as the organizing categories in that section. We are constantly running educational articles and book reviews being used for adult groups. We have been publishing the weekly John Shelby Spong articles since 2005. In the last four years we have built our third new website from scratch. It is full of educational and inspirational materials for all ages. It is one of the busiest religious websites in the country.

If someone had asked me where I thought this organization would be five years ago, I could not have imagined where we are. All of this has been accomplished with a small group of young, dedicated part-time staff, and their retired and sometimes tired volunteer president with no significant funding entity. Most of our income comes from small donors and sales. Every year we wonder if we can make it work for another year. We shuffle our work loads, the staff sometimes agreeing to donate their time. We try new things, and admittedly I sometimes wonder if it is all worth it. Are we really making a difference?

Yet our overworked and underpaid, yet still enthusiastic staff, insists we are not done. One of them recently told me: "We are just beginning to fly. This is no time to stop flapping our wings."

A Place of Higher Learning

Several years ago, during a social function, I had a chance to visit with Dr. Fred Register, the former Southern Conference Minister of the United Church of Christ. At that time Dr. Register had been retired for nearly ten years. He had been the Conference Minister for over 25 years and I believe one of the best in the nation. He was also known as an excellent speaker. Whenever it was time for him to give the annual sermon, no matter what else was going on, nearly everyone in the conference managed to get there for his talk.

I am sure Dr. Register was always a good preacher in his early days as a pastor in rural churches in the South. But I am certain his speaking ability stayed fresh because he never stopped educating himself. He was in his late fifties, when at a time when most people would be thinking about their upcoming retirement—for him that meant golf—he decided to go back to school and finish up his doctorate.

Dr. Register had a very special love for the church where I served as pastor. He had a lot to do with the planning, funding and birthing of this congregation in its earliest days. He recruited me for the job of pastor when there were less than 20 members. I think it was a last desperate gasp. But he knew how tough new church starts were. Over the years, we shared a common concern about the future of the larger church and spent many hours talking about changes we felt would have to be made if the progressive church was going to survive.

That last time we were together I asked Dr. Register something I had been curious about for some time. "Now that you have been out of the official ministry for nearly a decade and after all your years of study and observations, how do you feel about church today?" He stopped and gave my question some thought. He responded with his wonderful southern accent. It always made you feel he was never in a hurry.

"Well after studying the concept of God for over 70 years, I am certain I do not know who or what God is; frankly I am no longer certain who Jesus was; and I have become even less certain about the purpose of life. But I have found that I really like being around people who think these issues are important. That is why I still go to church every week."

I gave a lot of thought to Dr. Register's comments over the years. I suspect it had something to do with the realization I too would soon retire from the ministry. I wondered in those days if I would attend church if it was not my job. I must admit the first thing that came to my mind is "it better be a darn good one."

I feel very much like Dr. Register. I cannot imagine spending time with people who are not interested in the ultimate questions and how they affect our daily lives. There are few places in our society where one can wrestle with those ultimate issues other than in churches. While I am certain there are exceptions, most of us would be uncomfortable sitting down during lunch break, leaning over to our co-worker and casually asking, "Gee Helen, I was wondering what you think the meaning of life is?" Or shooting hoops and saying, "Say Bob, I was wondering. Do you think God is omnipotent or transcendent?" Or "Hey Larry, do you think God intercedes directly into history? Do you think of God as a thing, or a force or something with anthropomorphic qualities?"

You might like to know your kids have those kinds of conversations. They too wonder if God acts directly in history and whether God has any power to act in this world. These are not just hypothetical or philosophical questions. Kids want to know if there is a God. If so, why did that powerful God let all those people die in New York on 9/11? Why does God let thousands of little children die every day all over the world? I like to encourage bright young adults to share their feelings and to think about the different perspectives they hear in each other. I have felt for years that young children are naturally spiritual until we tell them that some things just are not real. We un-teach them.

But as children grow more curious again they like to be engaged in some of these conversations. From experience I know many of them will begin to enjoy or at least be entertained by these discussions. They don't want to be told what to believe. They do not want to memorize some dogma or creed they think they will have to believe. They want to learn, I hope, the difference between belief and faith, the difference between a verbal formulation of what we think we know with certainty as opposed to a trust in the ultimate divine reality that will always be a mystery.

It is challenging for young people to wrestle with these new concepts, to use new words and to try and articulate things of great mystery. But I have a hunch many kids will never be completely happy unless somewhere in their lives they find a place to wrestle with these ultimate questions with people they trust. When I have worked with young people I have explained that we are not trying to find the answers. Rather we are searching for the right questions and hopefully this will lead us to the right responses, responses that will probably change over the years.

But I wonder, in our competitive, materialistic, technologically dependent world, where else could our young people have these kinds of conversations. Where else can they feel comfortable asking questions about ultimate issues than in a safe, open spiritual community?

Let me share something else. I have discovered when adults take the time to share their feelings, their ideas, and their questions about the ultimate issues, something very special happens in the relationships. People begin to feel differently about those people who share their ideas about the great mysteries of life. The group changes when together they ponder, as Paul once wrote, what is honorable, what is just, what is pure, and what is godly. When get together with a faith exploration group, an adult education class, a grief recovery class and share our feelings and our ideas, something changes in the dynamic of the group. And sometimes something opens up in us that has been trying to get out for a long time.

We always learn something from a higher plane.

Breakfast with the Dalai Lama

I once had breakfast with Bishop Tutu and the Dalai Lama. Of course another 100 people attended this intimate affair. Nevertheless, I felt both honored and very fortunate to be given an opportunity to see and hear such extraordinary people. The prayer breakfast was held on the last day of a five-day event organized by a volunteer group called Seeds of

Compassion. Most of the events were conducted at the University of Washington campus in north Seattle. The breakfast was catered at a hotel in downtown Seattle.

The Dalai Lama anchored the gathering. His longtime friend, Bishop Tutu, joined him on the final day. When the two spiritual giants, both in their 70s, saw each other that morning for the first time in several years, they both shouted their welcomes across the room. As they approached each other, they laughed and giggled. In the last ten yards, surrounded by security people and people just trying to get close, they literally jumped up and down. Finally they embraced while laughing, and touching each other like very young school children on a playground. At one point the Dalai Lama pushed Bishop Tutu back a couple of feet, looked at him, and laughing he said, "My goodness, you have gotten fat!" They both started laughing again and Bishop Tutu playfully shaking his finger at his Holiness, said: "Now you start acting like a Holy man." Again there was joyful laughter by these two playful men. It was delightfully infectious. Those ten minutes of joyful expression were worth the sleep I had lost, the hour drive in traffic and a giant hunk out of my busy schedule that week.

The Seeds of Compassion organization is a very interesting organization and I believe it has a lot to tell those of us who are still trying to grow Christian churches. The organization came about through the collaboration of the Kirlin Foundation and the Venerable Tenzin Dhonden and many other religious, educational and spiritual people from the area. These dreamers wanted to bring "concrete public awareness, public will, and an empowering call to action to address our local and global need for the social and emotional well–being of children. As an outcome, they seek to bring social and emotional learning into families, to caregivers, and to schools so that all who touch the lives of children have the tools and empowerment to provide the foundation for kinder and more compassionate children, communities, and society." These quotes are from their brochure.

One of the fascinating things about this major event was that it was planned by religious leaders from over a dozen traditions. The breakfast event I attended was represented by 17 different traditions—from Roman Catholic to Wicca. Even so, there were many letters to the editor of the local newspaper complaining that the local children were allowed to attend these events on school days to be "indoctrinated" into the Buddhist religion. One writer complained that since Jesus knew more about compassion than Buddha, we should let our children out of school to hear the Sermon on the Mount. Sermon on the Mount? I wondered if she had read it. If this were not so sad, it would have been funny.

Although I was unable to attend some of the larger events, the ones I did attend were enough to get my head spinning. It is a powerful experience to sit with over 10,000 people to hear grounded, bright, spiritual people talk about the importance and the joy of learning to live more compassionately. And more significantly they focused on the importance of teaching our children the potential joys of living compassionately and working to create a more compassionate world together.

I listened to a couple of panel discussions that included youth and young adults along with such sage leaders as Sister Joan Chittister, Bishop Tutu, Roshi Joan Halifax, and the Dalai Lama. But for me that real star was a 12 year-old girl who comfortably shared her view that compassionate living is really a gift for the giver in front of 10,000 people. When she was done with her extemporaneous comments, I thought the Dalai Lama was going to jump out of his chair and give her his seat of honor. My confidence in our youth being able to handle the challenges that we have left them was dramatically improved.

The statistics alone for this amazing event should cause us all to pause and reflect. Over 150,000 people paid to attend these events over the five-day period. Over 100,000 others were turned away because the tickets were sold out. Tens of thousands of people have already viewed the webcast of the event on the Seeds of Compassion website. This, in itself, is pretty impressive in what is supposed to be one of the least religious areas in the United States.

I found the mix of people at these events fascinating. Not only were there thousands of school age children there, but the arena and the classrooms were full of young adults. These are from the same group of people we cannot seem to bribe, drag, scare or beg into our local churches across the country. I have become so accustomed to seeing grey hair like mine whenever I go to national and regional church events, it was pleasantly startling to discover I was in the minority. It was in fact exciting.

I leave you with some questions. What was it that instilled the desire in some 250,000 people to attend such an event? Why did so many young people take this event so seriously, attend the lectures, and participate in the workshops? What was it that got so many young adults in their 20s and 30s to take time off from work or play and attend these events? What was it that scared so many people who call themselves Christian? Wasn't that what Jesus was trying to teach?

CHAPTER NINE

Celebrating Christian Holidays

Giving Thanks as a Life Changing Dynamic

Jesus was not born into a privileged life. He was not born with a silver spoon in his mouth. He did not live under easy circumstances. Still, he lived in gratitude. In fact he made giving thanks for life a foundational dynamic of his teaching. He seemed surprised by other people's inability to live happy, fulfilling lives with little or no gratitude. *"Why do you worry so much about what you eat, what you wear?"*

He was asking this question of some pretty marginalized people who were obviously struggling to make ends meet. At one time in his ministry, he preached to the multitudes who came to the coastal plain near Jerusalem. He told them, *"Congratulations you poor! For God's domain belongs to you. Congratulations, you who are hungry! For you shall have a feast. Congratulations, you who weep! You will laugh."* (Luke 6:20-6)

So what gives with all of this? Is this guy some kind of a Pollyanna fool? Was he on drugs? Or does he know something so many of us seem to miss? What in the world did he have to be thankful for, for God's sake?

Of course we must remember Jesus was coming from a long tradition of offering thanks to Alaha or G_d in all things. It was and still is tradition for Jews to give thanks and be grateful for just about everything—even the difficult lessons in life. Judeo/Christian scriptures encourage us to give thanks or express our gratitude for our blessings in over 130 places. It is a foundational part of our tradition.

Paul suggests that Jesus' whole life was a statement of thanks for the experience of living in an intimate relationship with Alaha or God. Jesus lived in a state of gratitude for that experience and the relationship he had with the creator present in all life. It will provide for all of our needs if we trust it.

I believe Jesus teaches thankfulness or gratitude as a dynamic action or attitude that can change your life. Living with thankfulness is not just about things we have acquired or have been given. It is not even about good things that happened. Being in-thankfulness is a way of living. It is a way of being aware. It is a way of being conscious. It is a way of discovering a new perspective; a new reality.

I suspect one of the most difficult things to accept or see is the one-dimensional thinking we often are in. We tend to think in terms of the material. We become score keepers for life based on things we think of as measurable. We tend to be thankful when we get what we thought we wanted. We measure how many bad things happened this year, how many good things and we tend to focus on the bad things. Did I get the promotion? Did we get the house we wanted? Did I have a fight with my spouse? We compare ourselves to others to decide if we are happy or thankful. How did we match up this year? But there is seldom enough and when there is, it tends to be temporal or impermanent. What was enough last year, unfortunately often does not seem to be enough this year.

This way of being ignores the multiple dimensions of existence. It includes those things that bring us a more fulfilling happiness if we are open to them—beauty, grace, love, growth and intimacy, for example. These things are the very essence of life and living and they are constantly available. All too often, I suspect we pay less attention to what is happening in our relationships, to our souls, than we do to our financial balance sheet. We concern ourselves far too much with how we are matching up with others. In other words, we look to something outside of ourselves to measure if we are happy and thankful, rather than what is happening on the inside.

The second thing this kind of thinking ignores is that every day provides an abundance of lessons for life; every day can be a teacher. Let's face it. Most of us know some of our most painful experiences provide our greatest and most profound lessons. We don't necessarily choose to go through them. But we can decide to learn from them with a faith that says, "Someday I will look back on this and realize there was an incredible gift in this experience."

Nearly forty years ago, my wife and I almost went our separate ways. The strains of a failing business and a new child was the setting. The immaturity of our relationship was the cause. Suddenly we found ourselves totally broke, living in a borrowed trailer on the property of a friend. We cut firewood every day and hauled it to the closet town, Helena Montana. Hopefully we would sell at least one load so we could buy enough gas and groceries to get us through the next day.

It was cold and getting colder on the western slopes of Montana and our thirty-year old Air Stream travel trailer was never warm. Every day as we worked together, we talked about our relationship. We wondered how it could have gotten off the rails so easily. Every day we talked about how lucky we were to have friends that wanted to help us. And every day we gave thanks. Slowly our hearts began to heal, and our souls slowly opened. We remembered our relationship started as two best friends and not only did we find that again but we fell in love again. We learned an extraordinary lesson in those challenging eighteen months as vagabonds. Today, we agree the whole experience is a foundational part in our forty five year love affair.

The most difficult thing to understand about the dynamic of living in a state of thankfulness is that we are led by our intentions. Gary Zukav writes, *"What you intend is what you become."* He goes on to explain, *"The creation of physical experience through intention, the infusion of Light into form, energy into matter, soul into body, are all the same."* It is one process.

In other words, our motivations, our intentions, our very thoughts can impact what we become and what we experience as individuals. Think about that very real possibility. Our thoughts, our intentions, our motivations, and our attitudes can dramatically alter the future of our lives. We have control over those things. That can either be a very scary thought or very liberating one.

What if we started every day with gratitude? How might that impact the course of our lives, our experiences and our health?

After Piglet and Pooh had been walking in silence for a while, Piglet asked, *"When you wake up in the morning, Pooh, what is the first thing you say to yourself?"*

"What's for breakfast?" said Pooh.

"I say, I wonder what's going to happen exciting today?" said Piglet.

I am not sure who is going to have a better day, but I am certain Piglet is going to have a more exciting one.

I suspect most people would discover their day would go a little better if they started it with a prayer of thanks for what is going to come. Macrina Wiederkehr writes that she starts her day with the following prayer:

> Your roots have found me
> I am bursting with life
> I feel like a brand new bud
> Singing gratefully to you . . .
> . . . I will preach the gospel
> of silence joyfully
> as I burst forth hopefully
> into sacred space
> of this new day knowing full well
> this is only a pale glimmer
> of the Life I am becoming
> So Full of Life Am I!

Macrina Wiederkehr tells us that learning to live in gratitude is a way of being. It is a way of perceiving reality. It is a way of thinking as much as it is a way of doing. If we believe we have something to look forward to, to be thankful for, the chances are good that we will. In other words, not only is it good to give thanks for what has occurred, but modern science and spiritual teachers for eons have been telling us our future will be affected by our thankfulness for what will be.

When you celebrate Thanksgiving, why not make it a true holiday, a holy day. Think of the things you have to be thankful for in the moment. And give thanks. Think of the future with unlimited possibilities. Be thankful for the lessons and the gifts you will receive. Somewhere along the way you may you discover you are shaping what you are becoming by living in a state of thankfulness. And then you, like Macrina Wiederkehr, will know you are not only a glimmer of the life you are becoming, but you are full of life indeed. Happy Thanksgiving.

A Family Christmas Remembered

Try and imagine you are a four-year old child. On Christmas Eve there are still no packages, there is no Christmas tree and there are very few decorations. In those early days, shortly after WWII, this was not at all unusual. I have no memory of thinking it was strange. Those were tough economic times for just about everyone. We were going to my grandparents' house to celebrate Christmas with them as we did every year. I was told Santa might leave my present there.

But when this four-year old woke up on Christmas morning, there was a beautiful tree decorated with sparkling white lights. The tinsel was carefully strung over the branches so it could be removed just as carefully and saved for the next year. The little living room had lights and white cotton decoration seemed to glisten. Waking up to this beautiful scene was a wonder. It was magical, and I dare say, even mystical.

We were told by our parents, with shared surprise, that Santa must have done it. Years later I realized what an amazing feat my parents had pulled off since we had arrived at our home late the evening before. I did not know until just a few years before my father's death, that the primary reason for the late tree trimming was dad could get the tree for free after a certain hour on Christmas Eve.

But that did not take away from the magic filling our little house and our Christmas celebrations in those early years. I should be clear. This magic had little to do with presents and gifts under the tree. For one thing, as children we expected only one gift from Santa—if we were lucky. We always knew which one came from Santa because it was never wrapped. Whatever it was, it was inexpensive and simple compared to most children's expectations in our Western world today. Any gifts from our family were almost always utilitarian. They might include a new shirt, socks or pair of jeans that were at least one size too large so we could grow into them.

I am a lucky man for many reasons but one of those was my parents' and my extended family's desire to make our Christmas magical and spiritual. Our family gatherings during my childhood were a real celebration with aunts and uncles, cousins, grandparents and least a few family friends who joined us every year.

Over the years I have come to understand that whatever was going at these family events, it had something to do with that moment in history. We were still trying to get over a war responsible for killing 60 million people. Fortunately, my two uncles returned from the war without serious physical injuries. Few people had extra money beyond essentials, so gifting took some creativity. Yes, there was a lot of celebration but there was also a great deal of reflection. Yes, there was a lot of laughter but there were also tears. And there was a great sense of gratitude felt by everyone.

During the evening dinner, all the children were encouraged to put on a play, sing a song or do a reading. Can you imagine a kid growing up with 12 to 15 adults watching you with adoring eyes as you sang "Silent Night?" Or what it felt like when you stumbled through a poem and everyone cheered when you were done. That did not mean anyone was above a little teasing but even the loving teasing could make you feel important and acknowledged.

Everyone in my family had some church connection which gave us a spiritual influence. It brought us closer to the power of the Jesus story. It meant something to even the youngest child that a poor peasant girl could give birth to such a special man. For my dear conservative Presbyterian, Uncle Sam, I am certain that special man was God. No matter, everyone in the room had some kind of love for this baby Jesus.

Of course there was an added bonus. I think every one of my relatives sang in some church choir. When two to three dozen of us gathered for our Christmas celebrations, it sounded more like the Mormon Tabernacle Choir than a family gathering. At least that's the way I remember it. I have never been able to explain the feelings of joy and love that filled me as we stood around the huge table all facing each other and singing "O Holy Night" while we looked each other in the eyes with love.

I particularly remember one Christmas evening when I was in my teens. My adoring Granddad was across the table from me. He seemed to be staring directly into my eyes and smiling as we all sang. I think I was doing the same thing. At one point, I had the feeling he was looking past the teenage boy sitting across from him and was seeing the heir to his story. It felt like he was looking into my soul or possibly seeing the infinite. I know I have rarely felt anything like the unique love of that moment. I have never forgotten him.

Over the years I have thought a lot about those wonderful Christmas memories. My parents and almost all my aunts and uncles are now deceased. The memories still live on in our family gatherings which include siblings and cousins. I have tried to recall and explain why I felt those events were so special. I have concluded it must have been my experience of unconditional love. I often wonder what the world would be like if every kid had the opportunity to grow up with that kind of loving influence in their lives.

I still find Christmas to be magical and even mystical at times. When I use the word mystical I am talking about having an experience of the Infinite. For purposes of this article let me just say it is an experience of the divine spirit or divine presence. It is an experience when everything seems perfect and infinite, at least for the moment. It usually means experiencing a sense of absolute connectedness and well-being. For many, this kind of experience can be transforming.

After all, the entire Jesus story and all of its symbols metaphorically point to an in-breaking of the divine presence into our world and consciousness. Another way to say it might be, having an experience of the divine presence that is always there, the one spirit that connects all being-ness. I believe if we took the teachings of Jesus seriously and actually practiced them we could learn how to experience that Oneness, that Connection of the Infinite Mystery, on a regular basis.

Every Christmas still finds me together with at least part of my extended family celebrating what has become my favorite Holy Day again. Yes we will eat, drink, laugh and open a few more presents than all those decades ago. We will sing, read poems or tell stories. And, on occasion, we will cheer for a performance by a young child. Somewhere along the way we will probably sing "O Holy Night." Perhaps in that evening, my grandchild will smile and look me in the eyes and realize she is the heir to my story. I would hope she will always remember that Christmas. And just maybe she will have experienced the Infinite Mystery.

The Magic of Christmas

My wife and I were having a quiet dinner with some friends one winter's eve when we found ourselves going through what seems to have become an annual ritual. It always starts with someone announcing, "Can you believe it? Christmas is only X days away!" And in chorus the rest of us echoed, "You are kidding! How did that happen?" We have other little ditties that we sing like, "It seems like it was only a few months ago we were celebrating Easter." Or, "But I just put the Christmas decorations away from last year." Then for the closing song we always sing rather sadly, "It comes faster and faster every year."

I really don't know why we always seem to be so surprised year after year. I mean 12 months is 12 months, or ought to be. The retailers put up Christmas decorations earlier every year. We really should realize Christmas is near as soon as the swimwear goes on the 40 percent off rack. The old tradition of no Christmas decorations until after Thanksgiving is long gone. I suppose the surprise comes from a combination of the busy life styles we have created for ourselves, and for some of us, aging. Each year is just a little smaller piece of our whole life.

After we and our friends went through our ritual that night, we began to share some of our favorite Christmas stories. They were plentiful and a couple of them were remarkable. One person remembered the Christmas when her father got a three-day leave from the military service in Vietnam and surprised the entire family Christmas morning. Another one recounted going to bed on Christmas Eve night knowing he was the only kid on the block who did not have a Christmas tree. He woke up Christmas morning to a beautiful tree with a gift for each sibling under it. He knew it must have been Santa and he was magic.

But most of our favorite stories were about small and simple things like shared meals and laughter. I do not remember one person recounting a favorite Christmas story that had anything to do with receiving a particular gift. Of course everyone at this dinner table had grown up long before marketing people bombarded children with exhortations telling them what they must have in order to have a merry Christmas. Our Christmas expectations were based on our often unique family traditions. For most of this pre-elderly group, their traditions were simple.

As the evening progressed someone wistfully asked, "I wonder if we can ever capture the magic of Christmas again?" I have thought a lot about that over the last few years. I wondered if the magic of Christmas was ever shared in common with others over the years. After doing over 20 years of pastoral counseling, I am well aware Christmas for a lot of people has never been magical and may still be for some a time of painful memories.

I frankly do not know what I would do today if I were raising young children to shield them from the constant brainwashing they are subjected to from television, computer marketing and peer pressure. Our children grow up as consumers before they are even in school. At very early ages they are raised to believe they will not be happy, whole or content until they acquire certain things they have seen on their favorite television or video program.

It is the beginning of the insidious understanding, not unique to children, that we are valued more by what we have and what we accomplish, not by what we are. Barbie, Sponge Bob, and Dora the Explorer products are not bad in themselves, of course. But they are perfect examples of how marketing experts have created a need—a demand even—out of nothing. These demands quickly become the measurement of one's value or for one's in-ness for young children.

Christmas is no longer a religious celebration, nor is it even a family celebration. You might be surprised to know how few people realize Christmas means Christ's Mass. But now Christmas does not occur in the temples or in the churches as much as it does in the malls and on retail web pages. It is not led by the Christian pastors or priests but rather by the high priests of advertising.

The holiday is no longer about a young peasant girl quietly giving birth to a poor Jewish child. It is about big theaters, flying angels and large orchestras all available at a hefty ticket price of course. It is no longer about the mystical story of the birth of a baby who goes on to discover the presence of the living God within by emptying himself of secular power and pride. No, it is now a secular holiday worshiping the pride of ownership and power of position. This includes right beliefs. We now think of a good Christmas as one where retail sales are up which usually means the stock market is up as well. I suppose it should be no surprise that when our children are asked, "How was your Christmas?" their normal response is measured by what they got.

So have we lost the magic of Christmas for good? Let's just say that if it is still there, it may be buried under a pile of social realities and religious delusions. It may be covered with unhealthy life styles and materialistic idols.

It will not be easy for most of us to unpack something that has become so counter-culture.

Truthfully our treatment of Christmas is more about our lives than it is about a holiday. But it may be a good place to begin the change.

We could start by slowing down the pace and spending some quiet time reflecting with our families about the reason we call Christmas a holiday or holy day. We could take some time to retell the story of a poor peasant Jew who changed the course of human history by rejecting the social norms of his time, by practicing a compassionate, radically inclusive way of living. We could remind ourselves that the power of his way was in the giving up and not in the receiving. We might even do something radical and turn off the TV for a while and share these stories.

The real magic of Christmas is where it has always been. It is about honoring relationships and the love shared within them. It is about appreciating family and community when we slow down long enough to enjoy them. If we dig a little deeper, we just might discover the magic of Christmas. Like an ancient artifact, it may be worth more than we ever realized.

The Truth About Christmas Magic

A few months away from turning eight I was faced with what seemed like an overwhelming ethical dilemma for a kid my age. It was sometime around Christmas, and I was playing with a group of neighborhood friends. I believe I was one of the youngest in the group. And as I remember, I was always trying to keep up. At one point in our rough and tumble boy play, the subject of Santa Claus came up. Of course we all let it be known at the ripe old age of somewhere between eight and ten, we did not believe in Santa Claus. "Only babies believe in Santa Claus," we chanted like little warriors getting ready for battle. We certainly were not babies.

The problem was my sister. She is only 15 months younger than me and I have always been a bit protective of her. I knew and they knew Sally still believed in the real, physical Santa Claus who came down chimneys and left presents under the tree. It bothered me that my sometimes unkind little friends were making fun of her behind her back. She was almost seven years old and in the first grade and probably the only kid in her class holding onto her belief in the living Santa. At times the teasing drifted over to me. One day, after a couple of shoving matches with one of the more aggressive ten-year olds, I decided I needed to fix the problem. Admittedly, I was not looking forward to it and wondered if I was doing the right thing.

The next day while we were playing on the backyard swings, I said something like, "Hey, Sally, I think I should tell you the truth about Santa Claus." But I never got a chance to say anything more. She looked at me with horror and anger in her eyes and ran off with her hands over her ears. In tears now, she turned and yelled back at me, "You are just trying to ruin Christmas for me!"

Trust me, her concern had little to do with presents. In those postwar days, our Santa Claus had a very limited budget. Most of our gifts were utilitarian, maybe a new sweater, pants, or shoes. All three kids in my family got one Christmas gift and we never felt cheated or deprived. It was not the presents she was concerned about. It was the fear of losing the magic of Christmas, the essence of the holiday we all loved.

Christmas was a special time for our entire, extended family. It was always a joyous celebration for us. It meant playing wild games with cousins, getting hugs from favorite aunts and uncles, putting on plays, and singing songs for the 20 to 30 adults after dinner. It was the sensation of abundance with more food than we ever saw at one time appearing on the table. For me watching the preparation was even more magical. It meant the whole family singing Christmas carols in three-part harmony for hours around the two ping-pong sized tables after our feast. It meant a whole lot of affirmation and love, especially for the kids.

It was that celebratory spirit my little sister really loved about Christmas. The following Christmas she caved in to the peer pressure of her schoolmates. Santa Claus became a powerful myth symbolizing love and sharing for her and she had a wonderful Christmas as always.

For some reason I have been thinking a lot about that incident lately. I suppose I think about it every time Christmas rolls around. As president of a progressive Christian organization, it probably has something to do with the emails and comments suggesting I am trying to ruin Christianity. Some writers are downright nasty.

When asked to defend myself, I find myself in the same kind of fix I was in over 60 years ago. I wonder; "How much do I say? How much do they really want to hear?" Often, when I think someone is really interested, I suggest some excellent reading material. Frequently the response is "You are not a real Christian, so why should I listen to you?"

Like the rowdy friends of my youth, there are a lot of different kinds of people, including some excellent scholars today, who are telling us there really is no Santa Claus in Christianity. That is, there was no supernatural, magical Jesus, born without need of a human father, who was able to bring people back to life after they had died and could create sight in people who had been physically blind. There was no Jesus who believed he was God and had to be a divine sacrifice for the sins of the world. There was no Jesus buried in a tomb who came back to life in three days and ascended into heaven. There are more and more of those rowdy friends out there who have been doing excellent research, writing and speaking about these things for decades. They are not going to go away. Rowdies have a way of sticking around.

Who would have believed a decade ago, three of the top non-fiction best sellers in the last few years were written by authors who openly declared themselves to be proud atheists? Who would have believed the death of one of those bright authors, Christopher Hitchens, would be regarded as a great loss by scholars and commentators of many disciplines including well known theologians? Authors, like Richard Dawkins, *The God Delusion*, and Sam Harris, *Letter to a Christian Nation*, joined Hitchens on a direct frontal attack on the curious beliefs of traditional and conservative Christians.

But, let's be honest. Highly qualified Christian theologians and biblical scholars have argued for decades that we have not had it right. More recently Marcus Borg, a wonderful scholar and faith-filled man, suggests the historical Jesus was a Jewish mystic, healer, wisdom teacher, and prophet. Bishop John Shelby Spong describes the miracles of Jesus as mythic stories meant to demonstrate the messianic role his early followers believed he fulfilled. Robert Price, a superb New Testament scholar posits in his book, *The Incredible Shrinking Son of Man*, that there is little, if any, historicity in the Gospels. Even the name Jesus may very well have been ". . . retrojected into the past history of the character" . . . after his death.

Today these rowdies are featured on the newsstands, on the front pages of major periodicals, in our libraries and can be found teaching classes in our universities and colleges. Their books are selling all over the world. Ironically, it seems the only place they seem to be absent is in our churches.

There has been a lot of hand-wringing in our old-line churches in a strong counter by the traditional and conservative Christians. Some congregations cry out about people like me ruining the Christian faith. I cannot help but wonder if this crying out is similar to the cries of my little sister, as she ran off covering her ears. She was afraid I was going to ruin her Christmas when I told her something she had probably already figured out. How many people in our churches are holding their hands over their ears because they are afraid if they really listened, it would ruin their Christianity?

Frankly, I see all of all this turmoil as an opportunity to re-conceptualize and invigorate the Christian tradition. But I am a rowdy after all. You see for me the magic of Christianity is not in the miracles, or in the beliefs, or in the written word. It is not even so much in having the correct information about the historical Jesus. The magic of Christianity is in the living and being. It is more about praxis than it is about belief. It is more about trust than it is about blind faith. The transformative magic can only be discovered in the doing; by opening, not closing; by letting go, and not by clinging. It is not about trying to decide what is divine and what is not. It is about discovering the divine in all things. Or as Lloyd Geering suggests, only when the sacred and the secular are made one, will the Kingdom of God have come.

We can find the magic of Christianity by taking Jesus' teachings seriously and by living the compassionate path toward self-discovery. That is the way we uncover the essence of Christianity. That has always been the way we can discover who Jesus really was and in the process discover who and what we are. This seems to me to be a truly magical Christmas present and no rowdies are ever going to take that away from us.

Epic Change and Christmas—2008

Have you noticed what an amazing time in history we are all living in? I think we are a very lucky group of people to be witnessing and participating in such incredible changes in our country and in the world. I am not just referring to the fact that we elected our first non-Caucasian individual to the presidency, although I do think it is a reflection of the shift. Personally I am more excited about this man's character than I am about his mixed ethnic roots. No, I am referring here to what I believe is a seismic change of epic proportions. I hope I will be around long enough to be able to a have conversation with my grandchildren about this shift.

I think it's time to admit this country has been on a drunken orgy of greed and consumption. It has been fueled by sophisticated marketing, easy credit and assumption of privilege for decades. I would like to blame it on the government, corporations, investment bankers, the lending institutions, the stock brokers—the entire culture of our financial institutions. But in the quiet of the night, I realize there is plenty of culpability to go around.

I think we have known for a long time that something was wrong. But as long as we could continue to buy our flat screen TVs, our SUVs, our 3,000 square-foot houses and designer jeans, few of us wanted to rock the boat. Even though it did not seem right, few of us said much as long as the appraised value of our over-priced homes continued to go up. I am afraid far too many of us were addicted to a costly drug—consumerism. Too many of us were getting high on our things. But we have discovered, like a lot of other addictive drugs, we do not derive any long term happiness or contentment from our possessions. Consumerism is a lie.

I suspect we are now going to have to go through a painful period of withdrawal. I know of few social commentators or economists who believe things are going to go back to the way they were. What we had was not real. We discovered the emperor had no clothes—and never did have clothes.

Investment banks are a thing of the past, our million dollar houses are being sold on the auction block and new cars are stacking up on the docks with no place to go. CEOs are turning down their outrageous bonuses and managing partners of hedge funds are watching trillions of dollars evaporate. Hopefully, the new economy hoisted upon us by MBA grad schools for the last 25 years is finally dead.

Sadly, as always, it will be those on the lower end of the economic ladder who will suffer the most in this economic tsunami. For some it will be tragic and we must do everything in our power to minimize their suffering.

I find it a fascinating irony that this catastrophe is happening during the holiday season, the time when we honor the birth of Jesus. I have wondered what Jesus would think of our typical Christmas season which represents as much as 70 percent of annual retail sales for many of our largest retailers. I have often wondered how Jesus would have interpreted our frantic shopping during Christmas season in the new temples of our society—the shopping malls. Although no one from the first century could possibly have understood our wealthy culture and social system, it seems clear the teachings of Jesus warn us about getting lost in our acquisitions and hoarding of our possessions. They will never allow us to discover the things of true value—relationships, community, trust in the Spirit and love, for example.

Being an eternal optimist, I see a silver lining in all of this. And it is not just a theoretical lining, but one based on my observations. I have heard more and more people talking about what is really important in their lives and coming to some very different conclusions than they might have a year ago. I have listened to more than one family talk about how they are going to find creative ways to do Christmas differently. They are excited about planning experiences rather than buying gifts.

I recently sat with a group of friends while one of the men shared openly about the likelihood that he was going to lose his job, his pension and severance pay. It was a unique experience to hear a man be so open and candid about his situation. There was a measurable growth in the depth of the relationships in the group. I wondered if he would have been so candid, so open if there had not been so many others in the same or similar dilemma.

Some people are talking about getting smaller homes and simplifying their lives. Individuals in churches are working together to find ways to help those who are the most destitute in this economic chaos. Many people are reexamining their lives and openly trying to sort out what is truly important. Somehow all of this chaos got our attention. It woke us up, in a sense, and it appears it will continue to wake us up for some time to come.

Hard as this all may be, we are bound to see changes. I believe a lot of them are going to be good. Maybe we have broken our addiction and we will have more time to meet our neighbors and find out how they are doing. Maybe we will be more sensitive to the plight of others and we will begin to take action, both politically as well as personally. Maybe we will become more compassionate and discover when we reach out to others with love, we will feel, as in the famous Leonardo da Vinci mural, we are touching the finger of God. We may even begin to discover God incarnate in the eyes and hearts of so many others that we missed before.

Just maybe this Christmas we will find the real purpose of Christmas is not shopping or getting things. It is not about loud parties and street decorations. And it is not about crowded malls and Christmas bonuses. Just maybe we will discover the real purpose of Christmas is rebirthing the Christ Spirit that is always within us.

Light in the Midst of Darkness

I have always been an early riser. According to my parents I was this way as a very young child. My mother used to jokingly complain, "It was like you could not wait to start the day." Even as a teen I would often slip out of bed to watch the sun slowly climbing over the trees that bordered our Northeastern fence line. I suppose I am like my dad in this way. He was an early riser as well. I have some fond memories of just the two of us sitting in the kitchen together quietly talking and sharing a cup of hot chocolate before anyone else in the house was awake.

I presume this characteristic could simply be imprinted in my DNA. It may also be a result of those lovely experiences I had as a child. But early mornings are still important to me. Frankly, I still wake up wondering what wonderful or exciting things are going to happen that day. It is also the time when I do most of my creative thinking and writing. I still have special places where I go to quietly wait for a new day.

When I am struggling, maybe with grief, or trying to sort out something difficult in my life, I often go to a special spot and quietly wait for the new sun to appear. It always makes a significant difference in my being when I do this. My load feels lighter. My fears often dissolve. My grief can be transformed into hope. Over the years I have thought of all kinds of metaphors that may explain this phenomenon. I am reminded that it is a new dawn, or a new day. No matter how painful or dark my situation seems to be, as that sun comes over the horizon everything in my life begins to look and feel different. The new sun symbolizes a new beginning for me. I feel I have gained a new perspective. My internal darkness has dissolved into new light and I am comforted.

It is sad if not tragic that so many people in our crowded world now live in developed areas where they rarely experience real darkness. The constant glare from street lights, house lights, car lights, billboards, cell phones and computers keeps us hidden from the darkness. And therefore the slow but definitive transition from darkness into light is lost to so many and experienced by so few. Without that, it is difficult to appreciate the new light. This transition is one of the fundamental rhythms of nature. Whether we recognize it or not, we are part of nature.

The late John O'Donohue wrote in his wonderful book, *Anam Cara:* "*It is one of the tragedies of modern culture that we have lost touch with these primal thresholds of nature. The urbanization of modern life has succeeded in exiling us from this fecund kinship with our mother earth. Fashioned from the earth, we are souls in clay form. We need to remain in rhythm with our inner clay voice and longing. Yet this voice is no longer audible in the modern world. We are not even aware of our loss, consequently, the pain of our spiritual exile is more intense in being largely unintelligible . . . Just as darkness brings rest and release, so the dawn brings awakening and renewal. In our mediocrity and distraction, we forget that we are privileged to live in a wondrous universe. Each day the dawn unveils the mystery of this universe. Dawn is the ultimate surprise; it awakens us to the immense 'thereness' of nature. The wonderful subtle color of the universe arises to clothe everything . . . Colors bring out the depth of secret presence at the heart of nature.*" (pg. 2)

Our early ancestors took these transitions seriously. For one thing they were part of an agricultural society. Their lives were dependent on knowledge of the seasons and the life of the sun. That is why so many of the ancient religious expressions were based around the worship of the sun. When the sun sank into the horizon they could never be certain where it was going or if it was going to come back. This got particularly scary during the winter when provisions were dwindling and the daylight hours become shorter each day. This is why most cultures included the worship of the sun or Sun God. There was almost always a special celebration of the day or the week when it was clear the days were becoming longer again. In the Roman Empire when Christianity was becoming an institution, those celebrations came to be called the winter Solstice or Sol Invictus.

After living in the Pacific Northwest for nearly a decade, I must admit the Winter Solstice has taken on a much larger importance in my life. During the winter, wherever you are—unless, of course, you live on the equator—the time of daylight gets shorter. On the latitude where we now live, the changes are far more dramatic than other areas where I have lived. Over a period of six months, from late June to late December, we slowly lose approximately eight hours of sunlight during the day. Sunrises are much later and sunsets much earlier. We spend a lot more time in darkness during the winter months. Many of us wait, sometimes impatiently, for the morning light. You will meet very few people in this area who cannot tell you the exact date of the Winter Solstice. Many of us attend Solstice celebrations. Occasionally we actually get what it must have been like for people who were trying to survive off the land 2000 years ago.

The decision to celebrate Jesus' birth on December 25th was made in the early fourth century when Constantine was the Roman Emperor. Constantine was grounded in the cult of Sol Invictus. The date was selected for Jesus' birth in order to correspond with the Roman festival of Dies Natalis Solis Invicti, or Birthday of the Unconquered Sun. Make no mistake, it was both a political as well as a cultural decision that worked for the Roman Empire and for the new empire church. I find it both interesting and even ironic that the Yeshua movement was started, in part at least, as an anti-empire movement. Yet 300 years later it was absorbed and became a tool of the very thing the movement opposed and had cost Jesus his life. This would be a lot like Monsanto absorbing the Whole Foods Corporation which specializes in selling organic foods.

For decades, I have felt compelled to explain that December 25 was really not the date Jesus was born. I suspect I have ruined Christmas mornings for more than one parishioner. But I thought this was important to explain because it provided an example of how so many things in the Jesus story were changed to fit the bias of the authors. It also bothered me because it represented another example of how the powerful took over the leadership and interpretation of the Jesus story.

However, over the last few years, I have begun to think that celebrating Jesus' birthday on the same holiday of Sol Invictus or the Winter Solstice was actually a good idea and in some ways appropriate. I rarely quote from the Book of John because we know there is little authentic Yeshua history in this late Gospel. In fairness, the writer or writers of the book of John did have the perspective of how Yeshua teachings may have had a positive, even enlightening impact on his first century followers. Maybe that is why as I write this, I continue to hear John's voice whispering in my ear.

"In the beginning was the Word, and the Word was with God, and the Word was God. He was with God in the beginning. Through him all things were made; without him nothing was made that has been made. In him was life, and that life was the light of all mankind. The light shines in the darkness, and the darkness has not overcome it." (John 1:1-5)

Jesus entered the world in a dark time in human history, particularly for his own people, the Jews. I will not go into the gory details here but few of us can even begin to grasp how hopeless and dark the world must have seemed to those oppressed people. They were living under extraordinary conditions. Most of them had lost the titles to their family farms. Through brutal and unfair taxation they had become tenant farmers on the same land their families may have owned for centuries. They had to endure unfair and abusive behavior from the Roman Empire and its soldiers who enforced the restrictive laws of both the Romans and the Temple priests. They had to fear death constantly through execution or starvation. This must have seemed particularly unimaginable for people who believed their G-d was watching out for them.

It was into this great darkness that Yeshua entered the world. In spite of his humble beginning, somewhere along the way he managed to bring a new light, a new perspective to many of his followers. For some it became a dawning or an awakening unlike any other. In spite of how we have adjusted or retold the Jesus story over the centuries, this man's life continues to inspire, to guide, to cajole millions more people into an awakening. For many it is an awakening from sleep. For others it is awakening from the darkness of the emotional winter, the overwhelming sense of loss or the pain of recognizing an unfulfilling or wasted life. For 2000 years, his teachings have guided people to new awareness, a new dawning, and his teachings continue to be a light for those who are willing to live his compassionate ways. I must admit it now seems perfectly appropriate to me to celebrate this unique man's life and legacy during the time of year promising a new dawn and offering a new beginning.

I wish for each and every one of you an enlightened Christmas and a joy-filled New Year. And may I also wish you a very bright, merry Solstice. Let there be light.

The New Year: A Time for Reflection, Repentance

It's January and the holiday season is over once again. The Champagne bottles have been recycled, resolutions have already been broken and unwanted presents have been returned to the stores. We may now be wondering why we made such a big hoopla about another New Year Eve's party. Many of us have made big new resolutions hoping for some real change but may be feeling like nothing has really been altered. Some may have been expecting a new beginning but things feel like they always have. We may even be feeling a little let down, a bit empty. It is a new year but nothing seems to have changed.

At times like this, I wish more people who identify themselves as Christians or followers of Jesus knew more about the roots of their own tradition, Judaism. The Mother religion of our tradition has a very different kind of New Year called Rosh Hashanah. Jesus, or Yeshua, was a Galilean Jew. As should be expected, his teachings are heavily influenced by his own tradition and its teachers. For Jews, Rosh Hashanah is preceded by a long period of time for introspection. It's time for looking back at the mistakes of the past year and thinking about those whom they may have harmed. Ten days later, this intentional self-inspection ends with the holiest of holidays, Yom Kippur. The time in between is referred to as the Days of Awe or Days of Repentance.

Understand that this is not a passive review. You are expected to seek out those whom you may have harmed because of your actions or lack of actions, and ask for forgiveness. When possible you are expected to try and right the wrongs you committed. It is an active, spiritual endeavor. First you must take responsibility. Second you are called to try and rectify when possible. There is also a component giving the harmed one an opportunity to offer forgiveness. This process can go on for the entire ten days.

Repentance has become one of the most maligned and misunderstood words in the Christian tradition. When we think of the word we usually picture a TV evangelist pounding on the pulpit or shaking the Bible and yelling: "If you don't repent your sins, you are going to burn in hell!" For many of us this picture conjures up bad memories and even pain. Over the centuries in the traditional church, the word repentance came to mean: "*Fall on your knees and beg for forgiveness for your sins and ask Christ your Savior for forgiveness.*"

In Hebrew, however, the word repent or Te-shuvah simply means to turn or change course. The traditional implications of that instruction are far more complex. If you take it seriously, they are much more demanding. I would argue that repentance is a primary teaching of Jesus. For him it was not a one-time thing. It was something we must learn to do regularly as a way of life.

First, it assumes one is willing to take the time to review one's life over the past year and to be willing to ask, "Where have I caused harm or pain? Where have I done damage to another or to another's property?" Keep in mind, according to the Jewish tradition, not only should we take the entire ten days leading up to Yom Kippur to ponder our actions over the past year, but the tradition challenges its followers to start that process during all of Elul, the month preceding Rosh Hashanah.

I have often wondered why so many people try and maintain such busy lives with work, Facebook, emails, social clubs, and video games and then complain about their busy lives. Is it a subconscious effort to avoid reflecting on one's life, to avoid thinking about our actions? Are we just too busy to make amends or to say I am sorry? I find it interesting that so many people who tell me they cannot sit for 20 minutes to meditate often seem like the people who could best use that time for reflection and their own happiness.

The second challenge in this process is we must assume responsibility. I did it and I have to correct it. The devil did not make me do it. My sinful nature did not make me do it. Jesus is not going to forgive me or correct it. It was me, a child of the Universe. There is no third party to take care of this suffering. As part of the universe, if I want to be at peace with that Infinite Mystery and I want to experience a sense of ultimate unity, I must make amends whenever possible.

Unfortunately, Western civilization, especially in this country, has developed a culture of blame. The Republicans blame the Democrats and the

Democrats blame the Republicans. Children blame their siblings and adults blame anybody they can. Employees blame their bosses and bosses blame their employees. This is one of the few places in the world where you can drink alcohol until you are staggering drunk, trip on an uneven sidewalk and then successfully sue the city. "It is not my fault" seems to be a first response syndrome that often keeps us trapped in our own unhappiness.

Finally, once we take responsibility, the ancient tradition for repentance assumes we will do something to correct the infraction. That can be scary, humbling, and possibly costly, but the process is not complete until we do it.

I once gathered a group of people who wanted to study and practice the teachings of Jesus during the Lenten season. The second session was on repentance and I was surprised by how many people thought it meant to admit they were sorry and to ask for God's forgiveness. Most thought this could be done privately in a prayerful way. After we did a word study together they agreed it is a far more demanding idea than they originally thought. At one point, everyone decided that if they wanted to truly experience the gift of the teaching, it was going to require some action on their part.

We made the commitment to review our lives and pick one situation requiring our action or one place where we needed to make amends. The next week, we talked about our reflections and explained a situation we each needed to address. Then we were determined to actually try and make contact with those whom we had harmed and ask for forgiveness and correct what we could.

Three out of the 12 people actually made contact. As I recall, it went very well. Most of the others were unable to go through with making the contact. Some just decided they couldn't do it. Others . . . well you guessed it. They decided it wasn't their fault after all.

Now let's go back to our recently past New Year traditions. How different would we be feeling right now if we had spent the week before this New Year making amends with those whom we had harmed or with whom we had a conflict during the year? How different would we be feeling if we had slowed our pace enough for some serious reflection about our actions over the year and truly began to take responsibility for our sometimes unthoughtful behavior.

Jesus offered these teachings as a way to experience something he may have referred to as the Kingdom of God or the Commonwealth of God. Neil Douglas-Klotz suggests the term in Aramaic would best be translated as *Queendom of God* or *the Reign of Unity*. Whatever we call it, most scholars today are confident he was not referring to a place but rather an experience, something both internal and external. We can choose to ignore the tough and challenging teachings and party all we want on New Year's Eve. But if we really want to experience Sacred Unity, the Oneness of all, here and now, we might decide to take these challenging teachings a little more seriously and courageously. It is not easy I might add.

But it is still a new year and there is plenty of time to start a new-old tradition. The season of Lent might be a good time to start the process based on the real and challenging lessons of our common teacher, our Rabbani.

> Turn again! Return to unity with Unity,
> like the sea flowing back to shore, in ebb and tide.
> The empowering vision,
> the "I-Can" of the cosmos,
> the reign of all that vibrates,
> the queendom of heaven
> arrives at this moment!
> It draws near, touching us,
> Carrying us away,
> wrenching us back into rhythm
> with the vibration of One.

(An alternative reading of Matthew 3:2 and 4:17.
Neil Douglas-Klotz, *The Hidden Gospel*, 1999)

Lent: It All Starts With Repentance

Lent can be the most important season in the Christian tradition if we take advantage of it. I should explain that Lent was created by the early church fathers and is not necessarily biblical. I say not necessarily because there is nothing in the Bible establishing the 40 days prior to Easter, excluding

Sundays, as the Lenten season. They loosely represents the 40 days Jesus spent in the desert fasting and struggling with his inner demons sometimes represented as Satan.

Although Lent may not be technically biblical, it is certainly based on biblical concepts. Your common dictionary suggests Lent is a season of *"penitence and self-denial."* For most of us over the years we thought of Lent as a good time to give up something we knew in our hearts we should probably give up anyhow. So we used that time to give up things like sweets, red meat or alcohol. For many people, Lent is more about giving up forbidden fruit than it is about anything internal. How many of us over the years have had friends ask us, *"What are you giving up for Lent?"* The depth of our Lenten experience is reflected in this question.

In reality, Lent is founded on a rich and ancient tradition that predates the Roman church, Christianity, and even Jesus. In many ways, it is one more time Christianity mirrors her older sister, Judaism, with her High Holy days.

For Jews, Rosh Hashanah traditionally represents the day G-d created human beings, the most precious and privileged creatures on earth. Therefore, Rosh Hashanah is considered the birthday of humankind. It gets more personal after that. It is also a time when Jews re-proclaim G-d as the true Creator King and reaffirm their vow to serve G-d.

Here comes the hard part. This is when G-d reviews the status of every person and determines to see if he or she merits another year in this world. Every Jew is judged during Rosh Hashanah on his or her actions in the previous year. Although the judgment is inscribed, it is not sealed and can still be changed for another ten days. G-d waits until Yom Kippur to seal the book for the year. Don't you think most of us would behave a little differently if we thought this G-d was going to decide each year if he was going to renew the contract on our life based on an assessment of our behavior?

Some years ago, a painting contractor who was doing some work in our house came to do a walk through. He saw my books out around my desk and realized I was a minister. Turns out he was active in a Southern California mega-church and was an avid and activist Christian. It didn't take him too long before he was lecturing me on the problems with liberal Christians and those who pretend to be Christians. *"For one thing,"* he explained, *"they don't make it clear God expects you to go to church every week to be counted. If you are not counted,*" he continued with absolute authority, "*you are not going to heaven.*" If I had gotten that message out to our congregation we would have had a lot of nervous people. No wonder those churches grow.

But there is hope. We can make corrections that will help our status. According to Jewish tradition, we can repent—a word that can raise the hackles on the back of our necks. When we hear someone ask, "*Have you repented?*" it usually means something like, "*Have you confessed your sins to Jesus Christ so that you can be forgiven?*" Of course the sins we confess are usually thought of as the rules our Bible is supposed to have listed somewhere. Unfortunately only nuns, Baptist ministers and God knows for certain where they are. So repenting meant asking for forgiveness. "*I have broken a rule (sinned). Please forgive me.*" Some self-punishment is assigned and then I wait for grace.

For ancient Jews the word repent had a very different meaning. To repent meant to try and make amends and/or restitution to those we may have harmed, to ask for forgiveness and make a vow to change one's behavior. It was about taking corrective action in community. It was about assuming responsibility to turn one's life around.

This would have been the kind of repentance Jesus was referring to when he told his disciples to go out and teach it. Although repentance is an important word in both the Jewish as well as the Christians tradition, we Christians have really put a twist on the word. We have assumed it was much too passive a verb. We make too lightly of it today. We don't understand it has thousands of years of practice behind it.

There is another subtlety with this word worth noting. There were two very distinct perspectives in the development of Jewish thinking. Over the years I have referred to them as the priestly and the prophetic. When the priestly referred to sins or transgressions they usually meant breaking one of the many purity laws they deemed to be important. In other words it was something you did that you weren't supposed to do.

But when the prophets referred to sin they were usually referring to something one did not do, like feeding the hungry, clothing the naked or bringing the homeless into your home. There is no better example of this than my favorite passage from the Hebrew Scriptures, Isaiah 58. It is not surprising that the few times Jesus cited scripture it was almost always from the prophets.

Furthermore, words from ancient languages can be difficult to translate directly because they are often derived from a combination of root words. The meaning is seldom clear until it is used in context. However, some years ago I came up with what I hope is a workable translation for the word repent in our tradition: *"To reconsider ones actions, inactions or thoughts that have caused pain or disharmony, to accept responsibility for the damage or harm they have caused, change the direction or the course of one's life, and be transformed in the process."*

Now I need to make an admission here. I have run this translation by a couple of acquaintances who are serious biblical scholars. The best I have been able to get them to say is, *"interesting"* or just *"hummm. . . ."* So you may want to do your own word study.

What I do know for certain is when Jesus told his disciples to go and teach repentance it did not mean *"I am sorry Lord Jesus, please forgive me"* so one could then wait for forgiveness. It is not about who can claim to be the worst sinner and then wait for God or Jesus to forgive them only because of grace.

It is about decisions we make and actions we take or don't take. Jesus made it very clear that once you repent and once you take corrective action you are already forgiven. You are starting with a clean slate but the action is up to you.

There is another important component of this powerful dynamic that seems to get lost these days. Repentance assumes first and foremost that we accept responsibility for what we have done or have not done. The healing process starts with that assumption. Real freedom starts there, the joy of life starts there, divine peace starts right there. If we don't take responsibility we don't start the real healing and we don't make real changes.

It is not just about penitence, suffering and grace. It is about taking responsibility for what we have done or said or thought and taking responsibility for making whatever changes we need to make so we learn from our experience. Hopefully, do not repeat our mistakes. It is really up to us.

"It's not my fault" has become an epidemic lament in our country these days. We blame others for anything that goes wrong in our lives, for any mistakes we make, for any illness we might get or for any unhappy experience. Moral people in some of our most conservative churches blame their actions on Satan.

This is the only country in the world where someone can walk out of a bar completely inebriated, trip on a crack in the side walk and sue for millions and win. And then there's the woman who put a hot cup of coffee between her legs, spilled it and burned herself. She sued and was awarded $2.7 million dollars, though the final settlement was an unknown amount.

It is also the only country in the world where doctors spend more money every year on medical malpractice insurance than some of them spent on their entire medical school education. Jayson Blair, the sullied reporter from the *New York Times* who fabricated his stories and his sources, signed a lucrative book deal about his deceit. The reason he cheated, he said, was to prove himself as a young African American in a white world. Oliver North, master of the Iran/Contra scandal was pardoned and was then given his own ranting and raving program. I am still waiting for our former president to say he's sorry we killed hundreds of thousands of people looking for weapons of mass destruction.

We blame our parents. We blame our race. We blame our sexual orientation. We blame our kids. We blame the schools. We blame the government. We blame the economy. We blame our neighbor. We blame the communists. We blame the terrorists. We blame God. We blame the devil.

But here is something that true repentance can teach us. Real life healing cannot begin until we take responsibility for our actions, our words and even our thinking. As long as we are blaming others, nothing is going to change in our lives. Our gear shift is in park. We are not going to experience the joy and peace that has been promised to us. We will not experience life as fulfilling.

If I have learned nothing else in my years of working with people—rich, poor, black, white, yellow, straight, gay, male, or female—I learned we are ultimately responsible for our own happiness, contentment, love and peace. We cannot really experience these wonderful things until we discover life is a rare and precious opportunity and it is a continuing learning experience.

The Buddhists teach that most of us go through life living in a shack with a dusty, dirt floor. We seldom discover that under the dirt we are sitting on, a treasure is waiting to be discovered. Unfortunately too many of us waste our lives dealing with superficial issues. However, if we are willing to dig a little deeper we may discover the treasure we have been sitting on for most of our lives. Pull out the treasure and dust it off to discover what a treasure your life really is. Sounds a lot like Jesus discovering the treasures in the field doesn't it?

If we allow life to show us ourselves in new ways and we reconcile those lessons within ourselves, then we grow and change spiritually, emotionally and mentally. The experience can be transformational.

The Lenten season is a good time to dig a little deeper, to reflect on what we have learned about ourselves this past year. Look more closely at what is bothering us and then decide what we can change and what we cannot change and must therefore let go.

So my dear friends, we can talk about giving up chocolate and wine for Lent or we can meditate on what a rare and precious opportunity our life really is. We can sit on the dirt floor and complain or we can dig a little deeper and discover a rare and beautiful treasure. The opportunity is always there. The responsibility is ultimately ours.

A Lenten Journey

It is no mystery why the early followers of Jesus often referred to themselves as people of the way. The Greek word for way is hodos which is often translated into English as path or road. The writer of Mark, the first of the four biblical Gospels to be written, is devoted to explaining what this path was all about. For Mark, it is first and foremost about the importance of discipleship.

Mark starts with Jesus' baptism by John in the Jordon River. There is no birth story, no immaculate conception, no little town of Bethlehem, no baby in the manger and no wise men or shepherds. The central focus and theme of the book of Mark has to do with Jesus' own journey into Jerusalem. Everything prior to that journey is part of the build-up for that event. Everything after is a way of explaining its meaning. All of this leads to the ultimate question Mark asks of his readers, *"Will you follow him?"*

According to Mark's story, immediately after his initiation ceremony by John, Jesus goes out into the desert. There is no way to know if this is historically accurate. However, it seems likely there must have been a time when Jesus had to resolve his relationship with the Infinite Mystery we call God and decide how this was going to impact his actions. It is difficult, of course, to discern what the issues might have been in this young man's mind. Clearly he felt he had to do something to make a difference. His people were suffering beyond imagination. This could not have been part of God's plan.

He must have struggled with the options. Was it John's way, who may have been an early Zealot? Was it the way of the more radical Sicarii rebels? Was it the way of power and influence or was it the power of love and compassion?

Although Mark gives us little information about this struggle in the desert, it appears Jesus chose a path of giving up all attempts at earthly power, violence and further hatred. He chose the path of kenosis. Kenosis comes from the Greek word, kenosein and means letting go or emptying one's self. By emptying self, I refer here to letting go of those ego demands or needs. It means identifying and letting go of things that we all build around our real being for self-protection and a false sense of self-importance or power or status. It allows us to create a false image of ourselves and somehow hold ourselves above others. Holding on to these false images keeps us from discovering who we really are. The result is separation from others and from ourselves. It is clear not the path of radical egalitarianism Jesus chose to live and teach. This kind of spiritual path can open the heart and give one the courage to love recklessly.

The well-known poet, Rumi, once wrote that *"love is recklessness, not reason. Reason seeks profit."* In the same poem he writes, *"Having died to self-interest she (love) asks for nothing, love gambles away every gift God bestows."*

According to Mark, Jesus knows there is a great risk for him to go into Jerusalem under any circumstances. Jesus speaks three different times about the price of following him and what this kind of discipleship can mean.

The first of these three passages is probably the most explicit. It is found in Mark 8:34. *"If any of you want to become my follower, let them deny themselves and take up their cross and follow me."* Like so many other religious symbols and traditions over the course of time, the word cross has lost much of its meaning. Today we talk about our cross to bear as something life or God has put upon us. Our task is to somehow learn to put up with this burden with patience and without begrudging it. But for first century Jews, the word cross meant execution. It meant a horrible death. One can only imagine how that word would have felt to a potential follower of Jesus.

209

There were probably few words in those times that could generate greater dread. For decades thousands of people were executed on crosses in front of the city gates, often left alive to suffer for days. That dread of the cross would have been reinforced on a regular basis, especially during the time of Passover.

Thus for Mark, discipleship was to be taken seriously. It meant embarking on a path that could even lead to one's physical death. Being a follower is not to be taken lightly.

When we look at the entire story of Jesus, including his teachings as well as his life, it seems clear his path always presumed a spiritual death before one could experience new life or rebirth. His hodos required a death to the old before there could be a birth to a new way of seeing, a new way of understanding and experiencing life. The writer of the Fourth Gospel of John understood this clearly when he wrote of the need to be born again of water and the Spirit, if one wants to experience the Realm of God.

What is that new way? It is a way driven by love rather than fear, even the fear of death. Like so many of the great spiritual teachers throughout history, Jesus understood that we are motivated primarily by two energies. One is love and the other is fear. Nothing saps our ability to love and to be loved more than fear. In fact love and fear are diametrically opposed energies. One who is motivated by love cannot be hampered by fear. For most people this is a different way of living.

Far too many of us still see the world through a paradigm of scarcity. We see the world with limitations not abundance. We live in fear of not having enough. We want our share and a little extra for safety's sake. We feel the need to hoard and to protect. We want control so we can't be hurt. We want guarantees. We want protection. We want to know the destination before we start a journey. We limit our love to limit our potential hurt.

The way of Jesus was very different then and still is for most people. Jesus invites us onto a path of love without guarantees except that we will discover a new perspective and a new experience of life. He invites us into a relationship with the Universe, with Sacred Unity, with Alaha, Elohim, or the Infinite Mystery we call God. He says if we truly follow this path we can trust that all of our needs will be met. He assures us we can learn to live without anxiety and fear. "There is no fear in love, for perfect love casts out fear." (1 John 4:18)

During this season, if we take it seriously, we are asked—*invited really*—to journey with Jesus to our own Jerusalem wherever and whatever it is, without fear. If we want to experience the promised new life, we must be willing to take this journey. It will require some deep soul searching and a willingness to empty ourselves of those things, those thoughts, those emotions we hold onto out of insecurity, our hurts or our losses. Only when we empty ourselves, or self, can we be filled by the "water and the Spirit" John refers to. This is never easy and for many of us, it is a lifetime journey.

It is a path challenging us to focus on abundance and to be motivated by love. It is a way that does not give in to fear. It is a way that acknowledges our interconnectedness to all life. In spite of all of its short comings, it trusts that our lives are a gift and this world is truly marvelous and good.

A Reason to Celebrate Easter

Each spring, I attend the annual Westar Institute Meeting. I enjoy milling around with scholars and clergy, retired and otherwise, and interested followers of the Jesus Seminar. For me these events have become more like an annual homecoming than a scholarly pursuit. Of course, there are always plenty of opportunities to learn something new and to be stimulated by some clear thinking scholars. However, so many of them have become friends over the decades. I find myself looking forward more to visiting and catching up with them than I do sitting through another lecture likely focusing on nuance.

I probably need to make a confession. I was once told by a seminary professor whom I admired, that I did not pay enough attention to detail. He admitted I understood the material and I had unique ideas that seemed to interest others, even stimulated conversation. "But," he told me, "you do not spend enough time studying the details." In other words, I am more interested that the Book of Thomas was discovered than I am whether it was written before or after Mark. I like the book of Thomas.

The professor used a painting on his wall to demonstrate my faults. He said before he bought the painting he studied it and other paintings by the same artist until he understood why he was attracted to the artist and to that particular painting. Only then did he make the purchase.

"You," he said, accusingly, "would just look at the painting and decide you like it. Then you would buy it without analyzing it or even knowing why you liked it." So there you have it. I am short on details and long on big pictures or at least knowing what I like. It might even be knowing what makes sense to me. He agreed I still deserved an A in the class and I agreed not to take any more classes from him.

I share this because some people have found it surprising to hear that I love the Easter holy day. As a progressive clergy person from my first day in the pulpit over 30 years ago, I have always felt everything from Lent to Easter Sunday was the most important and exciting season for Christians. It is another opportunity to teach and even to practice the path of kenosis, to move beyond our familiar boundaries of mind and body and move into a larger mind, to let go and change. What is not exciting about that?

I often felt sorry for clergy who found it necessary to stay in an old and outdated paradigm, talking, praying and singing about the resuscitation of a body that had been buried in a tomb for three days. I cannot tell you how many times one of them would call me and ask what I was going to do about Easter with a sense of urgency and sometimes of panic. Far too many times they would find themselves trying to make sense out of something they no longer believe.

More importantly, I felt sad for the people who missed an opportunity to discover the powerful and life transforming path Jesus left us that is the very foundation of his teachings and his life. This path has been buried in the crust of creeds, camouflaged by power struggles and dogmas and reinterpreted by ego driven personalities.

Ironically, the very path of kenosis Jesus offered us is a path intended to free us of the confining and often conflicting mindset that allows our fears, our wants, our hungers, and other ego needs, to control and separate us. It is a path of self-emptying love available to us for centuries. The best part is there is no better time or way to investigate that mindset than during the period of Lent leading up to an Easter celebration.

Of course we all know the Lenten season is often wasted on prideful stunts like giving up sweets, sex, alcoholic drinks or meat. But the true kenotic path is much tougher for most of us. It really refers to emptying of self—of self-interest and even of self-preservation. It is about learning to love dangerously and recklessly without any expectations in return. It is about letting go of judgment and anger. It is about letting go of self-righteousness and becoming a willing servant. It is about letting go of power to control or even to influence for self-gain.

I want to be very clear. This path is not about who gives up the most nor is it the goal to make some giant, measurable sacrifice. It is not about making the biggest donation to the Easter fund. I am referring here to a path of self-discovery. It is a path to a discovery of who and what we already are but have not had the eyes to see or the ears to hear. It is about losing yourself in order to find yourself.

If we allow the Easter story to be what it was intended to be—an allegory, it makes a lot more sense than a story about a time in history that never did make sense. When we let the Easter story become a lesson instead of a piece of Christian history, we gain something important. We learn real freedom. New life happens when we are willing to give up our old ways of thinking and being and move toward a new self. It means, as we journey toward an awareness of our true selves—let alone another reality—we must first die to the old. I believe the author of John understood this when he put the words into Jesus' mouth that we had to die to be born from above or from Spirit.

Obviously, we do not have to wait for the Easter season to move toward this revelation. It can be a weekly, even daily practice. For most of us, this is a challenging path but what a wonderful reward to discover who we really are.

When we identify those things separating ourselves from others, we can discover we indeed are part of one connected universe both instant and eternal. When we let go of those things that are ego driven, even without realizing it, we can find something much more special. We truly are a beautiful part of the divine creation. We are indeed divine.

In spite of how we might feel about ourselves sometimes, no matter how isolated, no matter how alone, no matter how broken, no matter how separated we might have felt, the facts are, we have always been connected. We are part of a river that has flowed through time and space as vast as the universe itself.

This means there is more to you than you have probably given yourself credit for. This means you are capable of marvelous things you cannot even imagine. Hard as this may be to believe, you have the wisdom of the ages within you, dancing to the music of the Universal angels.

Easter, spring and Jesus' teachings are all about rebirth, the renewal of spirit, and transformation. They invite and encourage each one of us to dive back into the river of life, the river of wonder we sometimes call God and open ourselves to all kinds of new possibilities. That is the big picture and something to celebrate.

Easter: A Time for Celebration

Several years ago, my wife and I were having dinner with some good friends and their guests. Some of the guests were university professors and all of them were highly educated and informed people. At one point we got into a theological discussion. This was a very heady group and I wasn't sure some of those sitting there had any interest in a theological discussion. It did seem one guest was far more interested in what I was saying than the others, so I tried my best to offer a condensed version of my perspective on the birth of the Christian tradition. I tracked the movement's sometimes twisted theological trail into the creedal church of the fourth century. Just as I was about to wrap up my remarks on the subject so we could all get back to politics, the arts and the philosophy of education, he said he had just one more question.

With a rather quizzical look, he asked, "So what in the heck do you do with Easter?"

For centuries the church and Christians in general have been confused about the resurrection story. I explained that Easter is not about the physical resuscitation of a corpse. It is not about an amazing miracle that demonstrated Jesus of Nazareth was indeed the one and only Son of God. Nor is it the proof so many would like to have that there is life after death—for those who qualify of course. It is not even some kind of proof that God can break directly into history, in this dimension in some miraculous way. I realize some people will feel comforted there is a God just waiting for the right moment when "He" will come down from "up there"—wherever up there is—and fix things forever. I suspect that idea says more about our insecurities than it does about Jesus or some concept of God.

Easter is not about celebrating the raising of a dead body. It is about the constant offer for new life and a new world. It is the acknowledgement and celebration that there is a Life Force in our universe that is constantly working toward a more loving, fair and compassionate creation. Easter is a time when we can celebrate a faith in the path of Jesus, of Isaiah, of Hosea, and of Jeremiah, who all believed that conscious humans could ultimately respond to that life changing force we call God, change lives and change the world. We are celebrating hope in a God force that is ever present in our daily lives, a God that can be experienced every day when we are open to that understanding.

Actually there are a lot of other good reasons to celebrate Easter. One very good reason is that Jesus, the master and teacher, encouraged us to celebrate. Jesus assumed celebration was an important part of experiencing the Realm of God and learning to celebrate the gift of life was an important step to that experience.

I had a seminary professor, a New Testament scholar, who told his new students, "Although there may be a lot of things about Jesus we will never know, according to the Bible, we do know this man clearly liked to party."

Now maybe his way of partying was a little different than the kind of partying young people think of these days. For Jesus it meant getting together and eating and drinking and laughing, sharing stories and giving thanks for the abundance of life.

In the scriptures Jesus attends weddings and feasts of all kinds. He constantly used festive celebrations as teaching metaphors for what he might have referred to as God's Realm or the idea of Scared Unity. When there wasn't enough wine or food, scripture stories tell us, he made more. When the prodigal son returned, Jesus insisted the first thing that should happen was massive celebration. By his own admission, he was accused by others as being a glutton and a drunkard, though I am not sure Southern Baptists could be convinced of this fact. Jesus taught and demonstrated that we can connect and communicate with each other at a very different level when we break bread and celebrate together.

In his book, *Rabbi Jesus*, eminent New Testament scholar, Bruce Chilton, writes about how Jesus became a traveling Rabbi who would join festivities all across Galilee. According to Chilton, Jesus began to use festive celebrations as a way to bring purification to people instead of Temple rites or even the immersion practices of John the Baptist. Dr. Chilton writes that Jesus was invited to festivities to offer a unique blessing and teachings of the Kingdom of God. He writes, "As he wined and dined his way around Galilee, he developed a simple prayer:"

Abba, your name will be sanctified,
Your kingdom will come:
Give me today the bread that is coming,
And release my debts

Chilton writes that the Galileans understood the importance of these festive meals. They meant their land was clean and acceptable to God; they were pure and forgiven. Their bread was an emblem of God's Kingdom. As enthusiasm for Jesus' teaching banquets increased, Chilton explains, the demands on his time increased as well. According to Chilton this became a full-time endeavor.

Ultimately the source of Jesus' celebrative life style was his joyous trust in the presence of God's activity in all things. Time and time again we find him telling his followers "hey, don't sweat the small things. God is at work. Can't you see it?" Wouldn't that be an interesting way to live your life? To live as if it were true? Joachim Jeremias, a biblical scholar, calls this the *Great Assurance*. Somehow things are going to work out with God's purpose. Now that is something to celebrate.

Another reason we should celebrate Easter is because it comes in the spring. Many of our big festivals and holy days were originally founded on the natural, yet critical, seasonal changes. The changes in light, the sun and the weather were constant reminders to our ancestors that we are not in control. People who lived off the land were always reminded that their lives, their very survival was dependent on forces greater than they could control or even understand.

Today we have lost touch with our dependency on those dramatic seasonal changes. Certainly we have lost the excitement of the miracle of spring. Now we can go into the supermarket and find almost any kind of food year round, brought to us from all over the world. Over the tens of thousands of years, since human beings have tried to organize into motley, stumbling and bumbling forms of civilization, spring was always an extraordinary time. Each year as the earth slowly rotated on her axis, humans faced the same haunting mystery. "Will the gods send back the sun or will they leave us stranded in the dark without food or warmth?"

Every year, regardless of how forlorn, scared or helpless those folks might have felt, they had hope that spring would return. The days would begin to grow longer. Streams would flow with water. Temperatures warmed the soil and dead plants would come back to life. They would respond with a tremendous celebration of thanks, praise and gratitude. Somehow they knew they were part of a miracle. Stories were told of brave deeds, of death and loss, of victories and new life. All of this was seen and understood in the context of the cycles of life. Cycles became rituals and rituals became religion.

These days we have lost touch with those cycles. We have lost touch with the miracle. We have lost touch with this incredible and precious planet earth, so finely tuned, so interdependent and so fertile it can produce an abundance of air, food, water and shelter for all. That is, if we ever learn to appreciate it and care for it like the precious Mother provider she is. Spring is about hope and new beginnings. It has always been a reason to celebrate and it is still a reason to celebrate.

A third reason we celebrate Easter is because the resurrection actually did happen. Oh, it wasn't the resuscitation of a dead corpse as we may have thought at one time, but it was a resurrection of sorts. I think Paul was right on this one. It was a spiritual resurrection not a physical one. And that spirit continues to be manifested in churches, small groups and followers all over the world over 2000 years later. And I think one could argue even with all of its flaws, foibles and weaknesses, Jesus continues to live through us.

That spirit is manifested in people who in large part believe in the Spirit of love and compassion for others. It is in the people who have gathered over the centuries, operating on the assumption that God is within each and every one of us, often waiting to be discovered. It has been a body of people who have gathered with the belief that with faith they could change their situation in life and they could change their relationship with the Universe. It is a body of people who have formed over the centuries because of a belief that if we all work at it, if we learn to have a little more faith, someday the world will be a more just and compassionate place for every citizen of this planet. For an admittedly small part of that body, this even meant having compassion and seeking justice for every person, regardless of their color, their gender, their sexual orientation, their religious persuasion, their political party or even what car they drive.

If we decide to take Jesus seriously, along with a lot of other pretty special spiritual people over the eons, we might accept that we have God in our family tree. Wow what a thought! We have Divine cells floating around in our minds, our bodies and of course in our hearts. We must be pretty special. In fact in spite of how we might feel about ourselves sometimes, no matter how isolated, no matter how alone, no matter how broken, no matter how separated we might have felt, the facts are, we have always been connected. We are part of a river that has flowed through time and space as vast as the universe itself.

This means, there is more to you than you have probably given yourself credit for. This means you are capable of marvelous things you cannot even imagine. Hard as this may be to believe, you have the wisdom of the ages within you, dancing to the music of the Universal angels. What a wonder that is and what a day to celebrate.

My friends, Easter, spring and Jesus' teachings are all about rebirth, the renewal of spirit, and transformation. They invite and encourage each one of us to dive back into the River of Life, the River of Wonder we sometimes call God and open ourselves to all kinds of new possibilities. You are invited to celebrate the good news that as you swim in this wondrous, astonishing, and sometimes terrifying River of Life, you are not alone, nor have you ever been alone, nor will you ever be alone. And for that we celebrate.

What Are You Looking For?

In the resurrection story recorded in Luke, a group of women go to the burial place of Jesus to bring spices and oil to anoint his body. This is different than the story depicted in the book of John where only Mary Magdalene goes to the tomb. In the book of Mark three women, Mary Magdalene, Jesus' mother Mary and Salome go to his burial place. I point this out because, unlike the other gospel writers, Luke wanted his readers to understand that Jesus was not just the messiah for the Jews as depicted in Matthew. He wants his readers to know Jesus was the messiah, the anointed one, for the whole world.

Therefore, he has a large group of nameless women show up to anoint their fallen leader. It can be presumed some of these women were gentiles. This seems more like the Easter services we have in our churches these days when a whole extra group of people show up for their semi-annual church experience. I used to enjoy getting reacquainted with the Christmas and Easter segment of our congregation.

I have always liked Luke's version of the empty tomb visit by all these women. According to this version of the resurrection story, the women meet a couple of dazzling men inside the tomb. The women were terrified, of course, but then the men asked, *"Why are you here?"* Now on the surface that sounds like a dumb question, doesn't it? Why are we here? We are here to do what we always do with dead bodies.

According to the writer of Luke, the two men continue, *"He is not here. He is risen."* But unlike other writers of the gospels these fellows don't give the women any instructions about where to go to find him or meet him. Not in Galilee. Not in Emmaus. Not in Jerusalem. We just get the idea that he is gone . . . out there . . . somewhere.

Over the years, as I struggled with Easter sermons, I often found myself asking some of the same questions. Why am I here? Why are we all here? Are we standing in an empty tomb? As a scholar of scholars, I have wondered what I can do with the resurrection.

I once heard a professor of church history and a consultant for the Alban Institute challenge an audience mostly made up of clergy. He said, *"Churches are rapidly becoming the empty tombs of the Christian story."* Quoting from the same passage from Luke he suggested that more and more people are asking the same question as the two dazzling men, *"Why are you looking for the living among the dead?"*

Someone wrote me a couple of years ago, quoting from what he considered a scholarly publication: *"In the Christian faith, Easter is the most sacred of holy days because it commemorates the cornerstone of the miracle of the Christian faith; had Christ not risen, Christianity could never have flourished, since the man Jesus would not have been proven to be the Son-of-God Jesus."*

Did he say, "proven to be the son-of-God?" I don't know who wrote this commentary but clearly he has not read recently published books like the one written by Bernard Brandon Scott, *The Trouble with Resurrection*. (Polebridge Press, 2010)

I would also like to ask him why Buddhism and Islam have flourished. There is no incarnate God/son in either of these traditions. The only proof that what Buddha said was true was to try it and find out for oneself. The proof was in the practicing.

I don't know why it is so important for some people to think there is historical or even scientific proof that their religion is the only right one. Why do they need to think their guy was really the only one true God and not a prophet or enlightened teacher? Is it too much of a threat to accept that the message came from out of one's real experience of the Holy, the Sacred . . . God? Is their faith so weak it requires some perceived proof that 2,000 years ago there was a one-time miracle of a physical resurrection proving this? Of course this leaves out Lazarus and a whole lot of other resurrection stories. Let's face it, Greek, Egyptian and Middle Eastern mythologies all had some form of resurrection story. We just happen to call them mythology.

Modern scholarship has made these traditional Christian super-miraculous beliefs more difficult to accept as a form of proof. Furthermore, we have 2,000 years of history to observe how the arrogance of thinking one's religion is the only right religion has led to terrible atrocities and horrible consequences. No loving God would ever have endorsed these results. Over the years it has become clearer to me that any religion dividing people into the ins and outs cannot be an expression of anything we could call God the Creator, Sacred Unity or Alaha.

But you see I do believe the contemporary Christian story still has a resurrection. It is not about an historical event seen through the eyes of simple people who believed in a judging God that caused lightning, floods, wind and epidemics. Nor am I referring to evangelist gospel writers who wanted everyone to know how special Jesus was. Naturally, they used common terms of the day such as Son of God, son of man, messiah and the anointed one to let people know how special they thought he was. I say this not through the eyes of the First Century Jew. At that time there was no concept of a separation between body and soul or body and spirit. An experienced phenomenon had to be described in terms that were common concepts to their listeners . . . a physical resurrection.

The resurrection story reminds us there can be new life as an experienced phenomenon. Theologian Tom Harper suggests we should view the resurrection as a primordial myth. It is about dying to ourselves—our egocentric, self-centered, frightened selves—so we might experience new birth, new life with a radical new way of seeing reality. It is waking up with eyes to see and ears to hear the path Jesus established for his followers.

This Jesus story does offer a different kind of resurrection. Jesus told his seekers where to find him. He told them if they wanted to meet him, to go and do likewise. "*When you see a stranger and welcome him, I will be there. When you see someone naked and you clothe him or her, I will be there. And when you see someone hungry and you give him or her food, or when you see someone thirsty and you give him or her drink, I will be there. When you visit the sick or the imprisoned I will be there.*"

John Cobb, eminent theologian and father of Process Theology, suggests that whenever there is an expression of compassionate love, Christ is there. Christ, according to Dr. Cobb, is the creative transformation at work in us as human love.

The post-resurrected Christ is manifested in our love, in our compassion, and in our actions . . . not in history. Jesus is resurrected in spirit, not in body. As Paul put it, "*What goes into the earth is physical, what comes out is spiritual.*"

Resurrection is something to be experienced not debated. It is not an historical date; it is an expression and an experience of Profound Love. It can happen in your home, your work place, your neighborhood, wherever you encounter someone in need. It can happen when we unconditionally offer someone a hug, a kind word, or forgiveness. It can be experienced in our quiet repentance. Jesus didn't tell his disciples to meet him at the temple to pray or to hang out around an empty tomb and worship him. He told them to go and do likewise and he would meet them there.

So the question is still "What are you looking for?" Unfortunately if you are someone looking for proof of an historical event to bolster your faith or prove your beliefs, then you may not be satisfied with much you read here. But if you are looking for ways to experience God Incarnate, to find the sacred in your secular world, to learn to live a resurrected life now in this incredible place we call earth, then I suggest you try living it.

Just think what that kind of living could create in the world: a place where everyone listens to everyone; where everyone is treated with dignity regardless of their color, gender, sexual orientation or economic standing; where the poor have as much right to govern as the rich; where the insights of women are valued as much as the insights of men; and where there is a reverence for all life and shared abundance for all.

That's what the resurrection could mean. When that happens, when enough of us experience and believe it, then we can raise our voices together and shout with utter joy . . . Alleluia! Alleluia! Alleluia!

CHAPTER TEN

Creating Sacred Communities

Community Making

Several years ago, I was invited by a friend to attend a two-day workshop based on a program created by Scott Peck, the author of the well-known self-help book, *The Road Less Traveled*. This friend knew I was looking for ways to develop an active small group program in the congregation I was leading at the time. She was a facilitator for a new organization, Foundation for Community Encouragement. This inspired group planned to lead community-building workshops all over the country based on a newer book Peck wrote in 1987, *The Different Drum: Community Making and Peace*. Although this book was never as popular as his earlier books, I believe it is still one of the best books ever written about building true or sacred community. I had already read the book when my friend invited me to attend one of Peck's workshops. Since I had been impressed by the book, I agreed to go.

Scott Peck died in 2005 but the body of his work continues to inspire people all over the world. Most of what Peck wrote about in this book came out of his experiences in leading and observing literally thousands of workshops based on the lessons from the book *The Road Less Traveled*. That book, written nearly ten years earlier than *The Different Drum*, was still on the best seller list. It remained on that list for over two decades.

In *The Different Drum*, Peck argued that finding and fostering real community may be the only way the world—or at least her inhabitants—will survive the future. Peck believed there are certain identifiable characteristics of what he called a true community distinguishing it from what he called a pseudo-community. In true community, he writes, you find a "group of individuals who have learned how to communicate honestly with each other, whose relationships go deeper than their masks of composure, and who have developed some significant commitment to 'rejoice together, mourn together and to delight in each other and make each other's condition our own.'"

Peck wrote about the mystery of this kind of community comparing it with the mystery of electricity. "Like electricity," he writes, "[community] is profoundly lawful. Yet there remains something about it that is inherently mysterious, miraculous . . . unfathomable."

In the second half of the book Peck identifies the laws or principles guiding what he understands are stages of spiritual development.

- Pseudo-community: when everyone is just being nice to each other and pretending;

- Chaos: when people realize they have not been honest, that they were pretending and everything blows up;

- Emptiness: when we are willing to empty ourselves of our expectations, our prejudices, our need to control, our ideologies;

- Community happens: when we are willing to remove our defenses and to be vulnerable; it happens when we practice open listening and begin practice a level of honest communication that is unfortunately rare.

According to Peck, every community must go through these stages to evolve into a true community or a sacred community. At the time Peck wrote this book he was avoiding any identification as a religious person although he had experienced a religious connection earlier in his life. As a result, he attempted to avoid any religious connotations in the book. Yet, I believe he would have been comfortable with the term sacred communities.

So what do I mean by a sacred community or spiritual community, or as Peck would call it a true community? I refer here to an intentional community with an identifiable common purpose. Maybe that purpose is simply to grow spiritually as individuals. It is a community where one can transcend oneself and experience a sense of the interconnectedness of life. Jesus may have called this an experience of Sacred Unity. It is a community in which each member seeks to see and relate to the divine or the sacred in the other.

Felix Adler a Jewish philosopher once wrote, "The unique personality which is the real life in me, I cannot gain unless I search for the real life, the spiritual quality, in others. I am myself spiritually dead unless I reach out to the fine quality dormant in others. For it is only with the god enthroned in the innermost shrine of the other, that the god hidden in me, will consent to appear."

These communities do not necessarily have to be part of a religious body, but it can help. For example, Christian communities have rituals and practices designed to remind us that we are part of something bigger than ourselves, including those who have come before. The ritual can pull us into a connection of something much larger than ourselves or even the gathered group. Jesus was reported to have said when two or more are gathered in my name I will be there. The people of the early Christian communities apparently took this very seriously. We may be reminded we are surrounded by "a great cloud of witnesses," as the writer of Hebrews suggested.

I did once participate in something I would call a sacred community or true community. It was not part of a church or even a religious setting. While I was in seminary, over thirty years ago, I spent one year in a special program working in the inner city along with eleven other interns. Each one of us worked in some kind of a social center, homeless shelter or in an ethnic minority urban church. Two participants were in churches with outreach programs in neighborhoods few of us would have driven through by choice prior to this time. Our small group started with thirteen naïve students. We were all white, upper middle class, highly educated folks who were largely ignorant about poverty, homelessness and inner city culture in general.

By the end of first week, most of us were sorry we had signed up for the program. By the end of the third week, we were certain we had made a mistake. We were feeling isolated, lonely and lost. We got together three times a week for debriefing and classes. The teaching professors came to our sites for classes. By the end of the year, however, only one person had dropped out of the class. The rest of us were more than glad we had made the life changing decision to participate. For several years after seminary some of us would

225

get together and recount our memories. We all agreed it was one of the most important, perspective altering experiences of our lives.

The thing we all remembered as the most important part of the experience was not only what we learned living, working, worshiping, crying and laughing with people we had had little or no contact with before, but it was the unique nature of the community the twelve of us formed that had the greatest impact. It was a real introduction for me to experience such special communal relationships. By the end of the year, we had no secrets, no defenses and no agendas that kept us from openly and honestly communicating, caring, forgiving and even forgetting. If one of us was hurt we all cried. If one of us celebrated, we all celebrated.

We laughed, we cried, and sometimes we fought like alley cats. But we never made decisions or took an action that did not take into consideration the best interest of the entire group. We were deeply connected. At one point, I think I would have sacrificed just about anything for the sake of the others.

Scott Peck wrote about what can happen when we make this kind of commitment to the group and to each other. He writes "When I am with a group of human beings committed to hanging in there through both the agony and the joy of community, I have a dim sense that I am participating in a phenomenon for which there is only one word . . . The word is glory." Maybe that's what the Psalmist was feeling when he wrote Psalm 133. "How very good and pleasant it is, when kindred live together in unity!"

It seems Paul knew something about creating sacred communities and what it means to experience this kind of glory. I would guess a third of his writings are devoted to the formation and nurturing of these unique kinds of communities. The idea that we are all part of one body, each part dependent on the other is an absolutely brilliant metaphor. In Romans, Paul writes, ". . . all things work together for those who are called to purpose."

Paul understood all of parts of the body, of the community, were committed to a higher purpose. If they were going to be successful in their mission, they would have to lay aside their personal agendas, their bickering, their egos and work together toward the higher good.

The author of the Book of Acts suggests that the members of the first Christian communities believed they could be extraordinarily generous with each other. These early followers of Jesus saw themselves as companions who could trust each other and share all they had. Maybe more importantly, they sincerely believed their community existed for a higher purpose. They believed these communities existed for something far more important than the needs of any individual. They did not wonder so much what they were going to get out of it, but rather what they could give; they did not worry so much about who was in control, but rather about learning to give up control.

In his book, *The Birth of Christianity*, John Dominic Crossan explains that these new and growing "communities of resistance" as he calls them, were the very heart of the early Christian movement. According to Crossan, their communal living was a real thing. Maybe more importantly, it was a "calculated rejection and purposed replacement for the materialism and greed of Roman commercialization" of their society. It was, according to Crossan, one of the early church's most important statements to the world.

I know this all sounds pretty idealistic and there are plenty of hints that things were not always peaceful, sweet, wonderful and loving. Even these communities made up of people who were attempting to live with an intentional divine-consciousness, had their share of differences. But like a good marriage, the members found ways to work things out. Although there was conflict and even some pretty harsh conflicts at the time, most of these folks must have felt they were part of something special. They had made a commitment to hang in there through the agony and the joy. And because of that commitment, that trust, that vulnerability, I believe every once in a while many of them must have experienced the glory Scott Peck referred to.

Now let's be clear. The vast majority of people will not experience that glory, nor will they experience such intimacy. It's not because of lack of desire. But these kinds of relationships take time. They take energy. They take commitment. And they take risk. Probably most challenging, they require a willingness to look deeply within ourselves, questioning our true motivations, attitudes, desires and fears. In other words sacred relationships, or true intimacy, require a level of vulnerability few of us are willing to risk.

The idea of living as if we are one part of a whole is not a natural thing for most of us raised in our Western culture of rugged individualism. Where else in the world could a song be so everlasting popular as the famous Frank Sinatra hit, "I Did It My Way?" When we take an honest look at the way we design our busy lives, our need to acquire, our need to get ahead, or our need to be on top, we have to wonder where we are going to fit these kinds of things into our lives. Can we ever accept the idea of giving up control and working for a higher good? We are trained to be competitive, defensive, protective, and possessive. Vulnerability is not considered a highly regarded trait in our society.

On the other hand, we are talking about something that should be a natural way of being a human. At some level most people yearn for that kind of intimacy. Sadly, without experiencing this kind of intimate community in our lives, we are often separated from an experience of the Divine, from each other, and even from ourselves.

Sacred communities are just one form of sacred relationships. But they can be the key to experiencing Divine Spirit and a level of intimacy our souls crave. They are a one doorway into the experience of Sacred Unity or Oneness, even glory. However they take a commitment, an openness and a vulnerability that does not come easily. It is up to us.

On Sacred Communities

For the last 18 months, I have interviewed or corresponded with people who are either leading a small group or are part of a small group that meets on a regular basis for community and spiritual direction. I plan to continue to do this with more groups and in more depth. My hope is that we can gain more information from a variety of groups to see what is working and what is not. Most of the information I gained from these interviews so far comes from groups who have been meeting on a regular basis for more than a year. In a couple of cases they have been meeting for over a decade. I am certain I will be revising my thoughts on some of this but I wanted to share what I have learned so far.

There seem to be two distinct types of groups forming out there. One is primarily educational. Everyone agrees to read a book or an article usually written by a well-known scholar. They may meet once a month and discuss what they learned. They may meet weekly, go chapter by chapter and discuss the ideas in more depth. They may read something as scholarly as John Dominic Crossan or something as new age as Eckhart Tolle. For these groups the emphasis is on education and the focus is about the particular books. Many of them are interested in the changes that scholars have made in the interpretation of the Christian story.

The other type of group tends to focus on spiritual experience. They may read a book, even a scholarly book on occasion. However, they tend to be more interested in an inspirational reading. If they do use a book, it is often a book on spiritual discipline or practices. The members of these groups are more interested in their own spiritual development so they often focus on practice. They tend to meet more often. They often include a simple meal and almost always make time for guided meditation or silence together.

In both cases true community can develop simply by being together as an intentional community as long as there is opportunity for open discussion and sharing. However, the groups that have formed for the explicit purpose of spiritual experience appear to deal better with the challenges of sharing and openness. I refer here to the willingness to be vulnerable ultimately leading to greater intimacy and connectedness. That same willingness to be vulnerable allows us to see the divine or sacred in the other. And that can only happen when there is mutual trust among the participants.

There is one other caveat. The groups primarily gathering for spiritual experience tend to meet more often and appear to have longer lives as a group. I will try and watch that data for future reporting.

There are things I was able to mine from the respondents that seem to be common to all the groups who consider themselves successful. I will list them briefly:

- There needs to be some basic organization and some agreements about why you are there, what is your purpose and how you will settle differences. It is helpful to put these on paper and review them on a regular basis. It helps when someone new wants to join the group.

- There has to be some system of leadership. This may not be an inspiring teacher or what might have been the agreed upon figure head. But it is the one who deals with the calendar, follows up with emails, and makes certain someone is going to have a plan for the evening. It may be the one who plans the meals. There has to be someone who makes certain things happen in an organized way. Sometimes someone must let the group know there is an issue that needs to be addressed.

- All of the groups stating they were trying to create true or sacred community had some ritual. It may be a simple opening. "Let us all hold hands in silence before we start." It may be the way they chose to close the gathering. I was told by two different respondents that when their leadership changed due to a move in one case and a death in another, they stopped doing their simple group rituals. Interestingly they both shared with me that it changed the group. One respondent said they did not feel as close. The other said it was hard to get their group to settle in and to become more focused.

- Whenever possible, share a meal. I sincerely believe something changes in a small group dynamic when we break bread together. No one made this clearer than Jesus. Dom Crossan devoted an entire chapter in his in-depth book on the historical Jesus (*The Historical Jesus: The Life of a Mediterranean Jewish Peasant*) about the importance of the "Common Meal Tradition" to Jesus and his early followers. This is not just a nod to a tradition today. It is an exchange that can have a spiritual impact on the participants and a deepening of relationships.

Most of the groups agreed there should be a time to review how the group is doing and if any changes need to be made. After these groups had been around for a while, this appeared to just happen naturally.

I suspect you may sense I have an affinity for the second kind of group and you would be right. It may be because I have participated in both types and am now part of a small group formed around spiritual practices. Our stated and agreed upon purpose is to develop sacred community and to work toward truly open and loving relationships. We eat a simple meal and meditate together once a week. Most of us have been doing this for over eight years. We still feel blessed every time we are together. Yes, there have been issues over the years, but we worked them out with love and compassion. We are careful before we invite new participants to make certain they have the same goals and purpose for being there.

We have become extremely close as a family. We know that when any one of us stumbles, when any one has a serious illness in the group, when there is a death in our group, we will become the compassionate family we have created. There will be real, loving support for whoever needs it. It is an amazing comfort, especially at this stage of life.

There is a lot going on in the religions of the world today. As a result there are all kinds of scholarly breakthroughs and new discoveries. They are interesting and even challenging for those who are still trying to hang onto the old religion of our past or are searching for some new way to understand their faith. I personally have an affinity for the Jesus I have come to know over the last 40 years. I spent many of those years, like a host of others, deconstructing the old story built around the concept that Jesus was the substitutionary sacrifice for the sins of all humanity.

A couple of decades ago, it became clear to me that my need to focus on the deconstruction was over. I became far more interested in being a follower of the teacher I had come to know. I became engrossed in an attempt to define the teachings and the path Jesus left for us. I found it helps to lay those teachings next to the teachings of some of the other great teachers of history as well as some of our modern mystics and enlightened contemporary teachers. It was not so much that I wanted to find which one was correct or the best. I was interested in learning which teachings offer support to the others.

Somewhere along the way it occurred to me that if I wanted to learn just who Jesus really was, I had to intentionally practice his teachings to the best of my abilities. You see, I believe when practiced they can lead to a new awareness. Jesus might have called it being awake. It is a path that can lead to a clearer understanding of who we are and what we are not. It is learning in part to observe the observer of our life. It is seeing and experiencing the connectedness of all life. It is being awake. It is discovering that you are awareness.

We can talk all we want about how Christianity was changed in the Fourth Century, and about the many ways the Jesus story was twisted and turned to benefit the Empire. And yes, it is still used to benefit empire

231

thinking. But sooner or later, if we really want to know who Jesus was and what he was teaching; if we want to know who Buddha was and what was he teaching; if we want to know who Sri Krishna was and what he was teaching, we will need to start practicing those teachings. I am afraid there are far too many people who would prefer to debate the scholarship and forget to practice the teachings. It is like studying the way a Steinway piano is built but never learning how to play it. As a former piano teacher once told me, "no one learns how to play the piano, no matter how great it is without practice, practice, practice." In my personal opinion that is a lost opportunity.

So you might want to gather some friends together and ask them if they would like to form a group to study a path or paths that could lead to a new awareness; a new understanding of who and what they are. You might want to let them know you would like to learn how to play on the path . . . that you would really like to practice, practice, practice. You just might experience true community and in the process discover who you are.

Trying to String Things Together

My wife and I have been part of a small group that meets ten to twelve times a year. We may agree to read a book, get together and discuss it. We have read books like *The Seat of the Soul*, by Gary Zukav; *The New Earth*, by Eckhart Tolle; *Life After Death*, by Deepak Chopra; *Uncomfortable With Uncertainty*, by Pema Chodron. Our goal is to stretch ourselves

One time we gathered to watch a Nova production called *The Elegant Universe* hosted by Brian Greene. For several of us, the readings we had had shared in the past had an amazing impact on the way we saw our lives and even the way we lived them. But this PBS production stretched every one of us in some way or other. It is a place where *"reality meets science fiction"* as host Brian Greene put it. Simply stated, quantum theory is radically changing the way we understand our world, our universe. It is changing the way we understand truth, facts and our reality.

According to some of the best scientists in the world, our universe is composed entirely of vibrating strings of energy. Everything from the smallest measurable particle to the largest star in our universe is made from the same kind of material. Just like the strings of a cello or viola can make a multitude of sounds, quantum strings of energy create a multitude of forms. In ways we cannot understand—at least at this point—all these strings are inter-related and interdependent. In other words the great spiritual teachers, including Jesus, were right. We are all one interconnected whole. The universe is like one grand symphony orchestra playing beautiful music and we are part of that music.

If this is not enough to get your attention, these same scientists tell us there are at least 11 dimensions of reality, all part of our universe, all happening simultaneously. We may be participating in some way in any one of these at the same time. At any moment we are faced with an infinite number of possibilities that the course of our life might take us. This is happening with every living creature.

I am clearly not a scientist. I barely got through my high school physics class a very long time ago. And it is true that this is all still considered a theory. However, it is a highly regarded theory being adopted by the vast majority of active scientists today. Most of the disagreements, as I understand, are more of a nuance than a challenge to the basic premise. There is enough solid science supporting this theory that it can't help but test the limits of our minds and even our hearts if we really start thinking about it.

It seems to me the purpose of religion or spiritual practice is to draw closer to the great mystery of something we call God. Certainly that was the direction Jesus was pointing, although he would not have used the word God. We are hypothetically trying to get closer to an infinite mystery all the great spiritual teachers have pointed us to which actually lies within. Maybe we need this kind of thinking in order to get out of our myopic and limiting ways of engaging with life.

This experience was particularly on my mind after I received an email from an individual who wanted to let me know I was "destroying Christianity and defaming Jesus." He attached a copy of an article published on a very conservative, and apparently a very popular blog site called Worldview Times. He was not the only one who sent the blog to me but he was the only who highlighted parts with his own scathing comments.

The article was entitled "*A New Religion Masquerading as Christianity*," by Marsha West. West writes: "*PCs (Progressive Christians) reject the notion that the Bible is infallible and inerrant but accept that it has some truth sprinkled throughout. When a PC comes to accept the orthodox view of Christianity, his or her worldview crumbles."*

My "loving" friend highlighted the text I am quoting here. *"But in order to make the God of the Bible more acceptable to the popular culture, liberals must reinvent the wheel. To accomplish this they have to undermine Church doctrine. So doctrine is tinkered with, intentionally misrepresented, or scrapped altogether! What gets scrapped includes some of the essential doctrines of the faith for which the martyrs shed their blood!"*

He also wanted to make certain I did not miss this: *"And yet the Body of Christ has done little or nothing to stop liberals and cult leaders from taking over entire denominations. These men and women are false teachers! Usurpers! Heretics! Liars! Fakes!"* I presume there was a message there.

Finally there is the punch line of what was a long article. It was underlined by my friend, just to make certain I read every word. *"There is a terrible malady upon you and judgment is coming. Yes, judgment is coming. For this reason true followers of Jesus Christ must make God's invisible Kingdom visible to the unsaved—before it's too late."*

I wondered, as I read this material over a few times, what would the author of the article do with the string theory? What would her so-called world view become? How would her belief system and her operative myth line up with one set of clear cut and written rules and truth? How would she deal with the incongruities of her fixed, inerrant biblical perspective? And how would she handle the very real possibility that no matter how much she wiggles and squirms, we are all stuck together, playing one beautiful symphony as part of the same orchestra. Although, I must admit it felt to me more like she was clanging bell or a very loud pair of cymbals, out of sync and out of key. I suppose if I could develop a more expanded awareness, I would hear her as simply part of the contrast.

But what would anyone with her perspective do with the idea that time is not linear? In which dimension will the judgment day occur? Maybe we are already experiencing hell in another dimension or maybe we have already died in some other world. Who are the good guys and who are the bad guys if we are made of the same stuff and we are part of one big interdependent system? How would they ever be able to get rid of the "them/us" tribal mentality which has tortured civilization since the early Mesopotamia Valley days?

Ponder for the moment, the very real possibility that these scientists are correct. How might that change the way we look at our religions, our life, our understanding of reality and most of all our relationships? What kind of boxes have we created that keep us from "experiencing the infinite mind of God?" Which of these 11 dimensions might be heaven or is there such a place? If we are all made up of the same strings, which one is the God string? Could there be a difference between us and Jesus or Buddha? What is our relationship to all other life if we are all one and interdependent? What sounds of the strings can we make and do we have a choice? Where and what is God in this model? Why are we capable of asking these questions? Or you can read Genesis again . . . nothing about string theory there.

Where is the Kingdom of God?

Every major religious movement in history has started with an individual who had a profound, transformative, spiritual experience. This experience or series of experiences, transformed his or her perspective on reality and of self. Some may have called it enlightenment, others awakening, and others born again. As other people noticed differences in these individuals, they asked what had changed. I believe these changed individuals, probably with some reluctance, became teachers of a path. What is important to note for purposes of this article, is how many things these teachers had in common when they attempted to describe what they had experienced and what had changed in them. In spite of different cultures and different settings, the most common characteristic these new teachers described was a profound experience of a sense of Unity or Oneness with all Creation, Life, God, or possibly the Father. Jesus was no exception.

When Jesus tried to explain his experience of the Realm or Kingdom of God, he talked about what he experienced using metaphors and images of his times. Over the centuries, much has been lost in translations and because of contemporary ignorance of what these images were meant to portray. I believe we find the best insight of this phenomenon in the Book of Thomas since this book does not appear to have been redacted as heavily as other Gospels.

Thomas' Jesus states: *". . . the Kingdom is inside you and it is outside you. When you come to know yourselves, then you will be known, and you will see that you are children of the living father . . ."* (L22)

He also declares: *"When you make the two into one, and when you make the inner like the outer and the outer like the inner, and the upper like the lower, and when you make male and female into a single one, so that the male will not be male nor the female be female, when you make eyes in place of an eye, a hand in place of a hand, a foot in place of a foot, an image in place of an image, then you will enter the kingdom."* (L84)

In other words, Thomas' Jesus was not teaching people how they must behave or think so that they might end up in some wonderful place when they die. Rather he teaches a path which could enable the follower to experience something profound and transforming, something that will change one's way to view and relate to reality in the present moment. It was his assumption that what he experienced, we, the followers, might experience it as well.

What is this place, this experience? It is the experience of Oneness—Oneness with all Creation, with God, with the Father. It is the experience that according to Neil Douglas-Klotz, Jesus referred to as Sacred Unity.

So how do we have this experience? How do we gain this perspective of our reality according to the Jesus path? Some of those teachings are obvious. We must learn to trust the Universe. We must learn to take responsibility for our actions that have harmed others or ourselves and commit to changing our ways. We must learn to forgive, even our enemies. We must learn to love without conditions. These are the lessons we can garner in the classroom. But they only work when we practice them.

However, Jesus the Teacher was very clear. If we really want to experience the Sacred Unity, we have to come out of our classrooms, our homes and our hiding places of comfort. We must meet people in need wherever they are in order to offer true compassion to those who suffer, and those in need. He suggested we do this no matter how different from us they might be, even our tribal enemies. Real compassion means a willingness to share another's experience. It may mean self-sacrifice. It might even prove to be costly.

Let me be clear. This is not an ought or even some "Kantian categorical imperative." This is an opportunity to discover and experience Sacred Unity. It is a state of being where all divisions, all separations, all boundaries disappear. It can be the place where Oneness is experiential and transformative at the same time. We can be confident that Jesus lived in that state of being, in that reality. However we must not forget what he repeatedly told his students and followers: "Go and do likewise."

The Path of Jesus

I know of no spiritual path which does not presume some kind of significant personal transformation will occur if followed and practiced. By transformation, I mean to experience a change in our understanding of what is real and discovering who and what we really are as humans in this universe. It means getting in touch with our Eternal. The language may be different, the steps in a different order, the emphasis slightly unique. But I have found there are far more similarities than there are differences between most of the well know traditions. Their common goal is to learn how to live with a wide awake mind, an open heart and an absence of suffering. For many it also means cultivating the experience of joy.

I have explained in many places my understanding of Jesus' idea of God's Realm, or Kingdom or Heaven, or Sacred Unity. This was not a place where one goes after death but are rather descriptive words that refer to a state of mind. It is not a place but an experience of the Divine which is available to any of us in the here and now. And I believe Jesus laid out a path for us both by his teaching and his life which could lead one to a personal experience of this elevated state of mind. The Christian contemporaries refer to this as *illumination* brought on by *kenosis* or self-emptying. The Buddhist might call this enlightenment, *kensho* or *satori* achieved by meditation and living the Eightfold Path. A Hindu might use the term, *moksha* meaning freedom.

If we dig a little we can find some differences in these respective teachings intended to lead to transformation. I believe these may be more nuance than substance. For example, the Eastern teachers seem to put more emphasis on withdrawal, silence, meditation. Jesus path seems to emphasize more engaging, reaching out, risking. While we do know that Jesus went off to

237

pray frequently, it is not clear if he had an active meditation practice. It may simply have been assumed by his followers and even his culture at the time. My own presumption is that he did.

Let me be clear, I am referring here to the path and not the end goal. I am certain any Buddhist who is trying to live by the Nobel Eightfold Path is by nature engaging, reaching out and risking. What is common to all of these paths, in spite of their differences, is the assumption that if more people followed the path, they would become more awake to the suffering caused in large part by inequality. If more people became awake to these inequities, and lived with compassionate hearts, eventually the world would also be transformed. It is my sincere belief that Yeshua, in spite of his difficult situation, believed there could be a new, transformed world order.

ProgressiveChritianity.org is frequently challenged by those who believe we do not address social justice issues often enough or some would suggest, not at all. It should be obvious to anyone who actually reads our material, we do address social injustice and social issues. However, it has always been my belief that if we take on these issues and conflicts without an open heart, without some kind of internal transformation, it is too easy to become angry, add to the conflict and frankly be less effective. It is also a recipe for burnout.

In his book, *The Heart of Christianity*, Marcus Borg writes, "Christian life should be relational and transformational." According to Borg, there are really two transformations needed and they are "twins." He suggests one is a personal and spiritual, and the other is communal, social and political.

In other words, if we are going to be effective change agents for more a compassionate and just world, we must come at this change with open minds and open hearts. We first need to work on our own internal transformations through our own intentional path. Only then can our effort to transform our society and our world have any long term impact. This is what the early followers of Yeshua, people of The Way, believed. This was and still is the path or Way of Yeshua.

Clearly Jesus told us if we want to experience Sacred Unity, or the Realm of God, we need to go where there is pain and try to alleviate the suffering. But we are challenged to do this with an open and compassionate heart. Our hearts and our eyes will be opened when we reach out and actually serve. One reason he suggests that we serve is to gain this awareness, to become awake to the fact that these are "God's children." Compassionate serving, even sacrifice is part of the path. You cannot serve with a compassionate heart without eventually seeing those whom you are serving as your brother, your sister, your mother, your father, or eventually as yourself, even when it is "the least of these" whom you have compassionately served. All boundaries are erased. The served and the server become one. The ultimate goal however is to break down divisions and separation and move to a new understanding of our inter-connectedness and oneness.

Today some of the world's issues seem so big, the needs so great we can become frozen, often feeling helpless. We wonder if we can have any impact as an individual or even an organization. Much of this, I believe, is caused by "too much information." With television, social media and satellites we have instant knowledge of suffering everywhere and anywhere in the world, in 3D and color. With few exceptions, most thinking people in this country know the world does face a real, life ending, ecological disaster unless we make radical change in our behavior. What in the world can we do that would have any impact besides recycling and driving cars with better gas mileage?

On the other hand, in part because of our technical world and social media we are also given the opportunity today to experience oneness or inter-connectedness, which the world has never experienced before. Young people from over 25 countries go on our website every week. We have a whole generation of young adults who have grown up, in some ways, without geographic or language boundaries. They know what is going on in countries many of us never knew existed until recently. They travel with ease all over the world and communicate regularly with other young people in what we older folks might have referred as a foreign country. Many of them no longer see ethnic or racial differences any more than we might notice someone with blond or red hair.

They are inheriting a very different world than it was only fifty years ago. But they are still human and will have to overcome some of the weaknesses of the human condition in their attempt to forge their way. The survival of the human race may be dependent on their ability to move past the egoic mentality that has plagued our tiny planet for the last ten thousand years.

There must be a transformation in the world if the human race is going to survive. According to scientists, we can now actually calculate a deadline for human life on our planet, and it is not that far out there. Many young people all over the world are aware of this as well. Take a look at the movies and television programs today that are about end-times and the final survivalists. What a strange way it must be to grow up with this idea as a major influence.

So the question I leave you what can we do? Are we part of the problem? Do we have wise teachers today to help these young people while we can? Do we offer a model or a path for both personal and world transformation?

I believe we do and it is time we started making this clearer.

About the Author

A skeptic since his high school days, Fred Plumer was asked by the pastor of his church not to ask so many questions in church. He soon dropped out of the church. In college his major was political philosophy which introduced him to a wide variety of serious thinkers from Aristotle and Plato to Kant and John Locke to name just a few. He had a successful business life but was never quite fulfilled. He was always reading, seeking and finding people who wanted to discuss philosophy or religion with him. While in his thirties he joined a group led by a follower of Ouspensky, one of Gurdjieff's disciples.

After a tumultuous time in Colorado, owning and running a restaurant and a separate nightclub, Fred, Charron and their three-year-old daughter moved to Montana leaving everything behind. Following a healing experience in Montana that changed the course of his life, Fred went to the Pacific School of Religion where he signed up for a Master's program. However, this happened in the early eighties when Robert Funk was talking about something called the Jesus Seminar. One of the first members of the Seminar, Bill Culver Nelson, was the Minister in Residence in Fred's first year at the seminary. He gave Fred several books written by some of the earliest members of what would become the Jesus Seminar and insisted that Fred join him in one of their meetings so he could understand what was going on. It was a dream for a skeptic. Fred's world would never be the same again.

By the end of his second year, Fred changed his program to M.Div. and returned for his third year on an ordination track. He wondered if he could build a community around a more accurate representation of Jesus' life and teachings. In 1984 he was called to a new UCC church being started in Irvine (California) where he remained for over twenty years. It was the perfect location for a very progressive church and Fred's envelope-pushing theology and activism. In 2004 Fred "retired" took over leadership of ProgressiveChristianity.org, formally The Center for Progressive Christianity, founded by James Rowe Adams. He spends his time writing for ProgressiveChrilstianity.org, participating in his intentional community, and working with his two horses. Yes, Fred is seeking ways to communicate with horses now.